FEB 1 '90 DATE DUE			

THE DEFINITIVE TIME MACHINE

V I S I O N S

Harry M. Geduld, General Editor

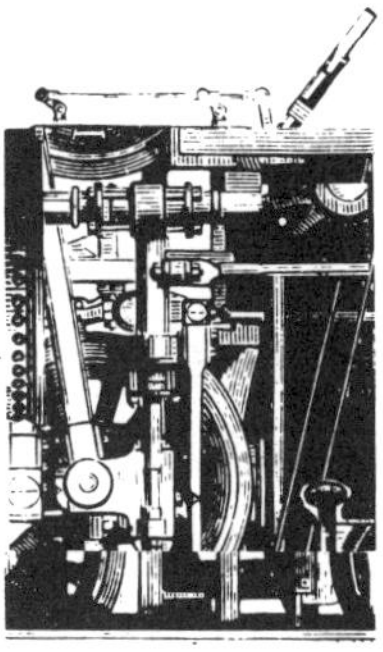

THE DEFINITIVE Time Machine

A Critical Edition of
H. G. Wells's Scientific Romance
With Introduction and Notes
by Harry M. Geduld

Indiana University Press BLOOMINGTON AND INDIANAPOLIS

MANUFACTURED IN THE UNITED STATES OF AMERICA

Library of Congress Cataloging-in-Publication Data

Wells, H. G. (Herbert George), 1866–1946.
'''The definitive Time machine.

(Visions)
Bibliography: p.
I. Geduld, Harry M.   II. Title.
III. Series: Visions (Bloomington, Ind.)
PR5774.T5   1987   823'.912   86–45940
ISBN 0–253–31611–1
ISBN 0–253–20427–5 (pbk.)

1 2 3 4 5 91 90 89 88 87

Wordsworth said,
"Dreams, books, are each a world."
The Time Machine is a *cosmic* dream,
and editing this great visionary story,
my favorite work of fiction since I read it
as a child, has been the realization of a
personal dream of many years.

This edition is dedicated

To the many Wells scholars whose work
has enriched my understanding and
appreciation of *The Time Machine*.

To my parents—with "gratitude and . . .
tenderness"—for putting me on the real
time machine and for giving me my first
copy of Wells's scientific romance.

To Marcus Stephen Geduld (one of my two
best-loved Time Travellers) who
encouraged me to undertake the project.

[*The Time Machine* is] "something new under the sun."
—London *Daily Chronicle* review (1895)

The Time Machine, The Island of Dr. Moreau, The Plattner Story, The First Men in the Moon. ... are the first books I read; perhaps they will be the last. I think they will be incorporated, like the fables of Theseus or Ahasuerus, into the general memory of the species and even transcend the fame of their creator or the extinction of the language in which they were written.
—Jorge Luis Borges, *Other Inquisitions*

The Time Machine ... will take its place among the great stories of our language. Like all excellent works it has meanings within its meaning. ...
—V. S. Pritchett, *The Living Novel*

Sir Ernest Barker recalled seeing Wells slumped in a chair at a reception, and he asked him how he was. "Poorly, Barker, poorly," he said. I asked him what he was doing. "Writing my epitaph." I asked him what it was. "Quite short," he said, "just this—God damn you all: I told you so."
—Norman and Jeanne Mackenzie,
H. G. Wells: A Biography

The end crowns all,
And that old common arbitrator, Time,
Will one day end it.
—Shakespeare, *Troilus and Cressida*

CONTENTS

Acknowledgments   IX

A Brief Chronology through 1895   X

Introduction   I

The Time Machine   29
(*Text of the Atlantic Edition, 1924*)

Notes   91

Probable Route of the Time Traveller   121

Select Bibliography   122

After *The Time Machine*   128

Adaptations and Spin-offs   130

A P P E N D I X E S

   I. *The Chronic Argonauts*   135

  II. The Second and Third Versions   153

  III. The *National Observer Time Machine*   154

  IV. The *New Review Time Machine*: Two Excerpts   175

  V. Correlation of the Holt Edition with the *New Review*   181
     Version and the Atlantic Edition

  VI. Correlation of the Heinemann Edition and the   183
     Atlantic Edition

  VII. The Time Traveller Visits the Past   184

  VIII. How to Construct a Time Machine, by Alfred Jarry   189

IX. Robert Paul and *The Time Machine*, by Terry Ramsaye   196

X. Hinton and Newcomb on the Fourth Dimension   204

XI. *Beowulf* and *The Time Machine*:   211
  A Note on Analogues, by Harry M. Geduld

XII. The Heaven of the Time-Machine, by Louis Untermeyer   214

Acknowledgments

For expert advice on specific questions and/or invaluable assistance in obtaining source material, I am particularly indebted to Professor Martin S. Burkhead (Astronomy Department, Indiana University), Mr. Anthony R. Guneratne, Professor James W. Halporn (Chairperson, Classical Studies Department, Indiana University), Mr. N. J. Pearce (Far Eastern Division, Victoria and Albert Museum, London), Professor Robert M. Philmus (English Department, Concordia University, Montreal), Professor Roger Shattuck (French Department, University of Virginia), and two old and valued friends—George Stover and Steve Vertlieb.

I am most grateful to the Literary Executors of the Estate of H. G. Wells for permission to include the early drafts of *The Time Machine* in this edition. Professor Roger Shattuck's translation of "How to Construct a Time Machine" from *Selected Works of Alfred Jarry* is reprinted here by kind permission of Grove Press, Inc. "Robert Paul and *The Time Machine*" from *A Million and One Nights* by Terry Ramsaye appears by permission of Simon & Schuster, Inc.

A Brief Chronology through 1895

1866 Sept. 21: Herbert George Wells (d. 1946), third son of Joseph Wells and Sarah (Neal) Wells, born in Bromley, Kent, England.

In this year Charles Darwin (1809–1882) is 57; his *Origin of Species* had been published seven years earlier. Thomas Henry Huxley (1825–1895), the most dedicated defender of the Darwinian theory of evolution and the most influential of Wells's mentors, is 41. Jules Verne (1828–1905) is 38; he had published his *Journey to the Center of the Earth* two years earlier.

1874–80 Wells attends the Bromley Academy, a private day school.

1880 Sarah Wells leaves her husband and becomes housekeeper at Up Park near Midhurst. Wells browses at will in the extensive library at Up Park.

1881 Wells has brief stints as a chemist's apprentice and as a pupil at Midhurst School. His mother arranges for him to become an apprentice at the Southsea Drapery Emporium, a period of misery that he will recapture vividly in *Kipps*.

1883 Quits his apprenticeship at the Drapery Emporium; becomes a pupil teacher at Midhurst School.

1884–87 Awarded a government scholarship that enables him to attend the Normal School of Science in South Kensington—where he studies under Thomas Henry Huxley.

1887 Suffers from a chronic pulmonary condition: the first of many serious bouts of illness.

1888 April through June: *The Chronic Argonauts*, the first version of *The Time Machine*, is serialized in the *Science Schools Journal*.

1891 July: Wells's article, "The Rediscovery of the Unique" is published in Frank Harris's *Fortnightly Review*.

October: Wells begins teaching biology at a crammer's: the University Correspondence College in Cambridge. One of his students (in 1892) is Amy Catherine Robbins who will become his second wife.

October 21: Marries his cousin, Isabel Mary Wells.

1893 *Text Book of Biology* and *Honours Physiography* (the latter co-authored with R. A. Gregory).

1894 Affair with Amy Catherine Robbins; separates from Isabel.
March through June: a serialized, unsigned, and unfinished version of *The Time Machine* appears in the *National Observer*.

1895 January: Divorces Isabel.
January through May: A completed version of *The Time Machine* is serialized in the *New Review*.
May 7: *The Time Machine* published in book form by Henry Holt & Co., New York.
May 29: *The Time Machine* published in book form by Heinemann, London.
October 27: Marries Amy Catherine Robbins, whom he nicknamed Jane. They will have two sons: George Philip Wells (b. 1901) and Frank Richard Wells (b. 1903).
Other publications this year include: *Select Conversations with an Uncle, The Wonderful Visit,* and *The Stolen Bacillus, and Other Incidents*.

Introduction

The Time Machine, H. G. Wells's earliest published work of fiction,[1] is widely regarded as the finest of his "scientific romances."[2] Never out of print since its original publication in book form in 1895 (when Wells was thirty), the work brought him instant acclaim as an important literary talent. Since 1895 it has appeared in innumerable editions and has been translated into virtually every language on earth.

Like *Alice in Wonderland* and *Gulliver's Travels*, *The Time Machine* embodies many levels of meaning and appeals to readers of virtually every age. Permanently established as a "classic" of its genre, Wells's novella was the first story to give a scientific cast to the notion of time travel,[3] an innovation which has become basic to much science fiction. It was also the first significant dystopia and one of the earliest visions of man's ultimate destiny to be based on serious scientific speculation.[4] Fifty years after its original publication, J. O. Bailey summed up its achievement in these words: "*The Time Machine* draws upon the sciences of biology, geology and astronomy; from them it brings a cosmic perspective to scientific fiction; and it deals with areas of the imagination that properly belong to no other kind of fiction."[5]

GESTATION

The genesis of *The Time Machine* vividly exemplifies Carl Rogers's definition of the creative process as "the emergence in action of a novel relational product, growing out of the uniqueness of the individual on the one hand, and the materials, events, people, or circumstances of his life on the other."[6]

Wells's novella absorbed, first of all, a wide range of childhood experiences involving his environment, his reading, his religious upbringing, and certain juvenile fears and fantasies. It was also shaped by various adult experiences, including his scientific training, his responses to what he perceived to be ominous late nineteenth-century social and political developments, his familiarity with a wide variety of literary material (from mythology and scientific and socialistic allegories on the one hand to the writings of his mentor, Thomas Henry Huxley, on the other), his critical sensitivity to the aesthetic cross-currents of the *fin-de-siècle*, and last but far from least, the encouragement of W. E. Henley, who urged him to rewrite his early drafts of the story and who published two revised, serialized versions of *The Time Machine* in the *National Observer* and the *New Review*.

As Alex Eisenstein has observed: "Wells's imagination transformed the objects of commonplace experience into the fundamental imagery of his fictions."[7] As far as *The Time Machine* is concerned those commonplace experiences centered initially on Atlas House (with its completely subterranean kitchen) where Wells was born and passed his early childhood and on Up Park where his mother lived and worked as a housekeeper and which he frequently visited during his boyhood. Wells's *Experiment in Autobiography* gives us highly memorable accounts of both places,[8] and several commentators have traced relationships between Atlas House and Up Park and various aspects (particularly the imagery, settings, and upper-and-lower world structure) of the remote future described in *The Time Machine*. Eisenstein, for example, explains how the "particular situation and character [of Atlas House] reflect[ed], to a large degree, the peculiar dichotomy of the world of A.D. 802,701,"[9] while Anthony West speaks of Wells's "descriptions of the loathly caverns inhabited by the light-fearing Morlocks" as a "purgative release" of his feelings about the basement quarters inhabited by his mother at Up Park.[10]

Childhood fears also left their mark on *The Time Machine*. At the age of seven, Wells, poring over a copy of John George Wood's *The Boy's Own Book of Natural History*,[11] "conceived a profound fear of the gorilla, of which there was a fearsome picture, which [i.e., the gorilla] came out of the dark and followed me noiselessly about the house. The half landing was a favorite lurking place for this terror. I passed it whistling, but wary and then ran for my life up the next flight."[12] Eisenstein remarks that the Morlocks were to "share all the insidious, nocturnal habits of the imaginary ape: like him, they emerged at night to ambush the dawdler from shadowed hideaways; they clambered up from lower levels to chase and terrorize small and youthful innocents."[13]

The imagery of the underworld of the Morlocks can also be linked to young Wells's fascination with certain dark or "forbidden" subjects. He discovered a garish depiction of Hell, an illustration in a devotional text (Christoph Christian Sturm's. *Reflections for Every Day of the Year on the Works of God*)[14] that his mother had tried to censor.[15] At this period, in secret he also cherished a fantasy of a subterranean world which he associated with sexual license: "At the age of seven . . . I had already between me and my bleak Protestant God, a wide wide world of snowy mountains, Arctic regions, tropical forests, prairies and deserts and high seas . . . about which I was prepared to talk freely, and cool and strange below it all a cavernous world of nameless goddess mistresses of which I never breathed a word to any human being."[16] Wells also retained lasting memories of strange, surly men invading Atlas House to haul sacks of coal through the shadowy kitchen to the coal-hole under the staircase.[17] This image coupled with the fact that from "his schooldays in Bromley he had disliked and feared the working class in a way wholly inappropriate to the son of a small tradesman"[18] points clearly to the psychic origins of the Morlocks and their predatory raids on the Eloi.

We know from the *Experiment in Autobiography* that young Wells read voraciously, not only the Bible and other religious texts (including *The Pilgrim's Progress*) imposed on him by his mother but also a wide variety of miscellaneous literature which he borrowed from the extensive library at Up Park. From Bunyan, "he learned much about English style and narrative technique which persisted into his stories."[19] Self-chosen books over which he pored included Tom Paine's *Common Sense*, Swift's *Gulliver's Travels*, and Plato's *Republic*, works that "represent three themes—radicalism and agnosticism, utopian satire and the idea of a rational society ruled by men of intellect—which played a predominant role in his ideas and his writings."[20] But the influence under which he claimed to have written *The Chronic Argonauts* (his first version of *The Time Machine*) was Hawthorne's *The Scarlet Letter*[21]—although, as Bernard Bergonzi points out, *The Chronic Argonauts* owes rather more to the opening pages of *The House of the Seven Gables*.[22]

A far stronger influence, discernible in all the later versions of *The Time Machine*, is that of *Gulliver's Travels*. In his 1934 "Preface" to a collection of *Seven Famous Novels* (including *The Time Machine*) Wells says nothing about Hawthorne but admits to an "early, profound and lifelong admiration for Swift [which] appears again and again in this collection, and is particularly evident in a predisposition to make the stories reflect upon contemporary political and social discussions."[23] Swiftian influences on *The Time Machine*—indeed, on much of Wells's early fiction—is a subject worthy of a long article; it must suffice here to notice Wells's fundamental indebtedness to *Gulliver's Travels* for his story's central situation: that of a lone voyager confronting alien civilizations whose nature and values reflect satirically, and comment darkly on, the misguided complacency of his contemporaries.

Wells refers to Bulwer-Lytton in *Experiment in Autobiography* without mentioning that novelist's *The Coming Race* (1871), the most widely read Victorian tale of a mysterious underworld.[24] However, he was probably as familiar with that work as he was with most nineteenth-century scientific and socialistic utopias, including William Morris's *News from Nowhere* and Edward Bellamy's *Looking Backward* (both 1888)—from both of which he was to borrow freely for *When the Sleeper Wakes* (1899).

A theme related to *The Time Machine*—that of the misunderstood scientist whose experiment results in totally unexpected consequences—was well established in British literature long before Wells: He could have encountered it in *Frankenstein* (1818) and *Dr. Jekyll and Mr. Hyde* (1886). As an adolescent Wells certainly read Stevenson[25] and it is hard to imagine that he would not also have dipped into Mary Shelley at the same period.[26]

A degree of self-idealization also seems evident in his depiction of the spare and solitary scientist of *The Time Machine*, but we must be extremely wary of any elaborate identification of the Time Traveller and H. G. Wells.[27]

Nevertheless, it was during his years at the Normal School, while he was studying to become a scientist, that he wrote *The Chronic Argonauts*. Wells explains the impetus thus: "In the students' Debating Society . . . I heard about and laid hold of the idea of a four dimensional frame for a fresh apprehension of physical phenomena, which afterwards . . . gave me a frame for my first scientific fantasia, the *Time Machine*."[28] The idea was derived from a paper on Time as the Fourth Dimension, presented by a fellow-student named E. A. Hamilton-Gordon. Hamilton-Gordon at first believed his ideas to be quite original, but when his paper was published in the *Science Schools Journal* for April 1887, he admitted that he had recently received a pamphlet by another writer entitled "What is the Fourth Dimension?" This "pamphlet" turned out to be "an almost exact counterpart" to his theory.[29] Hamilton-Gordon's admission probably drew Wells's attention to the piece—which was almost certainly an essay by C. H. Hinton (see notes 9 and 11 for chapter 1), an ingenious little treatise that would eventually leave its mark on the Time Traveller's exposition of four-dimensional geometry.

Several other influences are explicitly indicated in *The Time Machine*, most notably Simon Newcomb (see note 15 for chapter 1) and Sir George Darwin (chapter 5, note 21). Unmentioned, however, are several far stronger influences: those of Pierre Simon Laplace (whose cosmogonic theories are discernible in chapter 11 of *The Time Machine*); Lord Kelvin, formulator of the second law of thermodynamics (*The Time Machine* is a vivid depiction of the cosmic consequences of entropy, and Wells would place great emphasis on thermodynamics in his Introduction to the Random House edition of *The Time Machine*, 1931); and, above all, his teacher Thomas Henry Huxley, the great champion of Charles Darwin's evolutionary theories. Wells would acknowledge much later, in *Experiment in Autobiography*, that "that year I spent in Huxley's class [1884], was beyond all question, the most educational year of my life."[30]

In his "Preface" to *Seven Famous Novels* Wells describes *The Time Machine* as "a glimpse of the future that ran counter to the placid assumption of that time [the late Victorian period] that Evolution was a pro-human force making things better and better for mankind."[31] Wells studied biology and zoology under Huxley during a period when the latter was developing his own pessimistic conclusions about the fate of our planet and the destiny of the human race. These conclusions would be given their most elaborate formulation in the essay "The Struggle for Existence in Human Society" (1888) and the Romanes lecture on "Evolution and Ethics" (delivered by Huxley at Oxford in 1894). "If," Huxley conjectured, ". . . our globe has been in a state of fusion, and, like the sun, is gradually cooling down . . . then the time will come when evolution will mean an adaptation to an universal winter, and all forms of life will die out. . . ."[32] He advised mankind to have "no millennial anticipations" as far as evolution was concerned: "If for millions of years, our globe has taken the upward road, yet some time the summit will be reached and the downward route will be commenced. The most daring imagination will hardly venture upon the suggestion that the power and intelligence of man can ever arrest the procession of the great year."[33]

Huxley died in the same year that *The Time Machine* was first published in book form. At the Normal School Wells had spoken to his mentor only once, "holding open the door and exchanging a simple 'Good morning'."[34] But he was to pay homage to him in two ways: first, by fashioning, in the final chapters of *The Time Machine*, a profound and beautiful prose-poem out of his "cosmic pessimism";[35] second, by sending him a copy of the work with the following cover letter:[36]

> Lynton
> Mayburn Road
> Woking
>
> May 1895

Dear Sir:
I am sending you a little book that I fancy may be of interest to you. The central idea—of degeneration following security—was the outcome of a certain amount of biological study. I daresay your position subjects you to a good many such displays of the range of authors but I have this much excuse—I was one of your pupils at the Royal College of Science and finally [?]: The book is a very little one.

> I am, Dr Sir
> Very Faithfully yours
> H. G. Wells

Professor Huxley

PUBLICATION AND RECEPTION

Wells attempted at least five versions of *The Time Machine*, three of which appeared in print, in various periodical publications, before the work was first published in book form. The full history of these versions is long and complex. What follows is merely a brief summary of the publication history of *The Time Machine*.

First version. Between 1886 and 1893, Wells contributed sixteen articles and pieces of fiction to the *Science Schools Journal*, the students' magazine of the Royal College of Science. Among these early publications was *The Chronic Argonauts*, the first draft of what was to evolve into *The Time Machine*, serialized in issues 11, 12 and 13 (April, May, and June 1888).

"I began a romance, very much under the influence of Hawthorne," Wells recalled nearly half a century later. "I broke this off after three installments because I could not go on with it. That I could not go on with it marks a stage in my education in the art of fiction."[37] As Bergonzi notes, this immature essay in student writing "had only the bare idea of 'time travelling' and a few lines of dialogue in common with the later versions."[38] (Appendix I is the text of *The Chronic Argonauts*.)

Second and third versions. During the period 1889–1892 Wells rewrote the story, producing two separate versions. Unfortunately, neither of these is extant. But before they disappeared they were read by Professor A. Morley Davies who later recounted all that he could remember about them to Wells's biographer, Geoffrey West.[39] In 1906 Wells told an interviewer for the *New York Herald* that he had written *The Time Machine* in two weeks—information which does not square with what is known about the composition of any of the later versions.[40] The comment is tantalizing. Was Wells referring to the second or third versions—or even to another draft about which we have no information? (See Appendix II for Morley Davies's descriptions of the second and third versions.)

Fourth version. Early in 1894 Wells met W. E. Henley, editor of the *National Observer*. In response to Henley's invitation to him to contribute to that journal, Wells took up his time-travel story and extensively refurbished it. Wells noted in the "Preface' to volume I of the Atlantic Edition of his works: "A cleansing course of Swift and Sterne intervened before the idea was written again for Henley's *National Observer*." Henley may have asked him to write several *articles* on the subject of time-travel—that at least seems to be the implication of a letter Wells wrote to Morley Davies in March 1894 in which he speaks of "that old corpse of the Chronic Argo . . . being cut up into articles."[41] However, what Henley received and published was not a series of articles but a continuous narrative that bears significant resemblance to *The Time Machine* as it would appear in book form—though it is considerably shorter. This version of *The Time Machine* was serialized (unsigned) in seven issues of the *National Observer* during March through June 1894. It was terminated, unfinished, when Henley relinquished his editorship of the *National Observer*. Wells explains what occurred: Mr. Vincent, the new editor of that journal, "thought my articles queer wild ramblings and wound them up at once."[42]

The *National Observer Time Machine* goes beyond *The Chronic Argonauts* in providing an elaborate rationalization for time travel. In this version the Time Traveller describes his experiences in visiting the year 12,203 (not 802,701). He encounters the Eloi (who are not named) and the Morlocks (who are), but these degenerate subspecies have no contact with each another. There is no "Further Vision" of the world millions of years hence, but in the penultimate paragraph of the last episode the Time Traveller speculates on what might happen to the Earth after the extinction of man. For the reader with hindsight, the narrative seems pervaded with hints of later revisions—but it is also repeatedly interrupted by discussions of the Time Traveller's experiences. Indeed, his story seems to be recounted mainly to provide material for his skeptical and rather frivolous guests to comment on. Robert Philmus asserts that "Wells seems to have conceived the vision of the future in the *National Observer Time Machine* simply as an example appended to an argument against an unimaginative complacency which blinds man to the evolutionary prospects that may really await him."[43] (Appendix III is the text of this version of *The Time Machine*.)

Fifth version. Henley had encouraged Wells to develop his material, and when he took over the editorship of the *New Review* in December 1894, he proceeded to serialize yet another (this time complete) version of the story in five installments during January through May 1895. Wells received £100 for this expanded version of his story. In December 1894, he wrote his friend Elizabeth Healey: "You may be interested to know that our ancient *Chronic Argonauts* of the *Science Schools Journal* has at last become a complete story and will appear as a serial in the *New Review* for January. It's my trump card and if it does not come off very much I shall know my place for the rest of my career."[44]

Publication of this version of *The Time Machine* led to what were probably the earliest critical responses to Wells's prose fiction. Either W. T. Stead or Grant Richards declared in an unsigned critique published in the *Review of Reviews* (March 1895): "H. G. Wells, who is writing the serial in the *New Review*, is a man of genius. His invention of the Time Machine is good, but his description of the ultimate evolution of society . . . is gruesome and horrible to the last point. The story is not yet finished, but he has written enough to show that he has an imagination as gruesome as that of Poe."[45] Three months later the same journal described *The Time Machine* as "a very powerful story, which impresses the imagination more than anything of the kind since Richard Jefferies' marvellously powerful tale, *After London*."[46]

In retrospect we can see that the *New Review* text is even closer to the final (book) version than it is to the *National Observer* serialization. Philmus summarizes the contrasts between the fourth and fifth versions and the original book publication as follows: "If the principal defect of the *National Observer Time Machine* is the shapelessness and insubstantiality of the prophecy, that of the *New Review* is its failure to dramatize the contributory human causes of devolution. The [1895 book version published by] Heinemann . . . fuses the two serialized versions into a self-sufficient unity."[47] Nevertheless, the *New Review* text also contains material of considerable interest that does not show up in any other version. Two examples must suffice here. Embodied in the discussion of time travelling in chapter 1 ("The Inventor") are passages that appear to have been excerpted or adapted from "The Universe Rigid," an essay which Frank Harris had accepted for publication in his *Fortnightly Review* three years earlier and later rejected as "incomprehensible." Five paragraphs of chapter 13 ("The Further Vision") describe how the Time Traveller, arriving in a future far beyond 802,701, perceives creatures that look like rabbits or "some small breed of kangaroo" (evidently the descendants of the Eloi) being preyed upon by grotesque monsters resembling centipedes (apparently the descendants of the Morlocks). Bergonzi has published correspondence that suggests that this episode was added at Henley's suggestion and "as a result of the exigencies of serial publication."[48]

A vivid glimpse of Wells at work on this version is provided in *Experiment in Autobiography*: "I still remember writing that part of the story in which the *Time Traveller* returns to find his machine removed and his retreat cut off. I sat alone at the round table downstairs [at 23 Eardley Road, Sevenoaks] writing steadily in the luminous circle cast by a shaded paraffin lamp. Jane [who was to become Wells's second wife] had gone to bed and her mother had been ill all day. It was a very warm blue August night and the window was wide open. The best part of my mind fled through the story in a state of concentration before the Morlocks but some outlying regions of my brain were recording other things. . . . And outside in the summer night a voice went on and on, a feminine voice that rose and fell. It was Mrs.—I forget her name—our landlady in open rebellion . . . talking to a sympathetic neighbour in the next garden and talking through the window at me. I was aware of her and heeded her not, and she lacked the courage to beard me in my parlour. "Would I *never* go to bed? . . ." It went on and on. I wrote on grimly to that accompaniment. I wrote her out and she made her last comment with the front door well and truly slammed. I finished my chapter before I shut the window and blew out the lamp."[49]

(See Appendix IV for two excerpts from the *New Review Time Machine*.)

Sixth version: the Holt edition. The British edition of *The Time Machine* published by Heinemann in 1895 is often referred to as the first edition. In fact, it was not issued until 29 May 1895, whereas the American edition, published by Henry Holt and Co., was published on 7 May or earlier. The Holt version differs in a number of important respects and in numerous minor stylistic details from both the *New Review* text and the Heinemann version. For example, chapter 1 of the Holt text looks like a curious blend of passages from the *National Observer* and the *New Review* versions—although Philmus believes that the Holt text probably antedates the *New Review* version—and the *New Review* and Heinemann versions conclude with the memorable, poetic Epilogue, while the Holt text ends rather blandly with a terse account of what had become of the Time Traveller's guests during the period since his disappearance. (See Appendix V.) On the basis of textual collation, Bergonzi concludes: "there is a very strong probability that" the Holt version is "an early and un-revised version" of the *New Review* and Heinemann texts. "Wells may have virtually disowned the New York edition since it represented an unrevised text, and this may account for his subsequent silence about it."[50]

Seventh version. The Heinemann edition of 1895, the first British publication of *The Time Machine* in book form, is substantially the text that most readers today are familiar with. It was based primarily on the *New Review* version. Notable differences include (1) the opening of the first chapter which is based on the first *National Observer* article; (2) the omission of the "kangaroo" section noted above. As Philmus observes, the importance of this edition is that it "brings together in an aesthetic synthesis ideas that Wells had previously dealt with separately, by and large."[51]

The reviews of this edition ranged from guardedly positive to unre-servedly glowing. Richard Holt Hutton, in an unsigned review published in the *Spectator* (July 13, 1895), began by praising the book as "a very clever story"; but, as a critic with a strong Christian orientation, he felt constrained to denounce Wells's apparent indifference to religion and morality and to reject his speculations about the condition of man eight hundred thousand years hence. "We have no doubt that, so far as Mr. Wells goes, his warning is wise. But . . . we may expect with the utmost confidence that if the earth is still in existence in the year 802,701 A.D., either the A.D. will mean a great deal more than it means now, or else its inhabitants will be neither Eloi nor Morlocks. For in that case evil passions will by that time have led to the extinction of races spurred and pricked on by conscience and yet so frivolous or so malignant. Yet Mr. Wells's fanciful and lively dream is well worth reading, if only because it will draw attention to the great moral and religious factors in human nature which he appears to ignore."[52]

An unsigned review in the *Daily Chronicle* (27 July 1895) described *The Time Machine* as "a strikingly original performance" and the most "bizarre" work of fantasy since *The Strange Case of Dr. Jekyll and Mr. Hyde* (1886): "it grips the imagination as it is only gripped by genuinely imaginative work." The reviewer's only serious reservations concerned the 'machinery' of the story: "Wells . . . constantly forgets—or seems to forget—that his Traveller is journeying through *time*, and records effects which inevitably suggest travel through *space*."[53]

Novelist Israel Zangwill, in the *Pall Mall Gazette*, referred to Wells's story as a "brilliant little romance . . . a fine imaginative creation worthy of Swift, and possibly not devoid of satirical reference to 'the present discontents' . . . a vision far more sombre and impressive than the ancient imaginings of the Biblical seers." The only criticism he had to offer was that the "Time Traveller, a cool scientific thinker, behaves exactly like the hero of a commonplace sensational novel, with his frenzies of despair and his appeals to fate, when he finds himself in danger of having to remain in the year eight hundred and two thousand seven hundred and one . . . nor does it ever occur to him that in the aforesaid year he will have to repeat these painful experiences of his, else his vision of the future will have falsified itself. . . ."[54]

Eighth version. This is the text as it appears in volume I of the Atlantic Edition of the Works of H. G. Wells (1924). In a note prefacing this text, Wells mentions that he had come across a copy of *The Time Machine* "in which, somewhere [sic] about 1898 or 1899, he marked out a few modifications in arrangement and improvements in expression. Almost all these changes he has accepted, so that what the reader gets here is a revised definitive version a quarter of a century old."[55] The divergencies from the Heinemann edition are all minor.

The Atlantic edition provides the standard text of *The Time Machine* and is the version reprinted in this edition.

STRUCTURE

1. *Time Scheme.* The chronology of Wells's story is complicated and requires some explication. Hillyer, the Outer Narrator, is recounting the entire story three years after the events of chapters 2 and 12 (see the penultimate sentence of chapter 12). Chapter 1 occurs on a Thursday evening, exactly one week before chapter 2. Chapters 2 and 12 cover a single time period comprising the second Thursday evening (during which the Time Traveller gives his lengthy account of his journeys into the remote future) and the following day (when the Time Traveller disappears, possibly forever).

The Time Traveller, the Inner Narrator, starts his journeyings at 10:01 A.M. on the second Thursday morning [see opening of chapter 3]. He stops briefly at nearly 3:30 P.M. future time [see opening of chapter 3] before continuing on to 802,701 A.D. where he spends *eight days*. The chronology of his experiences in the future may be summarized thus:

Day One: The Time Traveller arrives in 802,701, sees the White Sphinx, and encounters the Eloi [chapters 3 and 4]. *Day Two*: His Time Machine disappears; he discovers some mysterious wells; at night he catches his first glimpse of a Morlock [chapter 5]. *Day Three*: He rescues Weena from drowning [chapter 5]. *Day Four*: In the morning he gets his first clear sight of a Morlock [chapter 5]. *Day Five*: Wandering south-west of Richmond, he observes the Palace of Green Porcelain in the distance [chapter 6]. *Day Six*: In the early morning he descends a well and discovers the world of the Morlocks. In the afternoon, accompanied by Weena, he heads for the Palace of Green Porcelain. They spend the night on a hillside [chapter 7]. *Day Seven*: At the Palace of Green Porcelain he discovers the decaying remains of books and arms himself with a lever and some matches. They pass the night in a forest, protected by a fire. The Morlocks attack. Weena disappears. Forest fire [chapter 9]. *Day Eight*: He returns to the White Sphinx. Just before sunset he finds the Time Machine and departs from 802,701 [chapter 10]. Thereafter he stops several times in the even more remote future. On a sloping beach at an unspecified but far distant time he sees "a thing like a huge white butterfly" and a "monstrous crab-like creature." He travels on a month and observes dozens more of these monsters. He moves on a hundred years and finds "the same crowd of earthy crustacea creeping in and out among the green weed and the red rocks." He travels on, "stopping ever and again, in great strides of a thousand years or more." More than thirty million years hence he witnesses "the old earth ebb away" and glimpses the last signs of life of earth ("a round thing, the size of football perhaps . . . tentacles trailed down from it") before returning to his own time [chapter 11].

He arrives back at "almost eight o'clock" on the second Thursday (see paragraph 5 of chapter 12). The very next day, after announcing his intention to return in half an hour with unassailable proof of time travel, he departs again (no one knows whither). Three years later he has still not returned, and Hillyer, the Outer Narrator, questions whether he will ever be seen again [chapter 12 and Epilogue].

2. *Plot*. Darko Suvin concisely describes the structure of *The Time Machine* as "a framework and three phantasmagoric evolutionary futures" which he names the "Eloi," the "crab," and the "eclipse" episodes.[56] These are indeed the main structural divisions, but it would be more precise to refer to them as "movements" or "segments" rather than episodes since each of these major structural divisions actually consists of a number of episodic sub-structures. The "Eloi" segment, for example, is composed of episodes of narrative action (providing the forward movements of the plot) alternating sporadically with episodes of physical description and episodes of interpretation (the Time Traveller's explanations of what he sees). The first five chapters present a series of unresolved episodes, provoking questions or problems for the Time Traveller (as well as the reader) whose "solutions" are deferred until later in the narrative. Thus the model Time Machine disappears (whither?); the Time Traveller suddenly appears before guests "in an amazing plight" (What has happened to him?); he journeys into the remote future (To what sort of world?); he encounters the Eloi (How can they be explained?); the Time Machine vanishes (Why? Who is responsible? How did it get inside the White Sphinx? What can be done about it?); the Time Traveller rescues

Weena from drowning (What sort of relationship will develop?); he catches
his first glimpses of the Morlocks (Who are they? What is their significance in the chain of events?).

Chapter 6 supplies the "hinge" or turning-point in this series of unresolved episodes. The climax of the chapter—the Time Traveller's experiences in the subterannean world of the Morlocks—is the first of a
series of *resolved* episodes. This terrifying adventure provides indubitable
explanations (as opposed to the Time Traveller's theories) of some of those
vexing questions raised earlier in the narrative. In particular, we now
know who must have stolen the Time Machine, and we suddenly understand the relationship of the Eloi and the Morlocks.

The "autonomous" episodes that follow recount the journey to the
Palace of Green Porcelain (chapter 7), the exploration of the Palace (8),
the conflict and fire in the woods (9), the finding of the Time Machine
and the escape from 802,701 (10). In these episodes, which collectively
form the second half of the "Eloi" segment, the interpretative material
diminishes—except for one passage at the start of chapter 10 where the
Time Traveller offers his final explanation of the world of the Eloi and
the Morlocks shortly before leaving it. Each of the two visions of the even
more remote future (chapter 11) is self-contained and predominantly descriptive with no significant interpretative passages. Wells is depicting
scenes rather than developing plot.

Suvin maintains that the "basic narrative rhythm" of *The Time Machine* is "characterized by growing pace and compression as the reader is
swept into the story, [and] the motivations and justifications [are] gradually dispensed with."[57] In the succession of the three episodes of the future
Suvin discerns "an exponentially regressing rhythm . . . [which] starts as
lento, with two sociobiological levels envisioned for 107 pages . . . continues as *presto*, with one biological level (mammal versus "amphibian")
and ends in abrupt *prestissimo* with four existential levels (land versus
sea animal; animal versus plant . . . organic existence versus sand, snow,
rocks, and sea; and existence of Earth versus eclipse) . . . within about
three pages."[58]

Some modification of this analysis seems necessary. We should distinguish first of all between rhythms that are developed to create narrative
effects and rhythms that underscore themes. Thematically the "Eloi"
segment is a *lento* movement, but its purely narrative rhythms are an
interplay of various tempi. In this connection the interpretative passages,
those "motivations and justifications" to which Suvin refers, actually
serve a double purpose: the Time Traveller's explanations of what he sees
frequently create suspense by interrupting the narrative. In chapter 5, for
example, we have a rapid succession of *presto* action-episodes (the Time
Machine disappears; the Time Traveller responds frantically to its disappearance; he discovers the mysterious "wells"; he rescues Weena from
drowning; he catches his first glimpses of the Morlocks). These episodes

are followed by a lengthy *lento* passage in which the Time Traveller speculates on the origins of the two species. As we noted earlier, in this part of the "Eloi" segment the successive action-episodes are deliberately left unresolved or unexplained or both. The effect on the reader is quite calculated. As the *lento* (interpretative) passage begins we are immediately torn between our desire to discover what happened next and our interest in determining what it all means. And Wells reinforces his intention of keeping us guessing and on the edge of our seats by opening chapter 6 with these words: "It may seem odd to you, but it was two days before I could follow up the new-found clue. . . ."

Suvin concludes his analysis by noticing that "telescoping and foreshortening" of the three visions of the future "powerfully contributes to and indeed shapes the effect of the logical or biological series."[59] This comment relates the pace of the three segments to the story's basic *themes*, an approach that leads Suvin to label the last two future visions as *presto* and *prestissimo*. But these terms do not accurately designate the pacing of the *narrative movement* in chapter 11 of *The Time Machine*. From the narrative standpoint both of the further visions are *lento* with variations, the first vision, building to the sinister advance of the crab, may be considered a *lento con moderato* (a relevant musical accompaniment would be the second movement of Vaughan Williams's *Symphony* no. 6) while the *lento* of the final vision of cosmic eclipse ends as a dying *pianissimo* (recalling the ineffable finale of the same symphony): "I saw the black central shadow of the eclipse sweeping towards me. In another moment the pale stars alone were visible. All else was rayless obscurity. . . ."

3. *Framework.* The Time Traveller's story is recounted within the context of an outer framing situation presented in chapters 1 and 2, the second half of 12, and the Epilogue. Crucial to a deeper understanding of *The Time Machine* is an awareness of the complex functions of this Chinese-box structure which Northrop Frye has described as the kind of "tale told in quotation marks." Frye observes that the effect of such a device is "to present the story through a relaxed and contemplative haze as something that entertains us without, so to speak, confronting us, as direct tragedy confronts us."[60] But the device has other effects and other functions.

Suvin has noticed how the "basic device of *The Time Machine* is an opposition of the Time Traveller's visions of the future to the ideal reader's norm of a complacent bourgeois class consciousness with its belief in linear progress. . . . The Victorian norm is set up in the framework of *The Time Machine* and supplemented by the Time Traveller's reactions."[61] But viewed from the (Huxleyan) evolutionary and cosmic perspective of the inner narrative, it is the frame situation with its display of blind complacency or bland indifference to the nightmarish future—and not the Time Traveller's story—that seems incredible. In other words, it is our civilization with its blinkered faith in the Advancement of Mankind (as represented in that "Victorian norm") which is set up to be viewed, through hindsight (and particularly from the standpoint of the story's Epilogue) as a "foolish heaping that must inevitably fall back upon and destroy its makers in the end."

Wells was not preaching to the converted: The typical original reader of *The Time Machine* was probably an incredulous bourgeois who would more easily have identified with the guests than with the Time Traveller. Keith Nettle explains how Wells attempts to overcome such incredulity in two phases: first, by using the tale-within-a-tale technique to tell that story to a fictional audience rather than directly to the reader; second, by using the fictional Outer Narrator and the other guests to anticipate and overcome the reader's potential disbelief. The "tale within a tale convention gives Wells several opportunities to make the Time Traveller's story seem more convincing. It enables him, for example, to make the Time Traveller insist upon telling his story without any doubts or objections (and therefore, implicitly, by his readers, too). . . . In the closing pages of the book several of the visitors again express incredulity . . . but Wells uses the [outer] narrator to state the lasting impression which the story leaves with the reader."[62]

The Time Traveller tells his listeners: "I cannot expect you to believe [my story] . . ." and he is right about most of his guests, but Hillyer, the Outer Narrator, tells us that his own "vast ignorance" of the future is "lit at a few casual places by the memory of his story." Of course, Wells wants his readers to suspend their disbelief while they are reading *The Time Machine*: hence the importance of the two opening chapters in providing validation for the fantastic inner narrative. This is achieved in two main ways: first, via the arguments for and against time-travel and the demonstration of the model Time Machine; second, via the "luxurious after-dinner atmosphere" (chapter 1)—which commentators have variously referred to as "complacent," "comfortable," "self-assured," "bourgeois," and "Dickensian."

Taken together, the arguments and the demonstration at the opening of the framework provide the most striking instance of that informed, pseudo-rationalization of the fantastic that is a recurrent technique of Wells's early fiction. Another notable example occurs in *The Invisible Man* (1897). Griffin, the hero of that novel, gives a fellow-scientist (Dr. Kemp) an apparently scientific explanation of the "theory" of invisibility and describes how he had made a cat invisible before trying the experiment on himself. Numerous folktales and legends had dealt with the theme of invisibility before *The Invisible Man*, but what made the novel's treatment of that topic uniquely different was that Wells gave the fantastic phenomenon an apparent scientific plausibility.

Wells himself explained his technique thus: "For the writer of fantastic stories to help the reader to play the game properly, he must help him in every possible unobtrusive way to *domesticate* the impossible hypothesis. He must trick him into an unwary concession to get some plausible assumption and get on with the story while the illusion holds. And that is where there was a slight novelty in my stories when they first appeared. Hitherto, except in exploration fantasies, the fantastic element was brought in by magic. . . . But by the end of the last century it had become difficult to squeeze even a momentary belief out of magic any longer. It occurred to me that . . . an ingenious use of scientific patter might with advantage be substituted. . . . I simply brought the fetish stuff up to date, and made it as near actual theory as possible. As soon as the magic trick has been done the whole business of the fantasy writers is to keep everything else human and real. Touches of prosaic detail are imperative and a rigorous adherence to the hypothesis. . . . So soon as the hypothesis is launched the whole interest becomes the interest of looking at human feelings and human ways, from the new angle that has been acquired."[63]

Yet another function of the framework is suggested at the opening of the first chapter. In the post-prandial atmosphere of coffee, brandy, and cigars, when (as Hillyer puts it) "thought runs free of the trammels of precision," there is a sense that almost any story, however fantastic, might seem *temporarily* plausible. This feeling is reiterated toward the end of the chapter where the Medical Man comments on the demonstration of the model Time Machine: "It sounds plausible enough tonight . . . but wait until tomorrow. Wait for the common sense of the morning." However, reliance on a plausibility that vanishes with the cigar smoke is not Wells's objective. He is after a different kind of credibility.

Throughout the framework, Wells concentrates on *undermining disbelief* rather than on creating plausibility. He does this in a variety of ways: *Emotional responses to reason.* Not one of the guests presents a convincing argument to counter the Time Traveller's exposition. They make jokes about it and indulge in petty name-calling. The Psychologist calls his ideas about time and time travel "wild extravagant theories"; the Medical Man contemptuously refers to the model Time Machine as "some sleight-of-hand trick" (even before he has seen it!); and the Editor dismisses the Time Traveller's story as a "gaudy lie." *Prejudiced judgments.* The Time Traveller's guests refuse to take him seriously because of his sense of humor. The Medical Man reminds everyone that he had played a practical joke on his guests the previous Christmas. Hillyer tells us: "The fact is, the Time Traveller was one of those men who are too clever to be believed . . . [he] had more than a touch of whim among his elements, and we distrusted him." But actually the most talkative guests are more frivolous than the Time Traveller. *Seriousness rejected by superficiality.* Except for Hillyer, the shallow thinking of the guests contrasts negatively with the profound issues raised by the Time Traveller. They listen to his story with rapt attention but consider it unworthy of

serious comment. *Unreasonable rejection of evidence.* The demonstration of the model Time Machine and the two flowers from the future are
promptly rejected even though none of the guests can satisfactorily account for them. *Non-expert opinion.* It is not an audience of fellow-sci-
entists or inventors that dismisses the Time Traveller's demonstration
and story. We may question his motives in choosing to demonstrate a
model that took him two years to make before such an audience and in
such a "non-scientific" environment—at the same time, we cannot consider his guests ideally qualified to judge the validity or significance of
the experiment.

Ultimately it is the framework that seals the "authenticity" of the
Time Traveller's story by revealing that it is being recollected three years
after the events of the opening chapter. By the Epilogue all the Outer
Narrator's initial doubts about time travel have been dispelled: he knows
now what the other guests did not know *then:* that the day after telling
his story the Time Traveller had disappeared—probably never to return.
The Outer Narrator has had a final conversation with him and has witnessed the second and last departure of the Time Machine (chapter 12).

No consideration of the framework of *The Time Machine* can afford
to ignore the actual role of the Outer Narrator, an aspect of the story that
has received close attention from Mark M. Hennelly, Jr. As Hennelly
notes, the Outer Narrator "does not simply narrate the tale . . . he is also
a character in it, one whose point of view naturally colors his narration,
whose sensibilities consequently transcend those of the caricatured and
wooden Dinner Guests, and who finally serves as a go-between, or me-
diator between the personalities of the Guests and the Time Traveller
and between the Time Traveller and the reader. In an important sense,
then, the Narrator is a surrogate for the reader. . . ."[64] Hennelly goes on
to remark, however, that despite the Outer Narrator's final editorializing,
the reader is left in an ambivalent position, "tempted either to believe
the Narrator's own ignorant yet guarded, optimistic prognosis for the
future or to accept the Traveller's ambiguous account of the 'unknown'."[65] The reader's difficulty is, in part, compounded by the fact that
we know so little about the personality through whose mind the entire
narrative is supposed to be filtered.

Biographically, the relationship between Hillyer and the Time Traveller can be compared in certain respects to that between Plato and Soc-
rates. In each case there is some identification between the shadowy
narrator and his "hero," but its full extent and precise nature remain
indefinable. The platonic parallel can, however, be extended further. Hillyer's sense of his own "inadequacy" in conveying the quality of the Time
Traveller's story (which was, in itself, a mere recollection of the real
experience) may be likened to the representation of man's imperfect perception of truth in the myth of the cave. Particularly relevant to this are
Hillyer's words in the Epilogue: "To me the future is still black and

blank—is a vast ignorance, lit at a few casual places by the memory of his story."

The analogies suggested here underscore the fact that the closing pages of *The Time Machine* shift the significance of the story onto a new level. In chapter 12 and the Epilogue first the Time Traveller and then Hillyer speak to higher levels of "truth" than any consideration of the veracity of either the tale or its teller. That higher level is the truth of fable, allegory, poetry, and vision to which the Time Traveller appeals in his impassioned speech to the guests: "No. I cannot expect you to believe it. Take it as a lie. Say I dreamed it in the workshop. Consider I have been speculating upon the destinies of our race until I have hatched this fiction. Treat my assertion of its truth as a *mere stroke of art* [italics mine] to enhance its interest. . . . Did I ever make a Time Machine, or a model of a Time Machine? Or is it all only a dream? They say life is a dream, a precious poor dream at times. . . . And where did the dream come from?"

The import of these words along with the other profound meanings of his story are symbolized finally in that unforgettable image of the poetic truth of the narrative with which the framework closes: two strange, shrivelled white flowers from a visionary but not impossible future.

THEMES AND INTERPRETATIONS

Wells develops five major themes in the course of the narrative. These themes and a spectrum of thematic interpretations will be the focus of this section.

Time travel. Wells makes time travel appear "scientific" by rationalizing its possibilities and by introducing the concept of a time *machine*. Time travel is, of course, a fundamental narrative device of *The Time Machine*—but it is also treated, for the first time in literature, as a phenomenon of intrinsic interest.

The Time Traveller speculates on the possible risks of time travel (he might blow himself and his apparatus "out of all possible dimensions—into the Unknown") and he describes "the peculiar sensations of time travelling" (it is simultaneously cinematic and sickening): see chapter 3, note 3. In comparison with innumerable later treatments of this theme by other writers, Wells's pre-Einsteinian conception of time travel does not involve any cause-and-effect time paradoxes. (The nearest he gets to this is a *space*-paradox short story, "The Remarkable Case of Davidson's Eyes" [1895], in which a character living in London suddenly discovers that he can see events happening in the Antipodes.)

Describing the experience of time travel also enables Wells to make a necessary but conveniently vague transition to the world of 802,701. In chapter 3 the Time Traveller catches tantalizing glimpses of progress ("huge buildings," "great and splendid architecture") and clear indications that man has conquered his environment ("I saw a richer green flow up the hillside and remain there without any wintry intermission.") Thereafter, time travel becomes the major device through which Wells is able to introduce the key themes of the narrative.

The repudiation of certain popular beliefs. "You must follow me carefully," says the Time Traveller to his guests at the start of chapter 1. "I shall have to controvert one or two ideas that are almost universally accepted." "One or two ideas" is an understatement. He begins by controverting Euclidean geometry and continues by questioning conventional conceptions of the nature of time. But the most serious challenge to his reactionary guests is the story he tells, which controverts two cherished Victorian beliefs: the conviction, on the one hand, that the present state of affairs is perfect and permanent, and the contradictory belief that man is proceeding along a path of infinite progress. However, the guests ignore his challenge. Not only do they avoid commenting on the story as a speculation upon "the destinies of our race," they even avoid discussing it as a story!

The inevitability and irresistible consequences of change. This theme is implicitly introduced as early as chapter 1. When the Medical Man insists that "you cannot move at all in Time, you cannot get away from the present moment," the Time Traveller retorts: "My dear sir, that is just where you are wrong. That is just where the whole world has gone wrong. We are always getting away from the present moment." The Time Traveller's words echo Thomas Henry Huxley's conviction that "the state of nature, at any time, is a temporary phase of a process of incessant change."[66] Like Huxley, Wells was convinced that man could not be permanently exempt from the process no matter how much he managed to subjugate nature. Hence in 802,701 the Time Traveller witnesses the irresistible erosion of what he believes had once been an "automatic civilization"; he speculates that "that perfect state had lacked one thing even for mechanical perfection—absolute permanency." In the more remote future he observes the same process of change irresistibly bringing about the extinction of man and the destruction of the solar system.

Speculations about the future. In chapters 3 through 10, the Time Traveller offers a succession of theories about what he observes in 802,701. Although he maintains that each of his theories eclipses the preceding one, each one actually *telescopes* into the next rather than cancelling it out, and (as will be seen in discussing interpretations) all the theories he advances may be viewed not only as speculations but also as Wellsian reactions to specific ideological cross-currents of the late nineteenth century.

The Time Traveller at first assumes that the beautiful but effete Eloi, their "physical slightness . . . their lack of intelligence and those abundant ruins," demonstrate the "fate of energy in security," that is, that all effort and purpose had become unnecessary when the human race had achieved a "perfect conquest of Nature." But he soon discards this theory as incorrect.

After his earliest encounters with the Morlocks he arrives at a second theory. The aristocratic-capitalist class (the Haves) and the working class (the Have-nots) must have evolved into two separate species: the former "armed with a perfected science and working to its logical conclusion the industrial system of today" had achieved not simply "a triumph over Nature but a triumph over Nature and the fellow-man." Above ground the Haves pursued "pleasure and comfort and beauty" and "had decayed to a mere beautiful futility" while below ground the Have-nots had increasingly "adapted to the conditions of their labour."

At length, following his descent into the underworld, the Time Traveller develops a third theory. He presumes that he has arrived at a turning-point in the relationship of the two degenerate species: "The Nemesis of the delicate ones was creeping on apace. Ages ago, thousands of generations ago, man had thrust his brother man out of the sunshine. And now that brother was coming back—changed!" He conjectures that "through the survival of an old habit of service" the Morlocks (the monstrous descendants of the Have-nots) continued to maintain the machinery and to provide for the basic needs of the Eloi (the weak and ineffectual descendants of the Haves). Whether all this is true or not, he does discover, to his horror, that the latter have become nothing more than fodder for the Morlocks. This discovery is one of the few certainties we are given about the world of 802,701, for the Time Traveller leaves that world without verifying any of his theories about it, commenting guardedly on his final speculation: "It may be as wrong an explanation as mortal wit could invent. It is how the thing shaped itself to me, and as that I give it to you."

Do we all go into the dark? Visions of a future "black and blank." Taken together the apocalyptic visions of chapter 11 and the (apparently) ambivalent words of the Epilogue convey the culminating theme of *The Time Machine*: That all that we know or can hope to know about what ultimately awaits the human race is either oblivion (the horror of the "great darkness") or almost total uncertainty ("a vast ignorance, lit at a few casual places by the memory of his story").

Published criticism has tended to follow rather clear-cut lines in interpreting the foregoing themes.

A Wellsian recoil from Victorian misoneism. This is Mark M. Hennelly, Jr.'s perception of *The Time Machine*, extrapolating from the Huxleyan theme of the inevitability of change. Noting that what all the character groupings in the work share is "the common flaw of *misoneism*—an obsessive hatred and fear of novelty and temporal change," Hennelly adds: "This taboo threat not only reappears throughout *The Time Machine*, but it is constantly enfleshed in the imagery and finally constitutes, of course, the tale's primary subject matter. As the Time Traveller learns, 'There is no intelligence where there is no change and no need of change'."[67]

A Marxian or anti-Marxian nightmare. Following Christopher Caudwell[68] many commentators have emphasized the Time Traveller's second and third speculations and read *The Time Machine* as a representation of Wells's view that social and evolutionary developments must inevitably invalidate the Marxian view of the future. A contrary view, expressed by Brian Aldiss, perceives *The Time Machine* as a quasi-Marxian treatment of the "great Victorian theme of the submerged nation, the hidden life awaiting the hour of its revenge."[69] Both interpretations have a degree of validity. The Morlocks are, presumably, descendants of the "submerged nation," but their devouring of the Eloi cannot be considered an act of conscious *revenge*. On the other hand, even though 802,701 is obviously not a fulfillment of the Marxian dream, the Time Traveller's speculations intimate that Marxian historical processes might well have contributed to the creation of that world.

Marx considered all history to be the history of class struggle. He believed that capitalists created their own class antagonists, the proletariat, by systematically exploiting and impoverishing the workers, and that this would eventually foment social revolution, leading to the overthrow of capitalism, and the global establishment of a classless society.

Clearly, this outcome of the class war is totally negated in *The Time Machine*. To better understand that negation we should notice that the Time Traveller suggests that two future-historical phases may have produced the Eloi and the Morlocks. The first is a phase in which the human race was separated "along lines of social stratification"; the second, a much longer phase during which the socially stratified classes (the Haves and the Have-nots) degenerated into two subspecies of humanity. Actually, it is only the first phase that directly controverts Marx's conception of the future—since Marx has nothing to say about man's eventual evolutionary development. Wells's different vision can be explained by his emphasis on Darwinian (or biological) rather than economic influences on class separation. His choice of vocabulary makes this patently evident. Thus, in chapter 5 The Time Traveller refers to the Workers "getting continually adapted" to labor conditions underground. In the same chapter, echoing the Darwinian idea of survival of the fittest, he theorizes that such of the workers "as were so constituted as to be miserable and rebellious would die; and, in the end, *the balance being permanent*, the survivors *would become as well adapted to the conditions* of underground life . . . as the Upper-world people were to theirs" (italics mine).

Now from Wells's Darwinian standpoint, survival of the fittest in such a situation would not necessarily point to the same outcome as the Marxian class struggle. *Both* classes could survive—each adapted to its own environment—and the descendants of the Have-nots would continue to maintain the descendants of the Haves in "their habitual needs, perhaps *through the survival of an old habit of service* . . . as a standing horse paws with his foot" (italics mine).

Finally, in place of the Marxian social revolution in which the expropriators would themselves be expropriated, Wells again envisions a Darwinian outcome. In 802,701, the struggle for survival focuses on the available supply of fresh meat. The Eloi are frugivorous (the creation of the "automatic civilization" had resulted in the extinction of animals) but the Morlocks are carnivorous (they are the descendants of workers who had needed as much strength as possible in toiling at the machines), and "when other meat failed them, the Morlocks had turned to what old habit had hitherto forbidden"—literally feeding on the descendants of those whose ancestors had only figuratively "devoured" the workers.

Through the Time Traveller, Wells does, of course, take sides. It might seem obvious for the Time Traveller to seek some common ground with the Morlocks—who at least share his interest in machinery, but as Bergonzi notices, his "gradual identification with the beautiful and aristocratic—if decadent—Eloi against the brutish Morlocks is indicative of Wells's own attitudes."[70] In this connection Bergonzi tellingly observes, "From his schooldays in Bromley . . . [Wells] had disliked and feared the working class in a way wholly inappropriate to the son of a small tradesman—as various Marxist critics have not been slow to remark."[71]

Wells's reaction to fin-de-siècle decadence. This approach underscores the Time Traveller's first theory. Just as the Morlocks have been interpreted as extrapolations of Wells's latent fear of the proletariat, so some critics, from Bergonzi onward, have seen the Eloi as embodiments of his contempt for certain ideals of the late nineteenth-century Aesthetic Movement. (Indeed, Bergonzi goes further, seeing in the opposition of the Eloi and the Morlocks not only the reflection of an opposition between aestheticism and utilitarianism but also "an opposition between . . . pastoralism and technology, contemplation and action, and ultimately, and least specifically, between beauty and ugliness, and light and darkness.")[72]

The Aesthetic Movement originated in France, but Wells would have been most familiar with its British manifestations in *The Yellow Book*, the drawings of Aubrey Beardsley, and the writings of Walter Pater and Oscar Wilde. Wells's hostility to the Aesthetes focused not on what Roger Shattuck has called "their preoccupation with vice and unnaturalness" but on their championing of artificiality and refinement of style at the expense of moral or utilitarian objectives (a philosophy summed up in the slogan "Art for art's sake"), and on their idealization of self-indulgence, sensuousness, eroticism, and languor. Wilde himself was rather gently satirized by Gilbert and Sullivan in *Patience* (1881). But the hothouse world of 802,701, with its "Dresden-china" Eloi depending mindlessly on the "service" of the Morlocks and its decaying Palace of Green Porcelain (housing a rotting library of "useful" knowledge), embodies a savage parody of the life-style implied in Wilde's flippant wish that he could live up to the quality of his china and by the famous words of Villiers de L'Isle-Adam: "Live? Our servants can do that for us."

Several passages of *The Time Machine* actually point to the Aesthetes as Wells's specific targets. The first Eloi to be described (end of chapter 3) is "a very beautiful and graceful creature, but indescribably frail" (cf. Des Esseintes, the aesthete-hero of Huysman's *Against the Grain*), and his flushed face reminds the Time Traveller of "the more beautiful kind of consumptive—that hectic beauty of which we used to hear so much" (the vocabulary echoes both Wilde's *The Picture of Dorian Gray* [1891] and contemporary descriptions of Aubrey Beardsley). In chapter 4, after detailing the androgyny, indolence, frivolity, and childish lack of interest displayed by the Eloi (critiques sometimes levelled against the Aesthetes), the Time Traveller launches into a (Wellsian) moral denunciation that is clearly directed at the Aesthetic Movement: "Under the new conditions of perfect comfort and security, that restless energy, that with us is strength, would become weakness. . . . I saw . . . the outcome of the last surgings of the now purposeless energy of mankind before it settled down into perfect harmony with the conditions under which it lived. . . . This has ever been the fate of energy in security; it takes to art and to eroticism, and then comes languor and decay." In short, the Time Traveller's speculation points to the *fin du globe* nightmare as a direct outcome of *fin de siècle* decadence.

A vision of the phenomena of retrogressive metamorphosis. The term is T. H. Huxley's in the "Prolegomena" to *Evolution and Ethics*, and he defines it as "progress from a condition of relative complexity to one of relative uniformity."[73] The relevance of the concept to *The Time Machine* has received particularly close attention from Darko Suvin in his *Metamorphoses of Science Fiction*. Suvin asks: "What if one were to take . . . literally [Huxley's] . . . sense of uneasiness about evolution and progress versus devolution and regress seriously . . . ? All that would be needed is to . . . imagine a canonic sociobiological "converging series of forms of gradually diminishing complexity" [quoting Huxley] unfolding as a devolution that retraverses the path of evolution backward to a *fin du globe*. That is what Huxley's heretical student did in *The Time Machine*. . . ."[74] Suvin examines Wells's extrapolations from Huxley first by representing diagrammatically the past, *evolutionary* phylogeny of life on earth and then by exploring its extensions in an elaborate and complex discussion of the phylogeny of future, *devolutionary* life-forms suggested in *The Time Machine*. Turning to the Eloi-Morlock chapters in particular, he observes: "The Time Traveller cannot be simply a representative Man, since he is faced with creatures that are maybe no longer *Homo sapiens*, but are certainly other races or species of the genus *Homo* (say *Homo eloii* and *Homo morlockius*). . . . the Time Traveller occupies an intermediate position between the two new species, a position isotopic with the position of the petty bourgeois Wells disdainful of a decadent upper class but horrifed and repelled by a crude lower class. . . . "[75]

A future black and blank: interpreting the final "message." Two critics provide particularly provocative commentaries on the closing pages of *The Time Machine*. Philmus maintains that "the Time Traveller himself does not appear to be wholly cognizant of the implications of his theories. If his etiology is correct, the cause of the degeneration he discovers exists in the present. Therefore, the burden of what he calls 'moral education' remains here and now; and his return to the world of 802,701 would appear to be either a romantic evasion . . . or a pessimistic retreat from a world 'that must inevitably fall back upon and destroy its makers.' "[76]

We must call into question Philmus's assumption that the Time Traveller returns to 802,701 as well as the conclusions he draws therefrom. The first paragraph of the Epilogue indicates that Hillyer is quite uncertain whither and how the Time Traveller disappeared. Just before his disappearance, the Time Traveller has equipped himself with a small camera and a knapsack, and he tells Hillyer: " 'I only want half an hour. . . . If you'll stop to lunch I'll prove to you this time travelling up to the hilt, specimen and all.' " Presumably if he *had* returned, as he intended, he would have assumed the burden of "moral education" which, unwittingly, he imparts to Hillyer. Certainly the Time Traveller's words are not those of a man planning either "a romantic evasion" or a "pessimistic retreat" from his own age.

By contrast, Frank McConnell examines the vexed contrast in the Epilogue between the Time Traveller's assertion of cosmic futility and Hillyer's words of comfort. He notes that readers are inclined to interpret those final words as "an exercise in fatuity, a falsely comforting conclusion to a book whose *real* conclusion is the Time Traveller's preceding vision of the end of the world in darkness and meaninglessness." McConnell counters this notion, arguing that the ending is deliberately ambiguous because Wells intends each reader to respond according to his/ her own pessimistic or optimistic outlook. "Wells *wants* the future to remain, however threatening or despairing aspects of it may appear, fundamentally 'black and blank'—black *and* white, that is, depending on the state of mind or soul with which we behold it. The two voices of *The Time Machine*, in other words, encapsulate between them that elementary tension between cosmic determinism and freedom of the will that we have seen at the heart of all speculation about the future of mankind."[77]

But if, as McConnell believes, Wells himself *wanted* the future to remain "black and blank" then we must indeed regard Hillyer as the one who provides the "real conclusion" to *The Time Machine*—since it is, after all, Hillyer and not the Time Traveller who views the future as "black and blank."

My own reading of the Epilogue offers an alternative to McConnell's interpretation. In *The Playwright as Thinker* Eric Bentley maintains that, as a vitalist, Bernard Shaw was a pessimist in the short run and an optimist in the long one. GBS cherished little or no faith in the capacity of man to solve his immediate political and economic problems. He did, however, believe that evolution was on the side of man or his successor, the Super- man. *Back to Methuselah*, Shaw's vision of the ultimate future, concludes with the words: "Of life only is there no end." By contrast, Wells could be described as an optimist in the short run and a pessimist in the long one: The optimist was dedicated to the Advancement of Mankind; the pessimist envisioned degeneration, catastrophe, or the cosmic process resulting in the inevitable doom of the human race.

This "philosophy" is quite evident in the closing pages of *The Time Machine*. Hillyer asserts that even if the Time Traveller's vision is true, "it remains for us to *live* as though it were not so" (italics mine). The Time Traveller, on the other hand, *knows* that his vision is true, yet it is his stated intention to return to his own time, presumably to undertake the moral education of his contemporaries. In brief, both men are dedi- cated to the potentials of mankind despite their doubts or certainties about the fate of the human race.

That this was also Wells's own conviction—and the ultimate message of *The Time Machine*—is clear from a letter he wrote to the *British Weekly*, 26 June 1939: "What," he asked, "have my books been from *The Time Machine* to *World Brain* and my *Fate of Homo Sapiens* (now in the press) but the clearest insistence on the insecurity of progress and the possibility of human degeneration and extinction? I think the odds are against man, but it is still worth fighting against them."[78]

NOTES

1. A brief account of Wells's creative work before *The Time Machine* appears in Bergonzi (1961, 24–25). See also Philmus and Hughes (1975) and Hughes and Philmus (1973, 98–114).

2. Wells uses this term in his preface to *Seven Famous Novels* (1934, ix). The British edition (London: Victor Gollancz, 1933) is actually titled *The Sci- entific Romances of H. G. Wells*.

In *Experiment in Autobiography* (1934, 172), Wells refers to *The Time Ma- chine* as "my first scientific fantasia"; elsewhere he speaks of it as "fiction of prophecy."

3. Robert Scholes and Eric S. Rabkin (1977, 19) note that "Wells took the notion of time travel, which had been very popular since [Edward Bellamy's] *Looking Backward*, and put it on a 'mechanical' basis. The importance of this is not in the vague, pseudoscientific rationale he provided for the time machine in his novel, but in the fact that it *was* a machine, which could move through time

under the control of its operator. The replacement of the dream, enchantment, mesmerization, hibernation or other method of reaching the future by a new mechanical agent, a time *machine*, changed the whole footing of time travel, opening up the past as well as the future, for imaginative investigation."

It is widely and erroneously believed that Wells invented the time-travel story. Earlier examples of time-travel literature include: (1) L. S. Mercier's *L'An Deux Mille Quatre Cent Quarante* (1771) in which a sleeper from the 18th century wakes up to find himself in a 25th-century Utopia. (2) Johan Herman Wessel's [Norwegian] *Anno 7603* (1781), a comedy in which a fairy takes two lovers into the distant future. (3) Washington Irving's "Rip Van Winkle" (1819). (4) Mary Griffith's "Three Hundred Years Hence" (1836) in which the hero, sealed in his chamber by an avalanche, is revived three centuries later. (5) "Missing One's Coach" [author anonymous], published in the *Dublin Literary Magazine* (1838), whose hero-narrator wanders into a time-warp and emerges a thousand years earlier during the era of the Venerable Bede. (6) Edgar Allan Poe's "A Tale of the Ragged Mountains" (1843). (7) Charles Dickens's *A Christmas Carol* (1843). (8) Edward Page Mitchell's *An Uncommon Sort of Spectre* (1879), in which a ghost from forty years on visits his father in the present. (9) Page Mitchell's "The Clock That Went Backwards," *The Sun* (New York), 18 September 1881: possibly the earliest story to deal with time paradoxes and a "time machine." (10) Robert Duncan Milne's "A Mysterious Twilight" (1885), a story about an experiment with electricity that results in the merging of separate time streams. (11) Camille Flammarion's *Lumen* (1887), perhaps the first work of fiction to deal with time reversal. (12) W. H. Hudson's *A Crystal Age* (1887). (13) Edward Bellamy's *Looking Backwards* (1888). (14) Mark Twain's *A Connecticut Yankee in King Arthur's Court* (1889). (15) William Morris's *News from Nowhere* (1890). (16) F. Anstey's *The Time Bargain* aka *Tourmalin's Time Cheques* (1891), a novel about a young man who receives time "credits" that allow him to time-travel at will. (17) J. H. Rosnyainé's "Another World" (1895), a tale of the Fourth Dimension.

Since the previous paragraph was first written, three more examples of time-travel literature earlier than Wells's have come to my attention. They are: Restif de la Bretonne's *Les Posthumes* (1802), a novel whose hero travels into the future; Eugene Mouton's "L'historioscope" (1883), a story about a machine that can see into the past; and Albert Robida's "Jadis chez aujourd'hui" (1890), a short story about time travel.

4. Another notable scientific speculation on this theme, Camille Flammarion's *La Fin du Monde* (1893–94), in English as *Omega: the Last Days of the World* (1894), was written either slightly earlier than or exactly contemporaneously with *The Time Machine*. See further chapter 5, note 23 and chapter 11, note 24.

5. See J. O. Bailey (1972, 81). (Bailey's book was first published by Argus Books, New York, 1947.)

Frank McConnell (1981,88) comments: "*The Time Machine* ... works as marvelously as it does as entertainment precisely because of the seriousness and complexity of the intellectual contradictions it incorporates."

6. Carl Rogers, "Towards a Theory of Creativity," in Harold H. Anderson, ed., *Creativity and its Cultivation* (New York: Harper and Brothers, 1959), 71.

7. Alex Eisenstein (1972, 125).

8. Wells, *Experiment*, 21–107.

9. Eisenstein (1972, 119).

10. Anthony West (1984, 226).

11. The work ran through many editions and it is impossible to say for certain which edition Wells saw. The 1861 reprint, the one he may well have dipped into, contained 330 engravings of animals.

12. Wells, *Experiment*, 54.

13. Eisenstein (1972, 123).

14. Like Wood's *Natural History*, Sturm's work also ran through many editions and there is no way of knowing which edition was owned by Sarah Wells, H.G.W.'s mother. Wells's memory may have failed him as far as this book was concerned. None of the copies I have consulted contains a picture of the devil, etc. But one engraving that appears in many editions depicts the nude figure of a wicked man recoiling in terror from the wrath of God, represented by a lightning-bolt.

15. Wells, *Experiment*, 29.

16. Ibid., 58.

17. Ibid., 22.

18. Bergonzi (1961, 56).

19. Norman and Jeanne Mackenzie (1973, 24).

20. Ibid., 38–39.

21. Wells, *Experiment*, 253–54. In the preface to volume 1 of the Atlantic edition of his works, Wells states that *The Chronic Argonauts*, the first version of *The Time Machine*, was "written obviously under the influence of Hawthorne and smeared with that miscellaneous allusiveness that Carlyle and many other of the great Victorians had made the fashion."

22. See Bergonzi (l961, 30–31).

23. Wells, *Seven Famous Novels*, viii.

24. On the possible influence of *The Coming Race* on *The Time Machine* see chapter 7, note 4 and Haight (1958, 325).

Brian Aldiss (1975, 125) perceptively remarks of the Morlocks that their *"vril* is flesh of Eloi"* (vril* being the beneficent force of the super-race in Bulwer-Lytton's novel).

Wells was probably familiar with Jules Verne's *Voyage au Centre de la Terre* (1864). Who was not? And he may also have been acquainted with some of the many other works about subterranean worlds published prior to (or contemporaneously with) *The Time Machine*. Among these (aside from Dante) were Ludwig Holberg's *The Journey of Niels Klim to the World Underground* (1741), Adam Seaborn's *Symzonia: A Voyage of Discovery* (1820), Mrs. J. Wood's *Pantaletta: A Romance of Sheheland* (1882), William R. Bradshaw's *The Goddess of Atvatabar* (1892), Will N. Harben's *Land of the Changing Sun* (1894), and John Uri Lloyd's *Etidorpha* (1895). We *do* know that Wells was familiar with Gabriel De Tarde's *Fragment d'Histoire Future* (1884): indeed he wrote a preface to *Underground Man* (1905), the first English translation of that work; but it is unclear whether he had already read De Tarde before writing *The Time Machine*.

On the literature of underground worlds see further L. Thomas Williams, *Journeys to the Center of the Earth: Descent and Initiation in Selected Science Fiction*, Ph.D. dissertation, Indiana University-Bloomington, 1983.

25. Wells, *Experiment*, 250.

26. Wells *does* refer to *Frankenstein* in his preface to *Seven Famous Novels*, viii.

27. See chapter 1, note 1.

28. Wells, *Experiment*, 172.

29. Bergonzi (1961, 30–31).

30. Wells, *Experiment*, 161.

31. Wells, *Seven Famous Novels*, ix.

32. Thomas Henry Huxley, "The Struggle for Existence in Human Society," in Huxley's *Evolution and Ethics and Other Essays* (New York: Greenwood Press, 1968), 199.

33. Huxley (1968, 85).

34. Mackenzie (1973, 57).

35. The term is taken from the title of an article by Mark R. Hillegas (1961, 655–63).

36. Wells quoted in David C. Smith, *H. G. Wells Desperately Mortal* (New Haven & London: Yale University Press, 1986), 48.

37. Wells, *Experiment*, 253.

38. Bergonzi (1960, 42).

39. Geoffrey West (1930, 291–92).

40. Bergonzi (1960, 42).

41. Bergonzi (1961, 40).

42. Wells, *Experiment*, 435.

43. Philmus (1976, 24).

44. Quoted in Geoffrey West (1930, 102).

45. The complete review is published in Patrick Parrinder (1972, 33). On Wells's debt to W. T. Stead, see J. D. Boylen, "W. T. Stead and the Early Career of H. G. Wells, 1895–1911," *Huntington Library Quarterly*, 32, no. 1 (Nov. 1974), 53–79.

46. Quoted in the New York edition of *Review of Reviews* (June 1895), 701–702.

47. Philmus (1976, 28).

48. Bergonzi (1960, 44–45).

49. Wells, *Experiment*, 436–37.

50. Bergonzi (1960, 49, 51).

51. Philmus (1976, 28).

52. See further Parrinder (1972, 34–37).

53. See further Parrinder (1972, 38–39).

54. See further Parrinder (1972, 40–41) and chapter 1, note 30.

55. Wells, "Preface to Volume I," *The Time Machine, The Wonderful Visit and Other Stories*, Atlantic Edition of the Works of H. G. Wells (New York: Charles Scribner's Sons, 1924), xxii.

56. Darko Suvin (1979, 231).

57. Ibid.

58. Suvin (1979, 232).

59. Ibid.

60. See further Northrop Frye, *Anatomy of Criticism* (Princeton: Princeton University Press, 1957), 202–203.

61. Suvin (1979, 223).

62. See Introduction to Keith Nettle (1966, *passim*).

63. Wells, *Seven Famous Novels*, viii.

64. Mark M. Hennelly, Jr. (1979, 157).

65. Ibid.

66. Huxley (1968, 5).

67. Hennelly (1979, 159).

68. See the essay on Wells in Caudwell's *Studies in a Dying Culture* (1938).

69. See further Brian Aldiss (1975, 108–109).

70. Bergonzi (1961, 56).

71. Ibid.

72. Bergonzi (1961, 61).

73. Huxley (1968, 6).

74. Suvin (1979, 225).

75. Suvin (1979, 239–240).

76. Philmus (1969, 534).

77. McConnell (1981, 87–88).

78. Quoted in Mackenzie (1973, 420).

The original Morlock: the picture in J. G. Wood's
Illustrated Natural History (1872) that terrified
Wells when he was eight. In Wood's book the picture
is captioned: GORILLA.—*Troglodytes Gorilla*,a
manifest association of underground (or cave) man
and ape.

H. G. WELLS:

The Time Machine

(Text of the Atlantic Edition, 1924)

The Time Machine

§ 1

The Time Traveller (for so it will be convenient to speak of him) was expounding a recondite matter to us. His grey eyes shone and twinkled, and his usually pale face was flushed and animated. The fire burned brightly, and the soft radiance of the incandescent lights in the lilies of silver caught the bubbles that flashed and passed in our glasses. Our chairs, being his patents, embraced and caressed us rather than submitted to be sat upon, and there was that luxurious after-dinner atmosphere when thought runs gracefully free of the trammels of precision. And he put it to us in this way—marking the points with a lean forefinger—as we sat and lazily admired his earnestness over this new paradox (as we thought it) and his fecundity.

"You must follow me carefully. I shall have to controvert one or two ideas that are almost universally accepted. The geometry, for instance, they taught you at school is founded on a misconception."

"Is not that rather a large thing to expect us to begin upon?" said Filby, an argumentative person with red hair.

"I do not mean to ask you to accept anything without reasonable ground for it. You will soon admit as much as I need from you. You know of course that a mathematical line, a line of thickness *nil*, has no real existence. They taught you that? Neither has a mathematical plane. These things are mere abstractions."

"That is all right," said the Psychologist.

"Nor, having only length, breadth, and thickness, can a cube have a real existence."

"There I object," said Filby. "Of course a solid body may exist. All real things——"

"So most people think. But wait a moment. Can an *instantaneous* cube exist?"

"Don't follow you," said Filby.

"Can a cube that does not last for any time at all, have a real existence?"

Filby became pensive. "Clearly," the Time Traveller proceeded, "any real body must have extension in *four* directions: it must have Length, Breadth, Thickness, and—Duration. But through a natural infirmity of the flesh, which I will explain to you in a moment, we incline to overlook this fact. There are really four dimensions, three which we call the three planes of Space, and a fourth, Time. There is, however, a tendency to draw an unreal distinction between the former three dimensions and the latter, because it happens that our consciousness moves intermittently in one direction along the latter from the beginning to the end of our lives."

"That," said a very young man, making spasmodic efforts to relight his cigar over the lamp; "that . . . very clear indeed."

"Now, it is very remarkable that this is so extensively overlooked," continued the Time Traveller, with a slight accession of cheerfulness. "Really this is what is meant by the Fourth Dimension, though some people who talk about the Fourth Dimension do not know they mean it. It is only another way of looking at Time. *There is no difference between Time and any of the three dimensions of Space except that our consciousness moves along it.* But some foolish people have got hold of the wrong side of that idea. You have all heard what they have to say about this Fourth Dimension?

"*I* have not," said the Provincial Mayor.

"It is simply this. That Space, as our mathematicians have it, is spoken of as having three dimensions, which one may call Length, Breadth, and Thickness, and is always definable by reference to three planes, each at right angles to the others. But some philosophical people have been asking why *three* dimensions particularly—why not another direction at right angles to the other three?—and have even tried to construct a Four-Dimensional geometry. Professor Simon Newcomb was expounding this to the New York Mathematical Society only a month or so ago. You know how on a flat surface, which has only two dimensions, we can represent a figure of a three-dimensional solid, and similarly they think that by models of three dimensions they could represent one of four—if they could master the perspective of the thing. See?"

"I think so," murmured the Provincial Mayor; and, knitting his brows, he lapsed into an introspective state, his lips moving as one who repeats mystic words. "Yes, I think I see it now," he said after some time, brightening in a quite transitory manner.

"Well, I do not mind telling you I have been at work upon this geometry of Four Dimensions for some time. Some of my results are curious. For instance, here is a portrait of a man at eight years old, another at fifteen, another at seventeen, another at twenty-three, and so on. All these are evidently sections, as it were, Three-Dimensional representations of his Four-Dimensioned being, which is a fixed and unalterable thing.

"Scientific people," proceeded the Time Traveller, after the pause required for the proper assimilation of this, "know very well that Time is only a kind of Space. Here is a popular scientific diagram, a weather record. This line I trace with my finger shows the movement of the barometer. Yesterday it was so high, yesterday night it fell, then this morning it rose again, and so gently upward to here. Surely the mercury did not trace this line in any of the dimensions of Space generally recognised? But certainly it traced such a line, and that line, therefore, we must conclude was along the Time-Dimension."

"But," said the Medical Man, staring hard at a coal in the fire, "if Time is really only a fourth dimension of Space, why is it, and why has it always been, regarded as something different? And why cannot we move about in Time as we move about in the other dimensions of Space?"

The Time Traveller smiled. "Are you so sure we can move freely in Space? Right and left we can go, backward and forward freely enough, and men always have done so. I admit we move freely in two dimensions. But how about up and down? Gravitation limits us there."

"Not exactly," said the Medical Man. "There are balloons."

"But before the balloons, save for spasmodic jumping and the inequalities of the surface, man had no freedom of vertical movement."

"Still they could move a little up and down," said the Medical Man.

"Easier, far easier down than up."

"And you cannot move at all in Time, you cannot get away from the present moment."

"My dear sir, that is just where you are wrong. That is just where the whole world has gone wrong. We are always getting away from the present moment. Our mental existences, which are immaterial and have no dimensions, are passing along the Time-Dimension with a uniform velocity from the cradle to the grave. Just as we should travel *down* if we began our existence fifty miles above the earth's surface."

"But the great difficulty is this," interrupted the Psychologist. "You *can* move about in all directions of Space, but you cannot move about in Time."

"That is the germ of my great discovery. But you are wrong to say that we cannot move about in Time. For instance, if I am recalling an incident very vividly I go back to the instant of its occurrence: I become absent-minded, as you say. I jump back for a moment. Of course we have no means of staying back for any length of time, any more than a savage or an animal has of staying six feet above the ground. But a civilised man is better off than the savage in this respect. He can go up against gravitation in a balloon, and why should he not hope that ultimately he may be able to stop or accelerate his drift along the Time-Dimension, or even turn about and travel the other way?"

"Oh, *this*," began Filby, "is all———"

"Why not?" said the Time Traveller.

"It's against reason," said Filby.

"What reason?" said the Time Traveller.

"You can show black is white by argument," said Filby, "but you will never convince me."

"Possibly not," said the Time Traveller. "But now you begin to see the object of my investigations into the geometry of Four Dimensions. Long ago I had a vague inkling of a machine———"

"To travel through Time!" exclaimed the Very Young Man.

"That shall travel indifferently in any direction of Space and Time, as the driver determines."

Filby contented himself with laughter.

"But I have experimental verification," said the Time Traveller.

"It would be remarkably convenient for the historian," the Psychologist suggested. "One might travel back and verify the accepted account of the Battle of Hastings, for instance!"

"Don't you think you would attract attention?" said the Medical Man. Our ancestors had no great tolerance for anachronisms."

"One might get one's Greek from the very lips of Homer and Plato," the Very Young Man thought.

"In which case they would certainly plough you for the Little-go. The German scholars have improved Greek so much."

"Then there is the future," said the Very Young Man. "Just think! One might invest all one's money, leave it to accumulate at interest, and hurry on ahead!"

"To discover a society," said I, "erected on a strictly communistic basis."

"Of all the wild extravagant theories!" began the Psychologist.

"Yes, so it seemed to me, and so I never talked of it until———"

"Experimental verification!" cried I. "You are going to verify *that*?"

"The experiment!" cried Filby, who was getting brain-weary.

"Let's see your experiment anyhow," said the Psychologist, "though it's all humbug, you know."

The Time Traveller smiled round at us. Then, still smiling faintly, and with his hands deep in his trousers pockets, he walked slowly out of the room, and we heard his slippers shuffling down the long passage to his laboratory.

The Psychologist looked at us. "I wonder what he's got?"

"Some sleight-of-hand trick or other," said the Medical Man, and Filby tried to tell us about a conjurer he had seen at Burslem; but before he had finished his preface the Time Traveller came back, and Filby's anecdote collapsed.

The thing the Time Traveller held in his hand was a glittering metallic framework, scarcely larger than a small clock, and very delicately made. There was ivory in it, and some transparent crystalline substance. And now I must be explicit, for this that follows—unless his explanation is to be accepted—is an absolutely unaccountable thing. He took one of the small octagonal tables that were scattered about the room, and set it in front of the fire, with two legs on the hearth rug. On this table he placed the mechanism. Then he drew up a chair, and sat down. The only other object on the table was a small shaded lamp, the bright light of which fell full upon the model. There were also perhaps a dozen candles about, two in brass candlesticks upon the mantel and several in sconces, so that the room was brilliantly illuminated. I sat in a low armchair nearest the fire, and I drew this forward so as to be almost between the Time Traveller and the fireplace. Filby sat behind him, looking over his shoulder. The Medical Man and the Provincial Mayor watched him in profile from the right, the Psychologist from the left. The Very Young Man stood behind the Psychologist. We were all on the alert. It appears incredible to me that any kind of trick, however subtly conceived and however adroitly done, could have been played upon us under these conditions.

The Time Traveller looked at us, and then at the mechanism. "Well?" said the Psychologist.

"This little affair," said the Time Traveller, resting his elbows upon the table and pressing his hands together above the apparatus, "is only a model. It is my plan for a machine to travel through time. You will notice that it looks singularly askew, and that there is an odd twinkling appearance about this bar, as though it was in some way unreal." He pointed to the part with his finger. "Also, here is one little white lever, and here is another."

The Medical Man got up out of his chair and peered into the thing. "It's beautifully made," he said.

"It took two years to make," retorted the Time Traveller. Then, when we had all imitated the action of the Medical Man, he said: "Now I want you clearly to understand that this lever, being pressed over, sends the machine gliding into the future, and this other reverses the motion. This saddle represents the seat of a time traveller. Presently I am going to press the lever, and off the machine will go. It will vanish, pass into future Time, and disappear. Have a good look at the thing. Look at the table too, and satisfy yourselves there is no trickery. I don't want to waste this model, and then be told I'm a quack."

There was a minute's pause perhaps. The Psychologist seemed about to speak to me, but changed his mind. Then the Time Traveller put forth his finger towards the lever. "No," he said suddenly. "Lend me your hand." And turning to the Psychologist, he took that individual's hand in his own and told him to put out his forefinger. So that it was the Psychologist himself who sent forth the model Time Machine on its interminable voyage. We all saw the lever turn. I am absolutely certain there was no trickery. There was a breath of wind, and the lamp flame jumped. One of the candles on the mantel was blown out, and the little machine suddenly swung round, became indistinct, was seen as a ghost for a second perhaps, as an eddy of faintly glittering brass and ivory; and it was gone—vanished! Save for the lamp the table was bare.

Every one was silent for a minute. Then Filby said he was damned.

The Psychologist recovered from his stupor, and suddenly looked under the table. At that the Time Traveller laughed cheerfully. "Well?" he said, with a reminiscence of the Psychologist. Then, getting up, he went to the tobacco jar on the mantel, and with his back to us began to fill his pipe.

We stared at each other. "Look here," said the Medical Man, "are you in earnest about this? Do you seriously believe that that machine has travelled into time?"

"Certainly," said the Time Traveller, stooping to light a spill at the fire. Then he turned, lighting his pipe, to look at the Psychologist's face. (The Psychologist, to show that he was not unhinged, helped himself to a cigar and tried to light it uncut.) "What is more, I have a big machine nearly finished in there" —he indicated the laboratory—"and when that is put together I mean to have a journey on my own account."

"You mean to say that that machine has travelled into the future?" said Filby.

"Into the future or the past—I don't, for certain, know which."

After an interval the Psychologist had an inspiration. "It must have gone into the past if it has gone anywhere," he said.

"Why?" said the Time Traveller.

"Because I presume that it has not moved in space, and if it travelled into the future it would still be here all this time, since it must have travelled through this time."

"But," said I, "if it travelled into the past it would have been visible when we came first into this room; and last Thursday when we were here; and the Thursday before that; and so forth!"

"Serious objections," remarked the Provincial Mayor, with an air of impartiality, turning towards the Time Traveller.

"Not a bit," said the Time Traveller, and, to the Psychologist: "You think. *You* can explain that. It's presentation below the threshold, you know, diluted presentation."

"Of course," said the Psychologist, and reassured us. "That's a simple point of psychology. I should have thought of it. It's plain enough, and helps the paradox delightfully. We cannot see it, nor can we appreciate this machine, any more than we can the spoke of a wheel spinning, or a bullet flying through the air. If it is travelling through time fifty times or a hundred times faster than we are, if it gets through a minute while we get through a second, the impression it creates will of course be only one-fiftieth or one-hundredth of what it would make if it were not travelling in time. That's plain enough." He passed his hand through the space in which the machine had been. "You see?" he said, laughing.

We sat and stared at the vacant table for a minute or so. Then the Time Traveller asked us what we thought of it all.

"It sounds plausible enough to-night," said the Medical Man; "but wait until to-morrow. Wait for the common sense of the morning."

"Would you like to see the Time Machine itself?" asked the Time Traveller. And therewith, taking the lamp in his hand, he led the way down the long, draughty corridor to his laboratory. I remember vividly the flickering light, his queer, broad head in silhouette, the dance of the shadows, how we all followed him, puzzled but incredulous, and how there in the laboratory we beheld a larger edition of the little mechanism which we had seen vanish from before our eyes. Parts were of nickel, parts of ivory, parts had certainly been filed or sawn out of rock crystal. The thing was generally complete, but the twisted crystalline bars lay unfinished upon the bench beside some sheets of drawings, and I took one up for a better look at it. Quartz it seemed to be.

"Look here," said the Medical Man, "are you perfectly serious? Or is this a trick—like that ghost you showed us last Christmas?"

"Upon that machine," said the Time Traveller, holding the lamp aloft, "I intend to explore time. Is that plain? I was never more serious in my life."

None of us quite knew how to take it.

I caught Filby's eye over the shoulder of the Medical Man, and he winked at me solemnly.

§ 2

I think that at that time none of us quite believed in the Time Machine. The fact is, the Time Traveller was one of those men who are too clever to be believed: you never felt that you saw all round him; you always suspected some subtle reserve, some ingenuity in ambush, behind his lucid frankness. Had Filby shown the model and explained the matter in the Time Traveller's words, we should have shown *him* far less scepticism. For we should have perceived his motives: a pork butcher could understand Filby. But the Time Traveller had more than a touch of whim among his elements, and we distrusted him. Things that would have made the fame of a less clever man seemed tricks in his hands. It is a mistake to do things too easily. The serious people who took him seriously never felt quite sure of his deportment: they were somehow aware that trusting their reputations for judgment with him was like furnishing a nursery with egg-shell china. So I don't think any of us said very much about time travelling in the interval between that Thursday and the next, though its odd potentialities ran, no doubt, in most of our minds: its plausibility, that is, its practical incredibleness, the curious possibilities of anachronism and of utter confusion it suggested. For my own part, I was particularly preoccupied with the trick of the model. That I remember discussing with the Medical Man, whom I met on Friday at the Linnæan. He said he had seen a similar thing at Tübingen, and laid considerable stress on the blowing out of the candle. But how the trick was done he could not explain.

The next Thursday I went again to Richmond—I suppose I was one of the Time Traveller's most constant guests—and, arriving late, found four or five men already assembled in his drawing-room. The Medical Man was standing before the fire with a sheet of paper in one hand and his watch in the other. I looked round for the Time Traveller, and—"It's half past seven now," said the Medical Man. "I suppose we'd better have dinner?"

"Where's ———?" said I, naming our host.

"You've just come? It's rather odd. He's unavoidably detained. He asks me in this note to lead off with dinner at seven if he's not back. Says he'll explain when he comes."

"It seems a pity to let the dinner spoil," said the Editor of a well-known daily paper; and thereupon the Doctor rang the bell.

The Psychologist was the only person besides the Doctor and myself who had attended the previous dinner. The other men were Blank, the Editor aforementioned, a certain journalist, and another—a quiet, shy man with a beard—whom I didn't know, and who, as far as my observation went, never opened his mouth all the evening. There was some speculation at the dinner table about the Time Traveller's absence, and I suggested time travelling, in a half jocular spirit. The Editor wanted that explained to him, and the Psychologist volunteered a wooden account of the "ingenious paradox and trick" we had witnessed that day week. He was in the midst of his exposition when the door from the corridor opened slowly and without noise. I was facing the door, and saw it first. "Hallo!" I said. "At last!" And the door opened wider, and the Time Traveller stood before us. I gave a cry of surprise. "Good heavens! man, what's the matter?" cried the Medical Man, who saw him next. And the whole tableful turned towards the door.

He was in an amazing plight. His coat was dusty and dirty, and smeared with green down the sleeves; his hair disordered, and as it seemed to me greyer—either with dust and dirt or because its colour had actually faded. His face was ghastly pale; his chin had a brown cut on it–a cut half healed; his expression was haggard and drawn, as by intense suffering. For a moment he hesitated in the doorway, as if he had been dazzled by the light. Then he came into the room. He walked with just such a limp as I have seen in footsore tramps. We stared at him in silence, expecting him to speak.

He said not a word, but came painfully to the table, and made a motion towards the wine. The Editor filled a glass of champagne, and pushed it towards him. He drained it, and it seemed to do him good: for he looked round the table, and the ghost of his old smile flickered across his face. "What on earth have you been up to, man?" said the Doctor. The Time Traveller did not seem to hear. "Don't let me disturb you," he said, with a certain faltering articulation. "I'm all right." He stopped, held out his glass for more, and took it off at a draught. "That's good," he said. His eyes grew brighter, and a faint colour came into his cheeks. His glance flickered over our faces with a certain dull approval, and then went round the warm and comfortable room. Then he spoke again, still as it were feeling his way among his words. "I'm going to wash and dress, and then I'll come down and explain things. . . . Save me some of that mutton. I'm starving for a bit of meat."

He looked across at the Editor, who was a rare visitor, and hoped he was all right. The Editor began a question. "Tell you presently," said the Time Traveller. "I'm—funny! Be all right in a minute."

He put down his glass, and walked towards the staircase door. Again I remarked his lameness and the soft padding sound of his footfall, and standing up in my place, I saw his feet as he went out. He had nothing on them but a pair of tattered, blood-stained socks. Then the door closed upon him. I had half a mind to follow, till I remembered how he detested any fuss about himself. For a minute, perhaps, my mind was wool gathering. Then, "Remarkable Behaviour of an Eminent Scientist," I heard the Editor say, thinking (after his wont) in head-lines. And this brought my attention back to the bright dinner table.

"What's the game?" said the Journalist. "Has he been doing the Amateur Cadger? I don't follow." I met the eye of the Psychologist, and read my own interpretation in his face. I thought of the Time Traveller limping painfully upstairs. I don't think any one else had noticed his lameness.

The first to recover completely from this surprise was the Medical Man, who rang the bell—the Time Traveller hated to have servants waiting at dinner—for a hot plate. At that the Editor turned to his knife and fork with a grunt, and the Silent Man followed suit. The dinner was resumed. Conversation was exclamatory for a little while, with gaps of wonderment; and then the Editor got fervent in his curiosity. "Does our friend eke out his modest income with a crossing? or has he his Nebuchadnezzar phases?" he inquired. "I feel assured it's this business of the Time Machine," I said, and took up the Psychologist's account of our previous meeting. The new guests were frankly incredulous. The Editor raised objections. "What *was* this time travelling? A man couldn't cover himself with dust by rolling in a paradox, could he?" And then, as the idea came home to him, he resorted to caricature. Hadn't they any clothes-brushes in the Future? The Journalist, too, would not believe at any price, and joined the Editor in the easy work of heaping ridicule on the whole thing. They were both the new kind of journalist—very joyous, irreverent young men. "Our Special Correspondent in the Day after To-morrow reports," the Journalist was saying—or rather shouting—when the Time Traveller came back. He was dressed in ordinary evening clothes, and nothing save his haggard look remained of the change that had startled me.

"I say," said the Editor hilariously, "these chaps here say you have been travelling into the middle of next week!! Tell us all about little Rosebery, will you? What will you take for the lot?"

The Time Traveller came to the place reserved for him without a word. He smiled quietly, in his old way. "Where's my mutton?" he said. "What a treat it is to stick a fork into meat again!"

"Story!" cried the Editor.

"Story be damned!" said the Time Traveller. "I want something to eat. I won't say a word until I get some peptone into my arteries. Thanks. And the salt."

"One word," said I. "Have you been time travelling?"

"Yes," said the Time Traveller, with his mouth full, nodding his head.

"I'd give a shilling a line for a verbatim note," said the Editor. The Time Traveller pushed his glass towards the Silent Man and rang it with his finger nail; at which the Silent Man, who had been staring at his face, started convulsively, and poured him wine. The rest of the dinner was uncomfortable. For my own part, sudden questions kept on rising to my lips, and I dare say it was the same with the others. The Journalist tried to relieve the tension by telling anecdotes of Hettie Potter. The Time Traveller devoted his attention to his dinner, and displayed the appetite of a tramp. The Medical Man smoked a cigarette, and watched the Time Traveller through his eyelashes. The Silent Man seemed even more clumsy than usual, and drank champagne with regularity and determination out of sheer nervousness. At last the Time Traveller pushed his plate away, and looked round us. "I suppose I must apologise, " he said. "I was simply starving. I've had a most amazing time." He reached out his hand for a cigar, and cut the end. "But come into the smoking-room. It's too long a story to tell over greasy plates." And ringing the bell in passing, he led the way into the adjoining room.

"You have told Blank, and Dash, and Chose about the machine?" he said to me, leaning back in his easy chair and naming the three new guests.

"But the thing's a mere paradox," said the Editor.

"I can't argue to-night. I don't mind telling you the story, but I can't argue. I will," he went on, "tell you the story of what has happened to me, if you like, but you must refrain from interruptions. I want to tell it. Badly. Most of it will sound like lying. So be it! It's true—every word of it, all the same. I was in my laboratory at four o'clock, and since then . . . I've lived eight days . . . such days as no human being ever lived before! I'm nearly worn out, but I shan't sleep till I've told this thing over to you. Then I shall go to bed. But no interruptions! Is it agreed?"

"Agreed," said the Editor, and the rest of us echoed "Agreed." And with that the Time Traveller began his story as I have set it forth. He sat back in his chair at first, and spoke like a weary man. Afterwards he got more animated. In writing it down I feel with only too much keenness the inadequacy of pen and ink—and, above all, my own inadequacy—to express its quality. You read, I will suppose, attentively enough; but you cannot see the speaker's white, sincere face in the bright circle of the little lamp, nor hear the intonation of his voice. You cannot know how his expression followed the turns of his story! Most of us hearers were in shadow, for the candles in the smoking-room had not been lighted, and only the face of the Journalist and the legs of the Silent Man from the knees downward were illuminated. At first we glanced now and again at each other. After a time we ceased to do that, and looked only at the Time Traveller's face.

§ 3

"I told some of you last Thursday of the principles of the Time Machine, and showed you the actual thing itself, incomplete in the workshop. There it is now, a little travel-worn, truly; and one of the ivory bars is cracked, and a brass rail bent; but the rest of it's sound enough. I expected to finish it on Friday; but on Friday, when the putting together was nearly done, I found that one of the nickel bars was exactly one inch too short, and this I had to get remade; so that thing was not complete until this morning. It was ten o'clock to-day that the first of all Time Machines began its career. I gave it a last tap, tried all the screws again, put one more drop of oil on the quartz rod, and sat myself in the saddle. I suppose a suicide who holds a pistol to his skull feels much the same wonder at what will come next as I felt then. I took the starting lever in one hand and the stopping one in the other, pressed the first, and almost immediately the second. I seemed to reel; I felt a nightmare sensation of falling; and, looking round, I saw the laboratory exactly as before. Had anything happened? For a moment I suspected that my intellect had tricked me. Then I noted the clock. A moment before, as it seemed, it had stood at a minute or so past ten; now it was nearly half past three!

"I drew a breath, set my teeth, gripped the starting lever with both hands, and went off with a thud. The laboratory got hazy and went dark. Mrs. Watchett came in and walked, apparently without seeing me, towards the garden door. I suppose it took her a minute or so to traverse the place, but to me she seemed to shoot across the room like a rocket. I pressed the lever over to its extreme position. The night came like the turning out of a lamp, and in another moment came to-morrow. The laboratory grew faint and hazy, then fainter and ever fainter. To-morrow night came black, then day again, night again, day again, faster and faster still. An eddying murmur filled my ears, and a strange, dumb confusedness descended on my mind.

"I am afraid I cannot convey the peculiar sensations of time travelling. They are excessively unpleasant. There is a feeling exactly like that one has upon a switchback—of a helpless headlong motion! I felt the same horrible anticipation, too, of an imminent smash. As I put on pace, night followed day like the flapping of a black wing. The dim suggestion of the laboratory seemed presently to fall away from me, and I saw the sun hopping swiftly across the sky, leaping it every minute, and every minute marking a day. I supposed the laboratory had been destroyed and I had come into the open air. I had a dim impression of scaffolding, but I was already going too fast to be conscious of any moving things. The slowest snail that ever crawled dashed by too fast for me. The twinkling succession of darkness and light was excessively painful to the eye. Then, in the intermittent darknesses, I saw the moon spinning swiftly through her quarters from new to full, and had a faint glimpse of the circling stars. Presently, as I went on, still gaining velocity, the palpitation of night and day merged into one continuous greyness; the sky took on a wonderful deepness of blue, a splendid luminous colour like that of early twilight; the jerking sun became a streak of fire, a brilliant arch, in space; the moon a fainter fluctuating band; and I could see nothing of the stars, save now and then a brighter circle flickering in the blue.

"The landscape was misty and vague. I was still on the hillside upon which this house now stands, and the shoulder rose above me grey and dim. I saw trees growing and changing like puffs of vapour, now brown, now green; they grew, spread, shivered, and passed away. I saw huge buildings rise up faint and fair, and pass like dreams. The whole surface of the earth seemed changed—melting and flowing under my eyes. The little hands upon the dials that registered my speed raced round faster and faster. Presently I noted that the sun belt swayed up and down, from solstice to solstice, in a minute or less, and that consequently my pace was over a year a minute; and minute by minute the white snow flashed across the world, and vanished, and was followed by the bright, brief green of spring.

"The unpleasant sensations of the start were less poignant now. They merged at last into a kind of hysterical exhilaration. I remarked indeed a clumsy swaying of the machine, for which I was unable to account. But my mind was too confused to attend to it, so with a kind of madness growing upon me, I flung myself into futurity. At first I scarce thought of stopping, scarce thought of anything but these new sensations. But presently a fresh series of impressions grew up in my mind—a certain curiosity and therewith a certain dread—until at last they took complete possession of me. What strange developments of humanity, what wonderful advances upon our rudimentary civilisation, I thought, might not appear when I came to look nearly into the dim elusive world that raced and fluctuated before my eyes! I saw great and splendid architecture rising about me, more massive than any buildings of our own time, and yet, as it seemed, built of glimmer and mist. I saw a richer green flow up the hillside, and remain there without any wintry intermission. Even through the veil of my confusion the earth seemed very fair. And so my mind came round to the business of stopping.

"The peculiar risk lay in the possibility of my finding some substance in the space which I, or the machine, occupied. So long as I travelled at a high velocity through time, this scarcely mattered; I was, so to speak, attenuated—was slipping like a vapour through the interstices of intervening substances!

But to come to a stop involved the jamming of myself, molecule by molecule, into whatever lay in my way; meant bringing my atoms into such intimate contact with those of the obstacles that a profound chemical reaction—possibly a far-reaching explosion—would result, and blow myself and my apparatus out of all possible dimensions—into the Unknown. This possibility had occurred to me again and again while I was making the machine; but then I had cheerfully accepted it as an unavoidable risk—one of the risks a man has got to take! Now the risk was inevitable, I no longer saw it in the same cheerful light. The fact is that, insensibly, the absolute strangeness of everything, the sickly jarring and swaying of the machine, above all, the feeling of prolonged falling, had absolutely upset my nerve. I told myself that I could never stop, and with a gust of petulance I resolved to stop forthwith. Like an impatient fool, I lugged over the lever, and incontinently the thing went reeling over, and I was flung headlong through the air.

"There was the sound of a clap of thunder in my ears. I may have been stunned for a moment. A pitiless hail was hissing round me, and I was sitting on soft turf in front of the overset machine. Everything still seemed grey, but presently I remarked that the confusion in my ears was gone. I looked round me. I was on what seemed to be a little lawn in a garden, surrounded by rhododendron bushes, and I noticed that their mauve and purple blossoms were dropping in a shower under the beating of the hailstones. The rebounding, dancing hail hung in a cloud over the machine, and drove along the ground like smoke. In a moment I was wet to the skin. 'Fine hospitality,' said I, 'to a man who has travelled innumerable years to see you.'

"Presently I thought what a fool I was to get wet. I stood up and looked round me. A colossal figure, carved apparently in some white stone, loomed indistinctly beyond the rhododendrons through the hazy downpour. But all else of the world was invisible.

"My sensations would be hard to describe. As the columns of hail grew thinner, I saw the white figure more distinctly. It was very large, for a silver birchtree touched its shoulder. It was of white marble, in shape something like a winged sphinx, but the wings, instead of being carried vertically at the sides, were spread so that it seemed to hover. The pedestal, it appeared to me, was of bronze, and was thick with verdigris. It chanced that the face was towards me; the sightless eyes seemed to watch me; there was the faint shadow of a smile on the lips. It was greatly weather-worn, and that imparted an unpleasant suggestion of disease. I stood looking at it for a little space—half a minute, perhaps, or half an hour. It seemed to advance and recede as the hail drove before it denser or thinner. At last I tore my eyes from it for a moment, and saw that the hail curtain had worn threadbare, and that the sky was lightening with the promise of the sun.

"I looked up again at the crouching white shape, and the full temerity of my voyage came suddenly upon me. What might appear when that hazy curtain was altogether withdrawn? What might not have happened to men? What if cruelty had grown into a common passion? What if in this interval the race had lost its manliness, and had developed into something inhuman, unsympathetic, and overwhelmingly powerful? I might seem some old-world savage animal, only the more dreadful and disgusting for our common likeness—a foul creature to be incontinently slain.

"Already I saw other vast shapes—huge buildings with intricate parapets and tall columns, with a wooded hillside dimly creeping in upon me through the lessening storm. I was seized with a panic fear. I turned frantically to the Time Machine, and strove hard to readjust it. As I did so the shafts of the sun smote through the thunderstorm. The grey downpour was swept aside and vanished like the trailing garments of a ghost. Above me, in the intense blue of the summer sky, some faint brown shreds of cloud whirled into nothingness. The great buildings about me stood out clear and distinct, shining with the wet of the thunderstorm, and picked out in white by the unmelted hailstones piled along their courses. I felt naked in a strange world. I felt as perhaps a bird may feel in the clear air, knowing the hawk wings above and will swoop. My fear grew to frenzy. I took a breathing space, set my teeth, and again grappled fiercely, wrist and knees, with the machine. It gave under my desperate onset and turned over. It struck my chin violently. One hand on the saddle, the other on the lever, I stood panting heavily in attitude to mount again.

"But with this recovery of a prompt retreat my courage recovered. I looked more curiously and less fearfully at this world of the remote future. In a circular opening, high up in the wall of the nearer house, I saw a group of figures clad in rich soft robes. They had seen me, and their faces were directed towards me.

"Then I heard voices approaching me. Coming through the bushes by the White Sphinx were the heads and shoulders of men running. One of these emerged in a pathway leading straight to the little lawn upon which I stood with my machine. He was a slight creature—perhaps four feet high—clad in a purple tunic, girdled at the waist with a leather belt. Sandals or buskins—I could not clearly distinguish which—were on his feet; his legs were bare to the knees, and his head was bare. Noticing that, I noticed for the first time how warm the air was.

"He struck me as being a very beautiful and graceful creature, but indescribably frail. His flushed face reminded me of the more beautiful kind of consumptive—that hectic beauty of which we used to hear so much. At the sight of him I suddenly regained confidence. I took my hands from the machine.

§ 4

"In another moment we were standing face to face, I and this fragile thing out of futurity. He came straight up to me and laughed into my eyes. The absence from his bearing of any sign of fear struck me at once. Then he turned to the two others who were following him and spoke to them in a strange and very sweet and liquid tongue.

"There were others coming, and presently a little group of perhaps eight or ten of these exquisite creatures were about me. One of them addressed me. It came into my head, oddly enough, that my voice was too harsh and deep for them. So I shook my head, and, pointing to my ears, shook it again. He came a step forward, hesitated, and then touched my hand. Then I felt other soft little tentacles upon my back and shoulders. They wanted to make sure I was real. There was nothing in this at all alarming. Indeed, there was something in these pretty little people that inspired confidence—a graceful gentleness, a certain childlike ease. And besides, they looked so frail that I could fancy myself flinging the whole dozen of them about like nine-pins. But I made a sudden motion to warn them when I saw their little pink hands feeling at the Time Machine. Happily then, when it was not too late, I thought of a danger I had hitherto forgotten, and reaching over the bars of the machine I unscrewed the little levers that would set it in motion, and put these in my pocket. Then I turned again to see what I could do in the way of communication.

"And then, looking more nearly into their features, I saw some further peculiarities in their Dresden-china type of prettiness. Their hair, which was uniformly curly, came to a sharp end at the neck and cheek; there was not the faintest suggestion of it on the face, and their ears were singularly minute. The mouths were small, with bright red, rather thin lips, and the little chins ran to a point. The eyes were large and mild; and—this may seem egotism on my part—I fancied even then that there was a certain lack of the interest I might have expected in them.

"As they made no effort to communicate with me, but simply stood round me smiling and speaking in soft cooing notes to each other, I began the conversation. I pointed to the Time Machine and to myself. Then, hesitating for a moment how to express time, I pointed to the sun. At once a quaintly pretty little figure in chequered purple and white followed my gesture, and then astonished me by imitating the sound of thunder.

"For a moment I was staggered, though the import of his gesture was plain enough. The question had come into my mind abruptly: were these creatures fools? You may hardly understand how it took me. You see I had always anticipated that the people of the year Eight Hundred and Two Thousand odd would be incredibly in front of us in knowledge, art, everything. Then one of them suddenly asked me a question that showed him to be on the intellectual level of one of our five-year-old children— asked me, in fact, if I had come from the sun in a thunderstorm! It let loose the judgment I had suspended upon their clothes, their frail light limbs, and fragile features. A flow of disappointment rushed across my mind. For a moment I felt that I had built the Time Machine in vain.

"I nodded, pointed to the sun, and gave them such a vivid rendering of a thunderclap as startled them. They all withdrew a pace or so and bowed. Then came one laughing towards me, carrying a chain of beautiful flowers altogether new to me, and put it about my neck. The idea was received with melodious applause; and presently they were all running to and fro for flowers, and laughingly flinging them upon me until I was almost smothered with blossom. You who have never seen the like can scarcely imagine what delicate and wonderful flowers countless years of culture had created. Then some one suggested that their plaything should be exhibited in the nearest building, and so I was led past the sphinx of white marble, which had seemed to watch me all the while with a smile at my astonishment, towards a vast grey edifice of fretted stone. As I went with them the memory of my confident anticipations of a profoundly grave and intellectual posterity came, with irresistible merriment, to my mind.

"The building had a huge entry, and was altogether of colossal di- mensions. I was naturally most occupied with the growing crowd of little people, and with the big open portals that yawned before me shadowy and mysterious. My general impression of the world I saw over their heads was of a tangled waste of beautiful bushes and flowers, a long-neglected and yet weedless garden. I saw a number of tall spikes of strange white flowers, measuring a foot perhaps across the spread of the waxen petals. They grew scattered, as if wild, among the variegated shrubs, but, as I say, I did not examine them closely at this time. The Time Machine was left deserted on the turf among the rhododendrons.

"The arch of the doorway was richly carved, but naturally I did not observe the carving very narrowly, though I fancied I saw suggestions of old Phœnician decorations as I passed through, and it struck me that they were very badly broken and weather-worn. Several more brightly clad people met me in the doorway, and so we entered, I, dressed in dingy nineteenth-century garments, looking grotesque enough, garlanded with flowers, and surrounded by an eddying mass of bright, soft-coloured robes and shining white limbs, in a melodious whirl of laughter and laughing speech.

"The big doorway opened into a proportionately great hall hung with brown. The roof was in shadow, and the windows, partially glazed with coloured glass and partially unglazed, admitted a tempered light. The floor was made up of huge blocks of some very hard white metal, not plates nor slabs, blocks, and it so much worn, as I judged by the going to and fro of past generations, as to be deeply channelled along the more frequented ways. Transverse to the length were innumerable tables made of slabs of polished stone, raised perhaps a foot from the floor, and upon these were heaps of fruits. Some I recognised as a kind of hypertrophied raspberry and orange, but for the most part they were strange.

"Between the tables was scattered a great number of cushions. Upon these my conductors seated themselves, signing for me to do likewise. With a pretty absence of ceremony they began to eat the fruit with their hands, flinging peel and stalks and so forth, into the round openings in the sides of the tables. I was not loth to follow their example, for I felt thirsty and hungry. As I did so I surveyed the hall at my leisure.

"And perhaps the thing that struck me most was its dilapidated look. The stained-glass windows, which displayed only a geometrical pattern, were broken in many places, and the curtains that hung across the lower end were thick with dust. And it caught my eye that the corner of the marble table near me was fractured. Nevertheless, the general effect was extremely rich and picturesque. There were, perhaps, a couple of hundred people dining in the hall, and most of them, seated as near to me as they could come, were watching me with interest, their little eyes shining over the fruit they were eating. All were clad in the same soft, and yet strong, silky material.

"Fruit, by the bye, was all their diet. These people of the remote future were strict vegetarians, and while I was with them, in spite of some carnal cravings, I had to be frugivorous also. Indeed, I found afterwards that horses, cattle, sheep, dogs, had followed the Ichthyosaurus into extinction. But the fruits were very delightful; one, in particular, that seemed to be in season all the time I was there—a floury thing in a three-sided husk—was especially good, and I made it my staple. At first I was puzzled by all these strange fruits, and by the strange flowers I saw, but later I began to perceive their import.

"However, I am telling you of my fruit dinner in the distant future now. So soon as my appetite was a little checked, I determined to make a resolute attempt to learn the speech of these new men of mine. Clearly that was the next thing to do. The fruits seemed a convenient thing to begin upon, and holding one of these up I began a series of interrogative sounds and gestures. I had some considerable difficulty in conveying my meaning. At first my efforts met with a stare of surprise or inextinguishable laughter, but presently a fair-haired little creature seemed to grasp my intention and repeated a name. They had to chatter and explain the business at great length to each other, and my first attempts to make the exquisite little sounds of their language caused an immense amount of amusement. However, I felt like a schoolmaster amidst children, and persisted, and presently I had a score of noun substantives at least at my command; and then I got to demonstrative pronouns, and even the verb 'to eat.' But it was slow work, and the little people soon tired and wanted to get away from my interrogations, so I determined, rather of necessity, to let them give their lessons in little doses when they felt inclined. And very little doses I found they were before long, for I never met people more indolent or more easily fatigued.

"A queer thing I soon discovered about my little hosts, and that was their lack of interest. They would come to me with eager cries of astonishment, like children, but like children they would soon stop examining me and wander away after some other toy. The dinner and my conversational beginnings ended, I noted for the first time that almost all those who had surrounded me at first were gone. It is odd, too, how speedily I came to disregard these little people. I went out through the portal into the sunlit world again so soon as my hunger was satisfied. I was continually meeting more of these men of the future, who would follow me a little distance, chatter and laugh about me, and having smiled and gesticulated in a friendly way, leave me again to my own devices.

"The calm of evening was upon the world as I emerged from the great hall, and the scene was lit by the warm glow of the setting sun. At first things were very confusing. Everything was so entirely different from the world I had known—even the flowers. The big building I had left was situate on the slope of a broad river valley, but the Thames had shifted, perhaps, a mile from its present position. I resolved to mount to the summit of a crest, perhaps a mile and a half away, from which I could get a wider view of this our planet in the year Eight Hundred and Two Thousand Seven Hundred and One A.D. For that, I should explain, was the date the little dials of my machine recorded.

"As I walked I was watchful for every impression that could possibly help to explain the condition of ruinous splendour in which I found the world—for ruinous it was. A little way up the hill, for instance, was a great heap of granite, bound together by masses of aluminium, a vast labyrinth of precipitous walls and crumbled heaps, amidst which were thick heaps of very beautiful pagoda-like plants—nettles possibly—but wonderfully tinted with brown about the leaves, and incapable of stinging. It was evidently the derelict remains of some vast structure, to what end built I could not determine. It was here that I was destined, at a later date, to have a very strange experience—the first intimation of a still stranger discovery—but of that I will speak in its proper place.

"Looking round with a sudden thought, from a terrace on which I rested for a while, I realised that there were no small houses to be seen. Apparently the single house, and possibly even the household, had vanished. Here and there among the greenery were palace-like buildings, but the house and the cottage, which form such characteristic features of our own English landscape, had disappeared.

" 'Communism,' said I to myself.

"And on the heels of that came another thought. I looked at the half dozen little figures that were following me. Then, in a flash, I perceived that all had the same form of costume, the same soft hairless visage, and the same girlish rotundity of limb. It may seem strange, perhaps, that I had not noticed this before. But everything was so strange. Now, I saw the fact plainly enough. In costume, and in all the differences of texture and bearing that now mark off the sexes from each other, these people of the future were alike. And the children seemed to my eyes to be but the miniatures of their parents. I judged, then, that the children of that time were extremely precocious, physically at least, and I found afterwards abundant verification of my opinion.

"Seeing the ease and security in which these people were living, I felt that this close resemblance of the sexes was after all what one would expect; for the strength of a man and the softness of a woman, the institution of the family, and the differentiation of occupations are mere militant necessities of an age of physical force. Where population is balanced and abundant, much child-bearing becomes an evil rather than a blessing to the State; where violence comes but rarely and offspring are secure, there is less necessity—indeed there is no necessity—for an efficient family, and the specialisation of the sexes with reference to their children's needs disappears. We see some beginnings of this even in our own time, and in this future age it was complete. This, I must remind you, was my speculation at the time. Later, I was to appreciate how far it fell short of the reality.

"While I was musing upon these things, my attention was attracted by a pretty little structure, like a well under a cupola. I thought in a transitory way of the oddness of wells still existing, and then resumed the thread of my speculations. There were no large buildings towards the top of the hill, and as my walking powers were evidently miraculous, I was presently left alone for the first time. With a strange sense of freedom and adventure I pushed on up to the crest.

"There I found a seat of some yellow metal that I did not recognise, corroded in places with a kind of pinkish rust and half smothered in soft moss, the arm rests cast and filed into the resemblance of griffins' heads. I sat down on it, and I surveyed the broad view of our old world under the sunset of that long day. It was as sweet and fair a view as I have ever seen. The sun had already gone below the horizon and the west was flaming gold, touched with some horizontal bars of purple and crimson.

Below was the valley of the Thames, in which the river lay like a band of burnished steel. I have already spoken of the great palaces dotted about among the variegated greenery, some in ruins and some still occupied. Here and there rose a white or silvery figure in the waste garden of the earth, here and there came the sharp vertical line of some cupola or obelisk. There were no hedges, no signs of proprietary rights, no evidences of agriculture; the whole earth had become a garden.

"So watching, I began to put my interpretation upon the things I had seen, and as it shaped itself to me that evening, my interpretation was something in this way. (Afterwards I found I had got only a half-truth—or only a glimpse of one facet of the truth.)

"It seemed to me that I had happened upon humanity upon the wane. The ruddy sunset set me thinking of the sunset of mankind. For the first time I began to realise an odd consequence of the social effort in which we are at present engaged. And yet, come to think, it is a logical consequence enough. Strength is the outcome of need; security sets a premium on feebleness. The work of ameliorating the conditions of life—the true civilising process that makes life more and more secure—had gone steadily on to a climax. One triumph of a united humanity over Nature had followed another. Things that are now mere dreams had become projects deliberately put in hand and carried forward. And the harvest was what I saw!

"After all, the sanitation and the agriculture of today are still in the rudimentary stage. The science of our time has attacked but a little department of the field of human disease, but, even so, it spreads its operations very steadily and persistently. Our agriculture and horticulture destroy a weed just here and there and cultivate perhaps a score or so of wholesome plants, leaving the greater number to fight out a balance as they can. We improve our favourite plants and animals—and how few they are—gradually by selective breeding; now a new and better peach, now a seedless grape, now a sweeter and larger flower, now a more convenient breed of cattle. We improve them gradually, because our ideals are vague and tentative, and our knowledge is very limited; because Nature, too, is shy and slow in our clumsy hands. Some day all this will be better organised, and still better. That is the drift of the current in spite of the eddies. The whole world will be intelligent, educated, and cooperating; things will move faster and faster towards the subjugation of Nature. In the end, wisely and carefully we shall readjust the balance of animal and vegetable life to suit our human needs.

"This adjustment, I say, must have been done, and done well; done indeed for all time, in the space of Time across which my machine had leaped. The air was free from gnats, the earth from weeds or fungi; everywhere were fruits and sweet and delightful flowers; brilliant butterflies flew hither and thither. The ideal of preventive medicine was attained. Diseases had been stamped out. I saw no evidence of any contagious diseases during all my stay. And I shall have to tell you later that even the processes of putrefaction and decay had been profoundly affected by these changes.

"Social triumphs, too, had been effected. I saw mankind housed in splendid shelters, gloriously clothed, and as yet I had found them engaged in no toil. There were no signs of struggle, neither social nor economical struggle. The shop, the advertisement, traffic, all that commerce which constitues the body of our world, was gone. It was natural on that golden evening that I should jump at the idea of a social paradise. The difficulty of increasing population had been met, I guessed, and population had ceased to increase.

"But with this change in condition comes inevitably adaptations to the change. What, unless biological science is a mass of errors, is the cause of human intelligence and vigour? Hardship and freedom: conditions under which the active, strong, and subtle survive and the weaker go to the wall; conditions that put a premium upon the loyal alliance of capable men, upon self-restraint, patience, and decision. And the institution of the family, and the emotions that arise therein, the fierce jealousy, the tenderness for offspring, parental self-devotion, all found their justification and support in the imminent dangers of the young. *Now*, where are these imminent dangers? There is a sentiment arising, and it will grow, against connubial jealousy, against fierce maternity, against passion of all sorts; unnecessary things now, and things that make us uncomfortable, savage survivals, discords in a refined and pleasant life.

"I thought of the physical slightness of the people, their lack of intelligence, and those big abundant ruins, and it strengthened my belief in a perfect conquest of Nature. For after the battle comes Quiet. Humanity had been strong, energetic, and intelligent, and had used all its abundant vitality to alter the conditions under which it lived. And now came the reaction of the altered conditions.

"Under the new conditions of perfect comfort and security, that restless energy, that with us is strength, would become weakness. Even in our own time certain tendencies and desires, once necessary to survival, are a constant source of failure. Physical courage and the love of battle, for instance, are no great help—may even be hindrances—to a civilised man. And in a state of physical balance and security, power, intellectual as well as physical, would be out of place. For countless years I judged there had been no danger of war or solitary violence, no danger from wild beasts, no wasting disease to require strength of constitution, no need of toil. For such a life, what we should call the weak are as well equipped as the strong, are indeed no longer weak. Better equipped indeed they are, for the strong would be fretted by an energy for which there was no outlet. No doubt the exquisite beauty of the buildings I saw was the outcome of the last surgings of the now purposeless energy of mankind before it settled down into perfect harmony with the conditions under which it lived—the flourish of that triumph which began the last great peace. This has ever been the fate of energy in security; it takes to art and to eroticism, and then come languor and decay.

"Even this artistic impetus would at last die away—had almost died in the Time I saw. To adorn themselves with flowers, to dance, to sing in the sunlight; so much was left of the artistic spirit, and no more. Even that would fade in the end into a contented inactivity. We are kept keen on the grindstone of pain and necessity, and, it seemed to me, that here was that hateful grindstone broken at last!

"As I stood there in the gathering dark I thought that in this simple explanation I had mastered the problem of the world—mastered the whole secret of these delicious people. Possibly the checks they had devised for the increase of population had succeeded too well, and their numbers had rather diminished than kept stationary. That would account for the abandoned ruins. Very simple was my explanation, and plausible enough—as most wrong theories are!

§ 5

"As I stood there musing over this too perfect triumph of man, the full moon, yellow and gibbous, came up out of an overflow of silver light in the north-east. The bright little figures ceased to move about below, a noiseless owl flitted by, and I shivered with the chill of the night. I determined to descend and find where I could sleep.

"I looked for the building I knew. Then my eye travelled along to the figure of the White Sphinx upon the pedestal of bronze, growing distinct as the light of the rising moon grew brighter. I could see the silver birch against it. There was the tangle of rhododendron bushes, black in the pale light, and there was the little lawn. I looked at the lawn again. A queer doubt chilled my complacency. 'No,' said I stoutly to myself, 'that was not the lawn.'

"But it *was* the lawn. For the white leprous face of the sphinx was towards it. Can you imagine what I felt as this conviction came home to me? But you cannot. The Time Machine was gone!

"At once, like a lash across my face, came the possibility of losing my own age, of being left helpless in this strange new world. The bare thought of it was an actual physical sensation. I could feel it grip me at the throat and stop my breathing. In another moment I was in a passion of fear and running with great leaping strides down the slope. Once I fell headlong and cut my face; I lost no time in stanching the blood, but jumped up and ran on, with a warm trickle down my cheek and chin. All the time I ran I was saying to myself, 'They have moved it a little, pushed it under the bushes out of the way.' Nevertheless, I ran with all my might.

All the time, with the certainty that sometimes comes with excessive dread, I knew that such assurance was folly, knew instinctively that the machine was removed out of my reach. My breath came with pain. I suppose I covered the whole distance from the hill crest to the little lawn, two miles, perhaps, in ten minutes. And I am not a young man. I cursed aloud, as I ran, at my confident folly in leaving the machine, wasting good breath thereby. I cried aloud, and none answered. Not a creature seemed to be stirring in that moonlit world.

"When I reached the lawn my worst fears were realised. Not a trace of the thing was to be seen. I felt faint and cold when I faced the empty space among the black tangle of bushes. I ran round it furiously, as if the thing might be hidden in a corner, and then stopped abruptly, with my hands clutching my hair. Above me towered the sphinx, upon the bronze pedestal, white, shining, leprous, in the light of the rising moon. It seemed to smile in mockery of my dismay.

"I might have consoled myself by imagining the little people had put the mechanism in some shelter for me, had I not felt assured of their physical and intellectual inadequacy. That is what dismayed me: the sense of some hitherto unsuspected power, through whose intervention my invention had vanished. Yet, of one thing I felt assured: unless some other age had produced its exact duplicate, the machine could not have moved in time. The attachment of the levers—I will show you the method later—prevented any one from tampering with it in that way when they were removed. It had moved, and was hid, only in space. But then, where could it be?

"I think I must have had a kind of frenzy. I remember running violently in and out among the moonlit bushes all round the sphinx, and startling some white animal that, in the dim light, I took for a small deer. I remember, too, late that night, beating the bushes with my clenched fists until my knuckles were gashed and bleeding from the broken twigs. Then, sobbing and raving in my anguish of mind, I went down to the great building of stone. The big hall was dark, silent, and deserted. I slipped on the uneven floor, and fell over one of the malachite tables, almost breaking my shin. I lit a match and went on past the dusty curtains, of which I have told you.

"There I found a second great hall covered with cushions, upon which, perhaps, a score or so of the little people were sleeping. I have no doubt they found my second appearance strange enough, coming suddenly out of the quiet darkness with inarticulate noises and the splutter and flare of a match. For they had forgotten about matches. 'Where is my Time Machine?' I began, bawling like an angry child, laying hands upon them and shaking them up together. It must have been very queer to them. Some laughed, most of them looked sorely frightened. When I saw them standing round me, it came into my head that I was doing as foolish a thing as it was possible for me to do under the circumstances, in trying to revive the sensation of fear. For, reasoning from their daylight behaviour, I thought that fear must be forgotten.

"Abruptly, I dashed down the match, and, knocking one of the people over in my course, went blundering across the big dining-hall again, out under the moonlight. I heard cries of terror and their little feet running and stumbling this way and that. I do not remember all I did as the moon crept up the sky. I suppose it was the unexpected nature of my loss that maddened me. I felt hopelessly cut off from my own kind—a strange animal in an unknown world. I must have raved to and fro, screaming and crying upon God and Fate. I have a memory of horrible fatigue, as the long night of despair wore away; of looking in this impossible place and that; of groping among moonlit ruins and touching strange creatures in the black shadows; at last, of lying on the ground near the sphinx and weeping with absolute wretchedness. I had nothing left but misery. Then I slept, and when I woke again it was full day, and a couple of sparrows were hopping round me on the turf within reach of my arm.

"I sat up in the freshness of the morning, trying to remember how I had got there, and why I had such a profound sense of desertion and despair. Then things came clear in my mind. With the plain, reasonable daylight, I could look my circumstances fairly in the face. I saw the wild folly of my frenzy overnight, and I could reason with myself. Suppose the worst? I said. Suppose the machine altogether lost—perhaps destroyed? It behooves me to be calm and patient, to learn the way of the people, to get a clear idea of the method of my loss, and the means of getting materials and tools; so that in the end, perhaps, I may make another. That would be my only hope, a poor hope perhaps, but better than despair. And, after all, it was a beautiful and curious world.

"But probably the machine had only been taken away. Still, I must be calm and patient, find its hiding-place, and recover it by force or cunning. And with that I scrambled to my feet and looked about me, wondering where I could bathe. I felt weary, stiff, and travel-soiled. The freshness of the morning made me desire an equal freshness. I had exhausted my emotion. Indeed, as I went about my business, I found myself wondering at my intense excitement overnight. I made a careful examination of the ground about the little lawn. I wasted some time in futile questionings, conveyed, as well as I was able, to such of the little people as came by. They all failed to understand my gestures; some were simply stolid, some thought it was a jest and laughed at me. I had the hardest task in the world to keep my hands off their pretty laughing faces. It was a foolish impulse, but the devil begotten of fear and blind anger was ill curbed and still eager to take advantage of my perplexity. The turf gave better counsel. I found a groove ripped in it, about midway between the pedestal of the sphinx and the marks of my feet where, on arrival, I had struggled with the overturned machine. There were other signs of removal about, with queer narrow footprints like those I could imagine made by a sloth. This directed my closer attention to the pedestal. It was, as I think I have said, of bronze. It was not a mere block, but highly decorated with deep framed panels on either side. I went and rapped at these. The pedestal was hollow. Examining the panels with care I found them discontinuous with the frames. There were no handles or keyholes, but possibly the panels, if they were doors, as I supposed, opened from within. One thing was clear enough to my mind. It took no very great mental effort to infer that my Time Machine was inside that pedestal. But how it got there was a different problem.

"I saw the heads of two orange-clad people coming through the bushes and under some blossom-covered apple-trees towards me. I turned smiling to them and beckoned them to me. They came, and then, pointing to the bronze pedestal, I tried to intimate my wish to open it. But at my first gesture towards this they behaved very oddly. I don't know how to convey their expression to you. Suppose you were to use a grossly improper gesture to a delicate-minded woman—it is how she would look. They went off as if they had received the last possible insult. I tried a sweet-looking little chap in white next, with exactly the same result. Somehow, his manner made me feel ashamed of myself. But as you know, I wanted the Time Machine, and I tried him once more. As he turned off, like the others, my temper got the better of me. In three strides I was after him, had him by the loose part of his robe round the neck, and began dragging him towards the sphinx. Then I saw the horror and repugnance of his face, and all of a sudden I let him go.

"But I was not beaten yet. I banged with my fist at the bronze panels. I thought I heard something stir inside—to be explicit, I thought I heard a sound like a chuckle—but I must have been mistaken. Then I got a big pebble from the river, and came and hammered till I had flattened a coil in the decorations, and the verdigris came off in powdery flakes. The delicate little people must have heard me hammering in gusty outbreaks a mile away on either hand, but nothing came of it. I saw a crowd of them upon the slopes, looking furtively at me. At last, hot and tired, I sat down to watch the place. But I was too restless to watch long; I am too Occidental for a long vigil. I could work at a problem for years, but to wait inactive for twenty-four hours—that is another matter.

"I got up after a time, and began walking aimlessly through the bushes towards the hill again. 'Patience,' said I to myself. 'If you want your machine again you must leave that sphinx alone. If they mean to take your machine away, it's little good your wrecking their bronze panels, and if they don't, you will get it back as soon as you can ask for it. To sit among all those unknown things before a puzzle like that is hopeless. That way lies monomania. Face this world. Learn its ways, watch it, be careful of too hasty guesses at its meaning. In the end you will find clues to it all.' Then suddenly the humour of the situation came into my mind:

the thought of the years I had spent in study and toil to get into the future age, and now my passion of anxiety to get out of it. I had made myself the most complicated and the most hopeless trap that ever a man devised. Although it was at my own expense, I could not help myself. I laughed aloud.

"Going through the big palace, it seemed to me that the little people avoided me. It may have been my fancy, or it may have had something to do with my hammering at the gates of bronze. Yet I felt tolerably sure of the avoidance. I was careful, however, to show no concern and to abstain from any pursuit of them, and in the course of a day or two things got back to the old footing. I made what progress I could in the language, and in addition I pushed my explorations here and there. Either I missed some subtle point, or their language was excessively simple—almost exclusively composed of concrete substantives and verbs. There seemed to be few, if any, abstract terms, or little use of figurative language. Their sentences were usually simple and of two words, and I failed to convey or understand any but the simplest propositions. I determined to put the thought of my Time Machine and the mystery of the bronze doors under the sphinx as much as possible in a corner of memory, until my growing knowledge would lead me back to them in a natural way. Yet a certain feeling, you may understand, tethered me in a circle of a few miles round the point of my arrival.

"So far as I could see, all the world displayed the same exuberant richness as the Thames valley. From every hill I climbed I saw the same abundance of splendid buildings, endlessly varied in material and style, the same clustering thickets of evergreens, the same blossom-laden trees and tree-ferns. Here and there water shone like silver, and beyond, the land rose into blue undulating hills, and so faded into the serenity of the sky. A peculiar feature, which presently attracted my attention, was the presence of certain circular wells, several, as it seemed to me, of a very great depth. One lay by the path up the hill, which I had followed during my first walk. Like the others, it was rimmed with bronze, curiously wrought, and protected by a little cupola from the rain. Sitting by the side of these wells, and peering down into the shafted darkness, I could see no gleam of water, nor could I start any reflection with a lighted match. But in all of them I heard a certain sound: a thud—thud—thud, like the beating of some big engine; and I discovered, from the flaring of my matches, that a steady current of air set down the shafts. Further, I threw a scrap of paper into the throat of one, and, instead of fluttering slowly down, it was at once sucked swiftly out of sight.

"After a time, too, I came to connect these wells with tall towers standing here and there upon the slopes; for above them there was often just such a flicker in the air as one sees on a hot day above a sun-scorched beach. Putting things together, I reached a strong suggestion of an extensive system of subterranean ventilation, whose true import it was difficult to imagine. I was at first inclined to associate it with the sanitary apparatus of these people. It was an obvious conclusion, but it was absolutely wrong.

"And here I must admit that I learned very little of drains and bells and modes of conveyance, and the like conveniences, during my time in this real future. In some of these visions of Utopias and coming times which I have read, there is a vast amount of detail about building, and social arrangements, and so forth. But while such details are easy enough to obtain when the whole world is contained in one's imagination, they are altogether inaccessible to a real traveller amid such realities as I found here. Conceive the tale of London which a negro, fresh from Central Africa, would take back to his tribe! What would he know of railway companies, of social movements, of telephone and telegraph wires, of the Parcels Delivery Company, and postal orders and the like? Yet we, at least, should be willing enough to explain these things to him! And even of what he knew, how much could he make his untravelled friend either apprehend or believe? Then, think how narrow the gap between a negro and a white man of our own times, and how wide the interval between myself and these of the Golden Age! I was sensible of much which was unseen, and which contributed to my comfort; but save for a general impression of automatic organisation, I fear I can convey very little of the difference to your mind.

"In the matter of sepulture, for instance, I could see no signs of crematoria nor anything suggestive of tombs. But it occurred to me that, possibly, there might be cemeteries (or crematoria) somewhere beyond the range of my explorings. This, again, was a question I deliberately put to myself, and my curiosity was at first entirely defeated upon the point. The thing puzzled me, and I was led to make a further remark, which puzzled me still more: that aged and infirm among this people there were none.

"I must confess that my satisfaction with my first theories of an automatic civilisation and a decadent humanity did not long endure. Yet I could think of no other. Let me put my difficulties. The several big palaces I had explored were mere living places, great dining-halls and sleeping apartments. I could find no machinery, no appliances of any kind. Yet these people were clothed in pleasant fabrics that must at times need renewal, and their sandals, though undecorated, were fairly complex specimens of metal-work. Somehow such things must be made. And the little people displayed no vestige of a creative tendency. There were no shops, no workshops, no sign of importations among them. They spent all their time in playing gently, in bathing in the river, in making love in a half-playful fashion, in eating fruit and sleeping. I could not see how things were kept going.

"Then, again, about the Time Machine: something, I knew not what, had taken it into the hollow pedestal of the White Sphinx. *Why?* For the life of me I could not imagine. Those waterless wells, too, those flickering pillars. I felt I lacked a clue. I felt—how shall I put it? Suppose you found an inscription, with sentences here and there in excellent plain English, and, interpolated therewith, others made up of words, of letters even, absolutely unknown to you? Well, on the third day of my visit, that was how the world of Eight Hundred and Two Thousand Seven Hundred and One presented itself to me!

"That day, too, I made a friend—of a sort. It happened that, as I was watching some of the little people bathing in a shallow, one of them was seized with cramp and began drifting downstream. The main current ran rather swiftly, but not too strongly for even a moderate swimmer. It will give you an idea, therefore, of the strange deficiency in these creatures, when I tell you that none made the slightest attempt to rescue the weakly crying little thing which was drowning before their eyes. When I realised this, I hurriedly slipped off my clothes, and, wading in at a point lower down, I caught the poor mite and drew her safe to land. A little rubbing of the limbs soon brought her round, and I had the satisfaction of seeing she was all right before I left her. I had got to such a low estimate of her kind that I did not expect any gratitude from her. In that, however, I was wrong.

"This happened in the morning. In the afternoon I met my little woman, as I believe it was, as I was returning towards my centre from an exploration, and she received me with cries of delight and presented me with a big garland of flowers—evidently made for me and me alone. The thing took my imagination. Very possibly I had been feeling desolate. At any rate I did my best to display my appreciation of the gift. We were soon seated together in a little stone arbour, engaged in conversation, chiefly of smiles. The creature's friendliness affected me exactly as a child's might have done. We passed each other flowers, and she kissed my hands. I did the same to hers. Then I tried talk, and found that her name was Weena, which, though I don't know what it meant, somehow seemed appropriate enough. That was the beginning of a queer friendship which lasted a week, and ended—as I will tell you!

"She was exactly like a child. She wanted to be with me always. She tried to follow me everywhere, and on my next journey out and about it went to my heart to tire her down, and leave her at last, exhausted and calling after me rather plaintively. But the problems of the world had to be mastered. I had not, I said to myself, come into the future to carry on a miniature flirtation. Yet her distress when I left her was very great, her expostulations at the parting were sometimes frantic, and I think, altogether, I had as much trouble as comfort from her devotion. Nevertheless she was, somehow, a very great comfort. I thought it was mere childish affection that made her cling to me. Until it was too late, I did not clearly know what I had inflicted upon her when I left her. Nor until it was too late did I clearly understand what she was to me. For, by merely seeming fond of me, and showing in her weak, futile way that she cared for me, the little doll of a creature presently gave my return to the neighbourhood of the White Sphinx almost the feeling of coming home; and I would watch for her tiny figure of white and gold so soon as I came over the hill.

"It was from her, too, that I learned that fear had not yet left the world. She was fearless enough in the daylight, and she had the oddest confidence in me; for once, in a foolish moment, I made threatening grimaces at her, and she simply laughed at them. But she dreaded the dark, dreaded shadows, dreaded black things. Darkness to her was the one thing dreadful. It was a singularly passionate emotion, and it set me thinking and observing. I discovered then, among other things, that these little people gathered into the great houses after dark, and slept in droves. To enter upon them without a light was to put them into a tumult of apprehension. I never found one out of doors, or one sleeping alone within doors, after dark. Yet I was still such a blockhead that I missed the lesson of that fear, and in spite of Weena's distress, I insisted upon sleeping away from these slumbering multitudes.

"It troubled her greatly, but in the end her odd affection for me triumphed, and for five of the nights of our acquaintance, including the last night of all, she slept with her head pillowed on my arm. But my story slips away from me as I speak of her. It must have been the night before her rescue that I was awakened about dawn. I had been restless, dreaming most disagreeably that I was drowned, and that sea-anemones were feeling over my face with their soft palps. I woke with a start, and with an odd fancy that some greyish animal had just rushed out of the chamber. I tried to get to sleep again, but I felt restless and uncomfortable. It was that dim grey hour when things are just creeping out of darkness, when everything is colourless and clear cut, and yet unreal. I got up, and went down into the great hall, and so out upon the flagstones in front of the palace. I thought I would make a virtue of necessity, and see the sunrise.

"The moon was setting, and the dying moonlight and the first pallor of dawn were mingled in a ghastly half-light. The bushes were inky black, the ground a sombre grey, the sky colourless and cheerless. And up the hill I thought I could see ghosts. Three several times, as I scanned the slope, I saw white figures. Twice I fancied I saw a solitary white, ape-like creature running rather quickly up the hill, and once near the ruins I saw a leash of them carrying some dark body. They moved hastily. I did not see what became of them. It seemed that they vanished among the bushes. The dawn was still indistinct, you must understand. I was feeling that chill, uncertain, early-morning feeling you may have known. I doubted my eyes.

"As the eastern sky grew brighter, and the light of the day came on and its vivid colouring returned upon the world once more, I scanned the view keenly. But I saw no vestige of my white figures. They were mere creatures of the half-light. 'They must have been ghosts,' I said; 'I wonder whence they dated.' For a queer notion of Grant Allen's came into my head, and amused me. If each generation die and leave ghosts, he argued, the world at last will get overcrowded with them. On that theory they would have grown innumerable some Eight Hundred Thousand Years hence, and it was no great wonder to see four at once. But the jest was unsatisfying, and I was thinking of these figures all the morning, until Weena's rescue drove them out of my head. I associated them in some indefinite way with the white animal I had startled in my first passionate search for the Time Machine. But Weena was a pleasant substitute. Yet all the same, they were soon destined to take far deadlier possession of my mind.

"I think I have said how much hotter than our own was the weather of this Golden Age. I cannot account for it. It may be that the sun was hotter, or the earth nearer the sun. It is usual to assume that the sun will go on cooling steadily in the future. But people, unfamiliar with such speculations as those of the younger Darwin, forget that the plants must ultimately fall back one by one into the parent body. As these catastrophes occur, the sun will blaze with renewed energy; and it may be that some inner planet had suffered this fate. Whatever the reason, the fact remains that the sun was very much hotter than we know it.

"Well, one very hot morning—my fourth, I think—as I was seeking shelter from the heat and glare in a colossal ruin near the great house where I slept and fed, there happened this strange thing: Clambering among these heaps of masonry, I found a narrow gallery, whose end and side windows were blocked by fallen masses of stone. By contrast with the brilliancy outside, it seemed at first impenetrably dark to me. I entered it groping, for the change from light to blackness made spots of colour swim before me. Suddenly I halted spellbound. A pair of eyes, luminous by reflection against the daylight without, was watching me out of the darkness.

"The old instinctive dread of wild beasts came upon me. I clenched my hands and steadfastly looked into the glaring eyeballs. I was afraid to turn. Then the thought of the absolute security in which humanity appeared to be living came to my mind. And then I remembered that strange terror of the dark. Overcoming my fear to some extent, I advanced a step and spoke. I will admit that my voice was harsh and ill-controlled. I put out my hand and touched something soft. At once the eyes darted sideways, and something white ran past me. I turned with my heart in my mouth, and saw a queer little ape-like figure, its head held down in a peculiar manner, running across the sunlit space behind me. It blundered against a block of granite, staggered aside, and in a moment was hidden in a black shadow beneath another pile of ruined masonry.

"My impression of it is, of course, imperfect; but I know it was a dull white, and had strange large greyish-red eyes; also that there was flaxen hair on its head and down its back. But, as I say, it went too fast for me to see distinctly. I cannot even say whether it ran on all-fours, or only with its forearms held very low. After an instant's pause I followed it into the second heap of ruins. I could not find it at first; but, after a time in the profound obscurity, I came upon one of those round well-like openings of which I have told you, half closed by a fallen pillar. A sudden thought came to me. Could this Thing have vanished down the shaft? I lit a match, and, looking down, I saw a small, white, moving creature, with large bright eyes which regarded me steadfastly as it retreated. It made me shudder. It was so like a human spider! It was clambering down the wall, and now I saw for the first time a number of metal foot and hand rests forming a kind of ladder down the shaft. Then the light burned my fingers and fell out of my hand, going out as it dropped, and when I had lit another the little monster had disappeared.

"I do not know how long I sat peering down that well. It was not for some time that I could succeed in persuading myself that the thing I had seen was human. But, gradually, the truth dawned on me: that Man had not remained one species, but had differentiated into two distinct animals: that my graceful children of the Upperworld were not the sole descendants of our generation, but that this bleached, obscene, nocturnal Thing, which had flashed before me, was also heir to all the ages.

"I thought of the flickering pillars and my theory of an underground ventilation. I began to suspect their true import. And what, I wondered, was this Lemur doing in my scheme of a perfectly balanced organisation? How was it related to the indolent serenity of the beautiful Upperworlders? And what was hidden down there, at the foot of that shaft? I sat upon the edge of the well telling myself that, at any rate, there was nothing to fear, and that there I must descend for the solution of my difficulties. And withal I was absolutely afraid to go! As I hesitated, two of the beautiful Upper-world people came running in their amorous sport across the daylight into the shadow. The male pursued the female, flinging flowers at her as he ran.

"They seemed distressed to find me, my arm against the overturned pillar, peering down the well. Apparently it was considered bad form to remark these apertures; for when I pointed to this one, and tried to frame a question about it in their tongue, they were still more visibly distressed and turned away. But they were interested by my matches, and I struck some to amuse them. I tried them again about the well, and again I failed. So presently I left them, meaning to go back to Weena, and see what I could get from her. But my mind was already in revolution; my guesses and impressions were slipping and sliding to a new adjustment. I had now a clue to the import of these wells, to the ventilating towers, to the mystery of the ghosts; to say nothing of a hint at the meaning of the bronze gates and the fate of the Time Machine! And very vaguely there came a suggestion towards the solution of the economic problem that had puzzled me.

"Here was the new view. Plainly, this second species of Man was subterranean. There were three circumstances in particular which made me think that its rare emergence above ground was the outcome of a long-continued underground habit. In the first place, there was the bleached look common in most animals that live largely in the dark—the white fish of the Kentucky caves, for instance. Then, those large eyes, with that capacity for reflecting light, are common features of nocturnal things— witness the owl and the cat. And last of all, that evident confusion in the sunshine, that hasty yet fumbling and awkward flight towards dark shadow, and that peculiar carriage of the head while in the light—all reinforced the theory of an extreme sensitiveness of the retina.

"Beneath my feet, then, the earth must be tunnelled enormously, and these tunnellings were the habitat of the new race. The presence of ventilating-shafts and wells along the hill slopes—everywhere, in fact, except along the river valley—showed how universal were its ramifications. What so natural, then, as to assume that it was in this artificial Underworld that such work as was necessary to the comfort of the day-light race was done? The notion was so plausible that I at once accepted it, and went on to assume the *how* of the splitting of the human species. I dare say you will anticipate the shape of my theory; though, for myself, I very soon felt that it fell far short of the truth.

"At first, proceeding from the problems of our own age, it seemed clear as daylight to me that the gradual widening of the present merely temporary and social difference between the Capitalist and the Labourer, was the key to the whole position. No doubt it will seem grotesque enough to you—and wildly incredible!—and yet even now there are existing circumstances to point that way. There is a tendency to utilise underground space for the less ornamental purposes of civilisation; there is the Metropolitan Railway in London, for instance, there are new electric railways, there are subways, there are underground workrooms and restaurants, and they increase and multiply. Evidently, I thought, this tendency had increased till industry had gradually lost its birthright in the sky. I mean that it had gone deeper and deeper into larger and ever larger underground factories, spending a still-increasing amount of its time therein, till, in the end—! Even now, does not an East-end worker lie in such artificial conditions as practically to be cut off from the natural surface of the earth?

"Again, the exclusive tendency of richer people—due, no doubt, to the increasing refinement of their education, and the widening gulf between them and the rude violence of the poor—is already leading to the closing, in their interest, of considerable portions of the surface of the land. About London, for instance, perhaps half the prettier country is shut in against intrusion. And this same widening gulf—which is due to the length and expense of the higher educational process and the increased facilities for and temptations towards refined habits on the part of the rich—will make that exchange between class and class, that promotion by intermarriage which at present retards the splitting of our species along lines of social stratification, less and less frequent. So, in the end, above ground you must have the Haves, pursuing pleasure and comfort and beauty, and below ground the Have-nots, the Workers getting continually adapted to the conditions of their labour. Once they were there, they would no doubt have to pay rent, and not a little of it, for the ventilation of their caverns; and if they refused, they would starve or be suffocated for arrears. Such of them as were so constituted as to be miserable and rebellious would die; and, in the end, the balance being permanent, the survivors would become as well adapted to the conditions of underground life, and as happy in their way, as the Upper-world people were to theirs. As it seemed to me, the refined beauty and the etiolated pallor followed naturally enough.

"The great triumph of Humanity I had dreamed of took a different shape in my mind. It had been no such triumph of moral education and general cooperation as I had imagined. Instead, I saw a real aristocracy, armed with a perfected science and working to a logical conclusion the industrial system of today. Its triumph had not been simply a triumph over Nature, but a triumph over Nature and the fellow man. This, I must warn you, was my theory at the time. I had no convenient cicerone in the pattern of the Utopian books. My explanation may be absolutely wrong. I still think it is the most plausible one. But even on this supposition the balanced civilisation that was at last attained must have long since passed its zenith, and was now far fallen into decay. The too-perfect security of the Upperworlders had led them to a slow movement of degeneration, to a general dwindling in size, strength, and intelligence. That I could see clearly enough already. What had happened to the Undergrounders I did not yet suspect; but, from what I had seen of the Morlocks—that, by the bye, was the name by which these creatures were called—I could imagine that the modification of the human type was even far more profound than among the 'Eloi,' the beautiful race that I already knew.

"Then came troublesome doubts. Why had the Morlocks taken my Time Machine? For I felt sure it was they who had taken it. Why, too, if the Eloi were masters, could they not restore the machine to me? And why were they so terribly afraid of the dark? I proceeded, as I have said, to question Weena about this Underworld, but here again I was disappointed. At first she would not understand my questions, and presently she refused to answer them. She shivered as though the topic was unendurable. And when I pressed her, perhaps a little harshly, she burst into tears. They were the only tears, except my own, I ever saw in that Golden Age. When I saw them I ceased abruptly to trouble about the Morlocks, and was only concerned in banishing these signs of human inheritance from Weena's eyes. And very soon she was smiling and clapping her hands while I solemnly burned a match.

§ 6

"It may seem odd to you, but it was two days before I could follow up the new-found clue in what was manifestly the proper way. I felt a peculiar shrinking from those pallid bodies. They were just the half-bleached colour of the worms and things one sees preserved in spirit in a zoological museum. And they were filthily cold to the touch. Probably my shrinking was largely due to the sympathetic influence of the Eloi, whose disgust of the Morlocks I now began to appreciate.

"The next night I did not sleep well. Probably my health was a little disordered. I was oppressed with perplexity and doubt. Once or twice I had a feeling of intense fear for which I could perceive no definite reason. I remember creeping noiselessly into the great hall where the little people were sleeping in the moonlight—that night Weena was among them—and feeling reassured by their presence. It occurred to me, even then, that in the course of a few days the moon must pass through its last quarter, and the nights grow dark, when the appearances of these unpleasant creatures from below, these whitened Lemurs, this new vermin that had replaced the old, might be more abundant. And on both these days I had the restless feeling of one who shirks an inevitable duty. I felt assured that the Time Machine was only to be recovered by boldly penetrating these underground mysteries. Yet I could not face the mystery. If only I had had a companion it would have been different. But I was so horribly alone, and even to clamber down into the darkness of the well appalled me. I don't know if you will understand my feeling, but I never felt quite safe at my back.

"It was this restlessness, this insecurity, perhaps, that drove me further and further afield in my exploring expeditions. Going to the south-westward towards the rising country that is now called Combe Wood, I observed far off, in the direction of nineteenth-century Banstead, a vast green structure, different in character from any I had hitherto seen. It was larger than the largest of the palaces or ruins I knew, and the façade had an Oriental look: the face of it having the lustre, as well as the pale-green tint, a kind of bluish-green, of a certain type of Chinese porcelain. This difference in aspect suggested a difference in use, and I was minded to push on and explore. But the day was growing late, and I had come upon the sight of the place after a long and tiring circuit; so I resolved to hold over the adventure for the following day, and I returned to the welcome and the caresses of little Weena. But next morning I perceived clearly enough that my curiosity regarding the Palace of Green Porcelain was a piece of self-deception, to enable me to shirk, by another day, an experience I dreaded. I resolved I would make the descent without further waste of time, and started out in the early morning towards a well near the ruins of granite and aluminium.

"Little Weena ran with me. She danced beside me to the well, but when she saw me lean over the mouth and look downward, she seemed strangely disconcerted. 'Good-bye, little Weena,' I said kissing her; and then, putting her down, I began to feel over the parapet for the climbing hooks. Rather hastily, I may as well confess, for I feared my courage might leak away! At first she watched me in amazement. Then she gave a most piteous cry, and, running to me, she began to pull at me with her little hands. I think her opposition nerved me rather to proceed. I shook her off, perhaps a little roughly, and in another moment I was in the throat of the well. I saw her agonised face over the parapet, and smiled to reassure her. Then I had to look down at the unstable hooks to which I clung.

"I had to clamber down a shaft of perhaps two hundred yards. The descent was effected by means of metallic bars projecting from the sides of the well, and these being adapted to the needs of a creature much smaller and lighter than myself, I was speedily cramped and fatigued by the descent. And not simply fatigued! One of the bars bent suddenly under my weight, and almost swung me off into the blackness beneath. For a moment I hung by one hand, and after that experience I did not dare to rest again. Though my arms and back were presently acutely painful, I went on clambering down the sheer descent with as quick a motion as possible. Glancing upward, I saw the aperture, a small blue disk, in which a star was visible, while little Weena's head showed as a round black projection. The thudding sound of a machine below grew louder and more oppressive. Everything save that little disk above was profoundly dark, and when I looked up again Weena had disappeared.

"I was in an agony of discomfort. I had some thought of trying to go up the shaft again, and leave the Underworld alone. But even while I turned this over in my mind I continued to descend. At last, with intense relief, I saw dimly coming up, a foot to the right of me, a slender loophole in the wall. Swinging myself in, I found it was the aperture of a narrow horizontal tunnel in which I could lie down and rest. It was not too soon. My arms ached, my back was cramped, and I was trembling with the prolonged terror of a fall. Besides this, the unbroken darkness had had a distressing effect upon my eyes. The air was full of the throb and hum of machinery pumping air down the shaft.

"I do not know how long I lay. I was roused by a soft hand touching my face. Starting up in the darkness I snatched at my matches and, hastily striking one, I saw three stooping white creatures similar to the one I had seen above ground in the ruin, hastily retreating before the light. Living, as they did, in what appeared to me impenetrable darkness, their eyes were abnormally large and sensitive, just as are the pupils of the abysmal fishes, and they reflected the light in the same way. I have no doubt they could see me in that rayless obscurity, and they did not seem to have any fear of me apart from the light. But, so soon as I struck a match in order to see them, they fled incontinently, vanishing into dark gutters and tunnels, from which their eyes glared at me in the strangest fashion.

"I tried to call to them, but the language they had was apparently different from that of the Over-world people; so that I was needs left to my own unaided efforts, and the thought of flight before exploration was even then in my mind. But I said to myself, 'You are in for it now,' and, feeling my way along the tunnel, I found the noise of machinery grow louder. Presently the walls fell away from me, and I came to a large open space, and, striking another match, saw that I had entered a vast arched cavern, which stretched into utter darkness beyond the range of my light. The view I had of it was as much as one could see in the burning of a match.

"Necessarily my memory is vague. Great shapes like big machines rose out of the dimness, and cast grotesque black shadows, in which dim spectral Morlocks sheltered from the glare. The place, by the bye, was very stuffy and oppressive, and the faint halitus of freshly shed blood was in the air. Some way down the central vista was a little table of white metal, laid with what seemed a meal. The Morlocks at any rate were carnivorous! Even at the time, I remember wondering what large animal could have survived to furnish the red joint I saw. It was all very indistinct: the heavy smell, the big unmeaning shapes, the obscene figures lurking in the shadows, and only waiting for the darkness to come at me again! Then the match burned down, and stung my fingers, and fell, a wriggling red spot in the blackness.

"I have thought since how particularly ill equipped I was for such an experience. When I had started with the Time Machine, I had started with the absurd assumption that the men of the Future would certainly be infinitely ahead of ourselves in all their appliances. I had come without arms, without medicine, without anything to smoke—at times I missed tobacco frightfully!—even without enough matches. If only I had thought of a Kodak! I could have flashed that glimpse of the Underworld in a second, and examined it at leisure. But, as it was, I stood there with only the weapons and the powers that Nature had endowed me with—hands, feet, and teeth; these, and four safety-matches that still remained to me.

"I was afraid to push my way in among all this machinery in the dark, and it was only with my last glimpse of light I discovered that my store of matches had run low. It had never occurred to me until that moment that there was any need to economise them, and I had wasted almost half the box in astonishing the Upperworlders, to whom fire was a novelty. Now, as I say, I had four left, and while I stood in the dark, a hand touched mine, lank fingers came feeling over my face, and I was sensible of a peculiar unpleasant odour. I fancied I heard the breathing of a crowd of those dreadful little beings about me. I felt the box of matches in my hand being gently disengaged, and other hands behind me plucking at my clothing. The sense of these unseen creatures examining me was indescribably unpleasant. The sudden realisation of my ignorance of their ways of thinking and doing came home to me very vividly in the darkness. I shouted at them as loudly as I could. They started away, and then I could feel them approaching me again. They clutched at me more boldly, whispering odd sounds to each other. I shivered violently, and shouted again—rather discordantly. This time they were not so seriously alarmed, and they made a queer laughing noise as they came back at me. I will confess I was horribly frightened. I determined to strike another match and escape under the protection of its glare. I did so, and eking out the flicker with a scrap of paper from my pocket, I made good my retreat to the narrow tunnel. But I had scarce entered this when my light was blown out, and in the blackness I could hear the Morlocks rustling like wind among leaves, and pattering like the rain, as they hurried after me.

"In a moment I was clutched by several hands, and there was no mistaking that they were trying to haul me back. I struck another light, and waved it in their dazzled faces. You can scarce imagine how nauseatingly inhuman they looked—those pale, chinless faces and great, lidless, pinkish-grey eyes!—as they stared in their blindness and bewilderment. But I did not stay to look, I promise you: I retreated again, and when my second match had ended, I struck my third. It had almost burned through when I reached the opening into the shaft. I lay down on the edge, for the throb of the great pump below made me giddy. Then I felt sideways for the projecting hooks, and, as I did so, my feet were grasped from behind, and I was violently tugged backward. I lit my last match . . . and it incontinently went out. But I had my hand on the climbing bars now, and, kicking violently, I disengaged myself from the clutches of the Morlocks, and was speedily clambering up the shaft, while they stayed peering and blinking up at me: all but one little wretch who followed me for some way, and well-nigh secured my boot as a trophy.

"That climb seemed interminable to me. With the last twenty or thirty feet of it a deadly nausea came upon me. I had the greatest difficulty in keeping my hold. The last few yards was a frightful struggle against this faintness. Several times my head swam, and I felt all the sensations of falling. At last, however, I got over the well-mouth somehow, and staggered out of the ruin into the blinding sunlight. I fell upon my face. Even the soil smelt sweet and clean. Then I remember Weena kissing my hands and ears, and the voices of others among the Eloi. Then, for a time, I was insensible.

§ 7

"Now, indeed, I seemed in a worse case than before. Hitherto, except during my night's anguish at the loss of the Time Machine, I had felt a sustaining hope of ultimate escape, but that hope was staggered by these new discoveries. Hitherto I had merely thought myself impeded by the childish simplicity of the little people, and by some unknown forces which I had only to understand to overcome; but there was an altogether new element in the sickening quality of the Morlocks—a something inhuman and malign. Instinctively I loathed them. Before, I had felt as a man might feel who had fallen into a pit: my concern was with the pit and how to get out of it. Now I felt like a beast in a trap, whose enemy would come upon him soon.

"The enemy I dreaded may surprise you. It was the darkness of the new moon. Weena had put this into my head by some at first incomprehensible remarks about the Dark Nights. It was not now such a very difficult problem to guess what the coming Dark Nights might mean. The moon was on the wane: each night there was a longer interval of darkness. And I now understood to some slight degree at least the reason of the fear of the little Upper-world people for the dark. I wondered vaguely what foul villainy it might be that the Morlocks did under the new moon. I felt pretty sure now that my second hypothesis was all wrong. The Upper-world people might once have been the favoured aristocracy, and the Morlocks their mechanical servants; but that had long since passed away. The two species that had resulted from the evolution of man were sliding down towards, or had already arrived at, an altogether new relationship. The Eloi, like the Carlovingian kings, had decayed to a mere beautiful futility. They still possessed the earth on sufferance: since the Morlocks, subterranean for innumerable generations, had come at last to find the daylit surface intolerable. And the Morlocks made their garments, I inferred, and maintained them in their habitual needs, perhaps through the survival of an old habit of service. They did it as a standing horse paws with his foot, or as a man enjoys killing animals in sport: because ancient and departed necessities had impressed it on the organism. But, clearly, the old order was already in part reversed. The Nemesis of the delicate ones was creeping on apace. Ages ago, thousands of generations ago, man had thrust his brother man out of the ease and the sunshine. And now that brother was coming back—changed! Already the Eloi had begun to learn one old lesson anew. They were becoming reacquainted with Fear. And suddenly there came into my head the memory of the meat I had seen in the Underworld. It seemed odd how it floated into my mind: not stirred up as it were by the current of my meditations, but coming in almost like a question from outside. I tried to recall the form of it. I had a vague sense of something familiar, but I could not tell what it was at the time.

"Still, however helpless the little people in the presence of their mysterious Fear, I was differently constituted. I came out of this age of ours, this ripe prime of the human race, when Fear does not paralyse and mystery has lost its terrors. I at least would defend myself. Without further delay I determined to make myself arms and a fastness where I might sleep. With that refuge as a base, I could face this strange world with some of that confidence I had lost in realising to what creatures night by night I lay exposed. I felt I could never sleep again until my bed was secure from them. I shuddered with horror to think how they must already have examined me.

"I wandered during the afternoon along the valley of the Thames, but found nothing that commended itself to my mind as inaccessible. All the buildings and trees seemed easily practicable to such dexterous climbers as the Morlocks, to judge by their wells, must be. Then the tall pinnacles of the Palace of Green Porcelain and the polished gleam of its walls came back to my memory; and in the evening, taking Weena like a child upon my shoulder, I went up the hills towards the south-west. The distance, I had reckoned, was seven or eight miles, but it must have been nearer eighteen. I had first seen the place on a moist afternoon when distances are deceptively diminished. In addition, the heel of one of my shoes was loose, and a nail was working through the sole—they were comfortable old shoes I wore about indoors—so that I was lame. And it was already long past sunset when I came in sight of the palace, silhouetted black against the pale yellow of the sky.

"Weena had been hugely delighted when I began to carry her, but after a time she desired me to let her down, and ran along by the side of me, occasionally darting off on either hand to pick flowers to stick in my pockets. My pockets had always puzzled Weena, but at the last she had concluded that they were an eccentric kind of vase for floral decoration. At least she utilised them for that purpose. And that reminds me! In changing my jacket I found . . ."

The Time Traveller paused, put his hand into his pocket, and silently placed two withered flowers, not unlike very large white mallows, upon the little table. Then he resumed his narrative.

"As the hush of evening crept over the world and we proceeded over the hill crest towards Wimbledon, Weena grew tired and wanted to return to the house of grey stone. But I pointed out the distant pinnacles of the Palace of Green Porcelain to her, and contrived to make her understand that we were seeking a refuge there from her Fear. You know that great pause that comes upon things before the dusk? Even the breeze stops in the trees. To me there is always an air of expectation about that evening stillness. The sky was clear, remote, and empty save for a few horizontal bars far down in the sunset. Well, that night the expectation took the colour of my fears. In that darkling calm my senses seemed preternaturally sharpened. I fancied I could even feel the hollowness of the ground beneath my feet: could, indeed, almost see through it the Morlocks in their anthill going hither and thither and waiting for the dark. In my excitement I fancied that they would receive my invasion of their burrows as a declaration of war. And why had they taken my Time Machine?

"So we went on in the quiet, and the twilight deepened into night. The clear blue of the distance faded, and one star after another came out. The ground grew dim and the trees black. Weena's fears and her fatigue grew upon her. I took her in my arms and talked to her and caressed her. Then, as the darkness grew deeper, she put her arms round my neck, and, closing her eyes, tightly pressed her face against my shoulder. So we went down a long slope into a valley, and there in the dimness I almost walked into a little river. This I waded, and went up the opposite side of the valley, past a number of sleeping houses, and by a statue—a Faun, or some such figure, *minus* the head. Here too were acacias. So far I had seen nothing of the Morlocks, but it was yet early in the night, and the darker hours before the old moon rose were still to come.

"From the brow of the next hill I saw a thick wood spreading wide and black before me. I hesitated at this. I could see no end to it, either to the right or the left. Feeling tired—my feet in particular, were very sore—I carefully lowered Weena from my shoulder as I halted, and sat down upon the turf. I could no longer see the Palace of Green Porcelain, and I was in doubt of my direction. I looked into the thickness of the wood and thought of what it might hide. Under that dense tangle of branches one would be out of sight of the stars. Even were there no other lurking danger—a danger I did not care to let my imagination loose upon— there would still be all the roots to stumble over and the tree-boles to strike against. I was very tired, too, after the excitements of the day; so I decided that I would not face it, but would pass the night upon the open hill.

"Weena, I was glad to find, was fast asleep. I carefully wrapped her in my jacket, and sat down beside her to wait for the moonrise. The hillside was quiet and deserted, but from the black of the wood there came now and then a stir of living things. Above me shone the stars, for the night was very clear. I felt a certain sense of friendly comfort in their twinkling. All the old constellations had gone from the sky, however: that slow movement which is imperceptible in a hundred human life- times, had long since rearranged them in unfamiliar groupings. But the Milky Way, it seemed to me, was still the same tattered streamer of star- dust as of yore. Southward (as I judged it) was a very bright red star that was new to me; it was even more splendid than our own green Sirius. And amid all these scintillating points of light one bright planet shone kindly and steadily like the face of an old friend.

"Looking at these stars suddenly dwarfed my own troubles and all the gravities of terrestrial life. I thought of their unfathomable distance, and the slow inevitable drift of their movements out of the unknown past into the unknown future. I thought of the great precessional cycle that the pole of the earth describes. Only forty times had that silent revolution occurred during all the years that I had traversed. And during these few revolutions all the activity, all the traditions, the complex organisations, the nations, languages, literatures, aspirations, even the mere memory of Man as I knew him, had been swept out of existence. Instead were these frail creatures who had forgotten their high ancestry, and the white Things of which I went in terror. Then I thought of the Great Fear that was between the two species, and for the first time, with a sudden shiver, came the clear knowledge of what the meat I had seen might be. Yet it was too horrible! I looked at little Weena sleeping beside me, her face white and starlike under the stars, and forthwith dismissed the thought.

"Through that long night I held my mind off the Morlocks as well as I could, and whiled away the time by trying to fancy I could find signs of the old constellations in the new confusion. The sky kept very clear, except for a hazy cloud or so. No doubt I dozed at times. Then, as my vigil wore on, came a faintness in the eastward sky, like the reflection of some colourless fire, and the old moon rose, thin and peaked and white. And close behind, and overtaking it, and overflowing it, the dawn came, pale at first, and then growing pink and warm. No Morlocks had approached us. Indeed, I had seen none upon the hill that night. And in the confidence of renewed day it almost seemed to me that my fear had been unreasonable. I stood up and found my foot with the loose heel swollen at the ankle and painful under the heel; so I sat down again, took off my shoes, and flung them away.

"I awakened Weena, and we went down into the wood, now green and pleasant instead of black and forbidding. We found some fruit wherewith to break our fast. We soon met others of the dainty ones, laughing and dancing in the sunlight as though there was no such thing in nature as the night. And then I thought once more of the meat that I had seen. I felt assured now of what it was, and from the bottom of my heart I pitied this last feeble rill from the great flood of humanity. Clearly, at some time in the Long-Ago of human decay the Morlocks' food had run short. Possibly they had lived on rats and such-like vermin. Even now man is far less discriminating and exclusive in his food than he was—far less than any monkey. His prejudice against human flesh is no deepseated instinct. And so these inhuman sons of men—! I tried to look at the thing in a scientific spirit. After all, they were less human and more remote than our cannibal ancestors of three or four thousand years ago. And the intelligence that would have made this state of things a torment had gone. Why should I trouble myself? These Eloi were mere fatted cattle, which the ant-like Morlocks preserved and preyed upon—probably saw to the breeding of. And there was Weena dancing at my side!

"Then I tried to preserve myself from the horror that was coming upon me, by regarding it as a rigorous punishment of human selfishness. Man had been content to live in ease and delight upon the labours of his fellow man, had taken Necessity as his watchword and excuse, and in the fulness of time Necessity had come home to him. I even tried a Carlyle-like scorn of this wretched aristocracy in decay. But this attitude of mind was impossible. However great their intellectual degradation, the Eloi and kept too much of the human form not to claim my sympathy, and to make me perforce a sharer in their degradation and their Fear.

"I had at the time very vague ideas as to the course I should pursue. My first was to secure some safe place of refuge, and to make myself such arms of metal or stone as I could contrive. That necessity was immediate. In the next place, I hoped to procure some means of fire, so that I should have the weapon of a torch at hand, for nothing, I knew, would be more efficient against these Morlocks. Then I wanted to arrange some contrivance to break open the doors of bronze under the White Sphinx. I had in mind a battering-ram. I had a persuasion that if I could enter those doors and carry a blaze of light before me I should discover the Time Machine and escape. I could not imagine the Morlocks were strong enough to move it far away. Weena I had resolved to bring with me to our own time. And turning such schemes over in my mind I pursued our way towards the building which my fancy had chosen as our dwelling.

§ 8

"I found the Palace of Green Porcelain, when we approached it about noon, deserted and falling into ruin. Only ragged vestiges of glass remained in its windows, and great sheets of the green facing had fallen away from the corroded metallic framework. It lay very high upon a turfy down, and looking north-eastward before I entered it, I was surprised to see a large estuary, or even creek, where I judged Wandsworth and Bettersea must once have been. I thought then—though I never followed up the thought—of what might have happened, or might be happening, to the living things in the sea.

"The material of the Palace proved on examination to be indeed porcelain, and along the face of it I saw an inscription in some unknown character. I thought, rather foolishly, that Weena might help me to interpret this, but I only learned that the bare idea of writing had never entered her head. She always seemed to me, I fancy, more human than she was, perhaps because her affection was so human.

"Within the big valves of the door—which were open and broken—we found, instead of the customary hall, a long gallery lit by many side windows. At the first glance I was reminded of a museum. The tiled floor was thick with dust, and a remarkable array of miscellaneous objects was shrouded in the same grey covering. Then I perceived, standing strange and gaunt in the centre of the hall, what was clearly the lower part of a huge skeleton. I recognised by the oblique feet that it was some extinct creature after the fashion of the Megatherium. The skull and the upper bones lay beside it in the thick dust, and in one place, where rain-water had dropped through a leak in the roof, the thing itself had been worn away. Further in the gallery was the huge skeleton barrel of a Brontosaurus. My museum hypothesis was confirmed. Going towards the side I found what appeared to be sloping shelves, and, clearing away the thick dust, I found the old familiar glass cases of our own time. But they must have been airtight, to judge from the fair preservation of some of their contents.

"Clearly we stood among the ruins of some latterday South Kensington! Here, apparently, was the Palæontological Section, and a very splendid array of fossils it must have been, though the inevitable process of decay that had been staved off for a time, and had, through the extinction of bacteria and fungi, lost ninety-nine hundredths of its force, was, nevertheless, with extreme sureness if with extreme slowness at work again upon all its treasures. Here and there I found traces of the little people in the shape of rare fossils broken to pieces or threaded in strings upon reeds. And the cases had in some instances been bodily removed—by the Morlocks as I judged. The place was very silent. The thick dust deadened our footsteps. Weena, who had been rolling a sea-urchin down the sloping glass of a case, presently came, as I stared about me, and very quietly took my hand and stood beside me.

"And at first I was so much surprised by this ancient monument of an intellectual age, that I gave no thought to the possibilities it presented. Even my preoccupation about the Time Machine receded a little from my mind.

"To judge from the size of the place, this Palace of Green Porcelain had a great deal more in it than a Gallery of Palæontology; possibly historical galleries; it might be, even a library! To me, at least in my present circumstances, these would be vastly more interesting than this spectacle of old-time geology in decay. Exploring, I found another short gallery running transversely to the first. This appeared to be devoted to minerals, and the sight of a block of sulphur set my mind running on gunpowder. But I could find no saltpetre; indeed, no nitrates of any kind. Doubtless they had deliquesced ages ago. Yet the sulphur hung in my mind, and set up a train of thinking. As for the rest of the contents of that gallery, though on the whole they were the best preserved of all I saw, I had little interest. I am no specialist in mineralogy, and I went on down a very ruinous aisle running parallel to the first hall I had entered. Apparently this section had been devoted to natural history, but everything had long since passed out of recognition. A few shrivelled and blackened vestiges of what had once been stuffed animals, desiccated mummies in jars that had once held spirit, a brown dust of departed plants; that was all! I was sorry for that, because I should have been glad to trace the patient readjustments by which the conquest of animated nature had been attained. Then we came to a gallery of simply colossal proportions, but singularly ill-lit, the floor of it running downward at a slight angle from the end at which I entered. At intervals white globes hung from the ceiling—many of them cracked and smashed—which suggested that originally the place had been artificially lit. Here I was more in my element, for rising on either side of me were the huge bulks of big machines, all greatly corroded and many broken down, but some still fairly complete. You know I have a certain weakness for mechanism, and I was inclined to linger among these; the more so as for the most part they had the interest of puzzles, and I could make only the vaguest guesses at what they were for. I fancied that if I could solve their puzzles I should find myself in possession of powers that might be of use against the Morlocks.

"Suddenly Weena came very close to my side. So suddenly that she startled me. Had it not been for her I do not think I should have noticed that the floor of the gallery sloped at all.* The end I had come in at was quite above ground, and was lit by rare slit-like windows. As you went down the length, the ground came up against these windows, until at last there was a pit like the 'area' of a London house before each, and only a narrow line of daylight at the top. I went slowly along, puzzling about the machines, and had been too intent upon them to notice the gradual diminution of the light, until Weena's increasing apprehensions drew my attention. Then I saw that the gallery ran down at last into a thick darkness. I hesitated, and then, as I looked round me, I saw that the dust was less abundant and its surface less even. Further away towards the dimness, it appeared to be broken by a number of small narrow footprints. My sense of the immediate presence of the Morlocks revived at that. I felt that I was wasting my time in this academic examination of machinery. I called to mind that it was already far advanced in the afternoon, and that I had still no weapon, no refuge, and no means of making a fire. And then down in the remote blackness of the gallery I heard a peculiar pattering, and the same odd noises I had heard down the well.

"I took Weena's hand. Then, struck with a sudden idea, I left her and turned to a machine from which projected a lever not unlike those in a signalbox. Clambering upon the stand, and grasping this lever in my hands, I put all my weight upon it sideways. Suddenly Weena, deserted in the central aisle, began to whimper. I had judged the strength of the lever pretty correctly, for it snapped after a minute's strain, and I rejoined her with a mace in my hand more than sufficient, I judged, for any Morlock skull I might encounter. And I longed very much to kill a Morlock or so. Very inhuman, you may think, to want to go killing one's own descendants! But it was impossible, somehow, to feel any humanity in the things. Only my disinclination to leave Weena, and a persuasion that if I began to slake my thirst for murder my Time Machine might suffer, restrained me from going straight down the gallery and killing the brutes I heard.

*It may be, of course, that the floor did not slope, but that the museum was built into the side of a hill.—ED. [Wells's note.]

"Well, mace in one hand and Weena in the other, I went out of that gallery and into another and still larger one, which at the first glance reminded me of a military chapel hung with tattered flags. The brown and charred rags that hung from the sides of it, I presently recognised as the decaying vestiges of books. They had long since dropped to pieces, and every semblance of print had left them. But here and there were warped boards and cracked metallic clasps that told the tale well enough. Had I been a literary man I might, perhaps, have moralised upon the futility of all ambition. But as it was, the thing that struck me with the keenest force the enormous waste of labour to which this sombre wilderness of rotting paper testified. At the time I will confess that I thought chiefly of the *Philosophical Transactions* and my own seventeen papers upon physical optics.

"Then, going up a broad staircase, we came to what may once have been a gallery of technical chemistry. And here I had not a little hope of useful discoveries. Except at one end where the roof had collapsed, this gallery was well preserved. I went eagerly to every unbroken case. And at last, in one of the really air-tight cases, I found a box of matches. Very eagerly I tried them. They were perfectly good. They were not even damp. I turned to Weena. 'Dance,' I cried to her in her own tongue. For now I had a weapon indeed against the horrible creatures we feared. And so, in that derelict museum, upon the thick soft carpeting of dust, to Weena's huge delight, I solemnly performed a kind of composite dance, whistling *The Land of the Leal* as cheerfully as I could. In part it was a modest *cancan*, in part a step-dance, in part a skirt-dance (so far as my tail-coat permitted), and in part original. For I am naturally inventive, as you know.

"Now, I still think that for this box of matches to have escaped the wear of time for immemorial years was a most strange, as for me it was a most fortunate thing. Yet, oddly enough, I found a far unlikelier substance, and that was camphor. I found it in a sealed jar, that by chance, I suppose, had been really hermetically sealed. I fancied at first that it was paraffin wax, and smashed the glass accordingly. But the odour of camphor was unmistakable. In the universal decay this volatile substance had chanced to survive, perhaps through many thousands of centuries. It reminded me of a sepia painting I had once seen done from the ink of a fossil Belemnite that must have perished and become fossilised millions of years ago. I was about to throw it away, but I remembered that it was inflammable and burned with a good bright flame—was, in fact, an excellent candle—and I put it in my pocket. I found no explosives, however, nor any means of breaking down the bronze doors. As yet my iron crowbar was the most helpful thing I had chanced upon. Nevertheless I left that gallery greatly elated.

"I cannot tell you all the story of that long afternoon. It would require a great effort of memory to recall my explorations in at all the proper order. I remember a long gallery of rusting stands of arms, and how I hesitated between my crowbar and a hatchet or a sword. I could not carry both, however, and my bar of iron promised best against the bronze gates. There were numbers of guns, pistols, and rifles. The most were masses of rust, but many were of some new metal, and still fairly sound. But any cartridges or powder there may once have been had rotted into dust. One corner I saw was charred and shattered; perhaps, I thought, by an explosion among the specimens. In another place was a vast array of idols—Polynesian, Mexican, Grecian, Phoenician, every country on earth I should think. And here, yielding to an irresistible impulse, I wrote my name upon the nose of a steatite monster from South America that particularly took my fancy.

"As the evening drew on, my interest waned. I went through gallery after gallery, dusty, silent, often ruinous, the exhibits sometimes mere heaps of rust and lignite, sometimes fresher. In one place I suddenly found myself near the model of a tin-mine, and then by the merest accident I discovered, in an air-tight case, two dynamite cartridges! I shouted 'Eureka,' and smashed the case with joy. Then came a doubt. I hesitated. Then, selecting a little side gallery, I made my essay. I never felt such a disappointment as I did in waiting five, ten, fifteen minutes for an explosion that never came. Of course the things were dummies, as I might have guessed from their presence. I really believe that, had they not been so, I should have rushed off incontinently and blown sphinx, bronze doors, and (as it proved) my chances of finding the Time Machine, all together into non-existence.

"It was after that, I think, that we came to a little open court within the palace. It was turfed, and had three fruit-trees. So we rested and refreshed ourselves. Towards sunset I began to consider our position. Night was creeping upon us, and my inaccessible hiding-place had still to be found. But that troubled me very little now. I had in my possession a thing that was, perhaps, the best of all defences against the Morlocks— I had matches! I had the camphor in my pocket, too, if a blaze were needed. It seemed to me that the best thing we could do would be to pass the night in the open, protected by a fire. In the morning there was the getting of the Time Machine. Towards that, as yet, I had only my iron mace. But now, with my growing knowledge, I felt very differently towards those bronze doors. Up to this, I had refrained from forcing them, largely because of the mystery on the other side. They had never impressed me as being very strong, and I hoped to find my bar of iron not altogether inadequate for the work.

§ 9

"We emerged from the palace while the sun was still in part above the horizon. I was determined to reach the White Sphinx early the next morning, and ere the dusk I purposed pushing through the woods that had stopped me on the previous journey. My plan was to go as far as possible that night, and then, building a fire, to sleep in the protection of its glare. Accordingly, as we went along I gathered any sticks or dried grass I saw, and presently had my arms full of such litter. Thus loaded, our progress was slower than I had anticipated, and besides Weena was tired. And I began to suffer from sleepiness too; so that it was full night before we reached the wood. Upon the shrubby hill of its edge Weena would have stopped, fearing the darkness before us; but a singular sense of impending calamity, that should indeed have served me as a warning, drove me onward. I had been without sleep for a night and two days, and I was feverish and irritable. I felt sleep coming upon me, and the Morlocks with it.

"While we hesitated, among the black bushes behind us, and dim against their blackness, I saw three crouching figures. There was scrub and long grass all about us, and I did not feel safe from their insidious approach. The forest, I calculated, was rather less than a mile across. If we could get through it to the bare hillside, there, as it seemed to me, was an altogether safer resting-place; I thought that with my matches and my camphor I could contrive to keep my path illuminated through the woods. Yet it was evident that if I was to flourish matches with my hands I should have to abandon my firewood; so, rather reluctantly, I put it down. And then it came into my head that I would amaze our friends behind by lighting it. I was to discover the atrocious folly of this proceeding, but it came to my mind as an ingenious move for covering our retreat.

"I don't know if you have ever thought what a rare thing flame must be in the absence of man and in a temperate climate. The sun's heat is rarely strong enough to burn, even when it is focussed by dewdrops, as is sometimes the case in more tropical districts. Lightning may blast and blacken, but it rarely gives rise to widespread fire. Decaying vegetation may occasionally smoulder with the heat of its fermentation, but this rarely results in flame. In this decadence, too, the art of fire-making had been forgotten on the earth. The red tongues that went licking up my heap of wood were an altogether new and strange thing to Weena.

"She wanted to run to it and play with it. I believe she would have cast herself into it had I not restrained her. But I caught her up, and, in spite of her struggles, plunged boldly before me into the wood. For a little way the glare of my fire lit the path. Looking back presently, I could see, through the crowded stems, that from my heap of sticks the blaze had spread to some bushes adjacent, and a curved line of fire was creeping up the grass of the hill. I laughed at that, and turned again to the dark trees before me. It was very black, and Weena clung to me convulsively, but there was still, as my eyes grew accustomed to the darkness, sufficient light for me to avoid the stems. Overhead it was simply black, except where a gap of remote blue sky shone down upon us here and there. I struck none of my matches because I had no hand free. Upon my left arm I carried my little one, in my right hand I had my iron bar.

"For some way I heard nothing but the crackling twigs under my feet, the faint rustle of the breeze above, and my own breathing and the throb of the blood-vessels in my ears. Then I seemed to know of a pattering about me. I pushed on grimly. The pattering grew more distinct, and then I caught the same queer sounds and voices I had heard in the Underworld. There were evidently several of the Morlocks, and they were closing in upon me. Indeed, in another minute I felt a tug at my coat, then something at my arm. And Weena shivered violently, and became quite still.

"It was time for a match. But to get one I must put her down. I did so, and, as I fumbled with my pocket, a struggle began in the darkness about my knees, perfectly silent on her part and with the same peculiar cooing sounds from the Morlocks. Soft little hands, too, were creeping over my coat and back, touching even my neck. Then the match scratched and fizzed. I held it flaring, and saw the white backs of the Morlocks in flight amid the trees. I hastily took a lump of camphor from my pocket, and prepared to light it as soon as the match should wane. Then I looked at Weena. She was lying clutching my feet and quite motionless, with her face to the ground. With a sudden fright I stooped to her. She seemed scarcely to breathe. I lit the block of camphor and flung it to the ground, and as it split and flared up and drove back the Morlocks and the shadows, I knelt down and lifted her. The wood behind seemed full of the stir and murmur of a great company!

"She seemed to have fainted. I put her carefully upon my shoulder and rose to push on, and then there came a horrible realisation. In manœuvering with my matches and Weena, I had turned myself about several times, and now I had not the faintest idea in what direction lay my path. For all I knew, I might be facing back towards the Palace of Green Porcelain. I found myself in a cold sweat. I had to think rapidly what to do. I determined to build a fire and encamp where we were. I put Weena, still motionless, down upon a turfy bole, and very hastily, as my first lump of camphor waned, I began collecting sticks and leaves. Here and there out of the darkness round me the Morlocks' eyes shone like carbuncles.

"The camphor flickered and went out. I lit a match, and as I did so, two white forms that had been approaching Weena dashed hastily away. One was so blinded by the light that he came straight for me and I felt his bones grind under the blow of my fist. He gave a whoop of dismay, staggered a little way, and fell down. I lit another piece of camphor, and went on gathering my bonfire. Presently I noticed how dry was some of the foliage above me, for since my arrival on the Time Machine, a matter of a week, no rain had fallen. So, instead of casting about among the trees for fallen twigs, I began leaping up and dragging down branches. Very soon I had a choking smoky fire of green wood and dry sticks, and could economise my camphor. Then I turned to where Weena lay beside my iron mace. I tried what I could to revive her, but she lay like one dead. I could not even satisfy myself whether or not she breathed.

"Now, the smoke of the fire beat over towards me, and it must have made me heavy of a sudden. Moreover, the vapour of camphor was in the air. My fire would not need replenishing for an hour or so. I felt very weary after my exertion, and sat down. The wood, too, was full of a slumbrous murmur that I did not understand. I seemed just to nod and open my eyes. But all was dark, and the Morlocks had their hands upon me. Flinging off their clinging fingers I hastily felt in my pocket for the match-box, and—it had gone! Then they gripped and closed with me again. In a moment I knew what had happened. I had slept, and my fire had gone out, and the bitterness of death came over my soul. The forest seemed full of the smell of burning wood. I was caught by the neck, by the hair, by the arms, and pulled down. It was indescribably horrible in the darkness to feel all these soft creatures heaped upon me. I felt as if I was in a monstrous spider's web. I was overpowered, and went down. I felt little teeth nipping at my neck. I rolled over, and as I did so my hand came against my iron lever. It gave me strength. I struggled up, shaking the human rats from me, and, holding the bar short, I thrust where I judged their faces might be. I could feel the succulent giving of flesh and bone under my blows, and for a moment I was free.

"The strange exultation that so often seems to accompany hard fighting came upon me. I knew that both I and Weena were lost, but I determined to make the Morlocks pay for their meat. I stood with my back to a tree, swinging the iron bar before me. The whole wood was full of the stir and cries of them. A minute passed. Their voices seemed to rise to a higher pitch of excitement, and their movements grew faster. Yet none came within reach. I stood glaring at the blackness. Then suddenly came hope. What if the Morlocks were afraid? And close on the heels of that came a strange thing. The darkness seemed to grow luminous. Very dimly I began to see the Morlocks about me—three battered at my feet— and then I recognised, with incredulous surprise, that the others were running, in an incessant stream, as it seemed, from behind me, and away through the wood in front. And their backs seemed no longer white, but reddish. As I stood agape, I saw a little red spark go drifting across a gap of starlight between the branches, and vanish. And at that I understood the smell of burning wood, the slumbrous murmur that was growing now into a gusty roar, the red glow, and the Morlocks' flight.

"Stepping out from behind my tree and looking back, I saw, through the black pillars of the nearer trees, the flames of the burning forest. It was my first fire coming after me. With that I looked for Weena, but she was gone. The hissing and crackling behind me, the explosive thud as each fresh tree burst into flame, left little time for reflection. My iron bar still gripped, I followed in the Morlocks' path. It was a close race. Once the flames crept forward so swiftly on my right as I ran that I was outflanked and had to strike off to the left. But at last I emerged upon a small open space, and as I did so, a Morlock came blundering towards me, and past me, and went on straight into the fire!

"And now I was to see the most weird and horrible thing, I think, of all that I beheld in that future age. This whole space was as bright as day with the reflection of the fire. In the centre was a hillock or tumulus, surmounted by a scorched hawthorn. Beyond this was another arm of the burning forest, with yellow tongues already writhing from it, completely encircling the space with a fence of fire. Upon the hillside were some thirty or forty Morlocks, dazzled by the light and heat, and blundering hither and thither against each other in their bewilderment. At first I did not realise their blindness, and struck furiously at them with my bar, in a frenzy of fear, as they approached me, killing one and crippling several more. But when I had watched the gestures of one of them groping under the hawthorn against the red sky, and heard their moans, I was assured of their absolute helplessness and misery in the glare, and I struck no more of them.

"Yet every now and then one would come straight towards me, setting loose a quivering horror that made me quick to elude him. At one time the flames died down somewhat, and I feared the foul creatures would presently be able to see me. I was even thinking of beginning the fight by killing some of them before this should happen; but the fire burst out again brightly, and I stayed my hand. I walked about the hill among them and avoided them, looking for some trace of Weena. But Weena was gone.

"At last I sat down on the summit of the hillock, and watched this strange incredible company of blind things groping to and fro, and making uncanny noises to each other, as the glare of the fire beat on them. The coiling uprush of smoke streamed across the sky, and through the rare tatters of that red canopy, remote as though they belonged to another universe, shone the little stars. Two or three Morlocks came blundering into me, and I drove them off with blows of my fists, trembling as I did so.

"For the most part of that night I was persuaded it was a nightmare. I bit myself and screamed in a passionate desire to awake. I beat the ground with my hands, and got up and sat down again, and wandered here and there, and again sat down. Then I would fall to rubbing my eyes and calling upon God to let me awake. Thrice I saw Morlocks put their heads down in a kind of agony and rush into the flames. But, at last, above the subsiding red of the fire, above the streaming masses of black smoke and the whitening and blackening tree stumps, and the diminishing numbers of these dim creatures, came the white light of the day.

"I searched again for traces of Weena, but there were none. It was plain that they had left her poor little body in the forest. I cannot describe how it relieved me to think that it had escaped the awful fate to which it seemed destined. As I thought of that, I was almost moved to begin a massacre of the helpless abominations about me, but I contained myself. The hillock, as I have said, was a kind of island in the forest. From its summit I could now make out through a haze of smoke the Palace of Green Porcelain, and from that I could get my bearings for the White Sphinx. And so, leaving the remnant of these damned souls still going hither and thither and moaning, as the day grew clearer, I tied some grass about my feet and limped on across smoking ashes and among black stems, that still pulsated internally with fire, towards the hiding-place of the Time Machine. I walked slowly, for I was almost exhausted, as well as lame, and I felt the intensest wretchedness for the horrible death of little Weena. It seemed an overwhelming calamity. Now, in this old familiar room, it is more like the sorrow of a dream than an actual loss. But that morning it left me absolutely lonely again—terribly alone. I began to think of this house of mine, of this fireside, of some of you, and with such thoughts came a longing that was pain.

"But, as I walked over the smoking ashes under the bright morning sky, I made a discovery. In my trouser pocket were still some loose matches. The box must have leaked before it was lost.

§ 10

"About eight or nine in the morning I came to the same seat of yellow metal from which I had viewed the world upon the evening of my arrival. I thought of my hasty conclusions upon that evening and could not refrain from laughing bitterly at my confidence. Here was the same beautiful scene, the same abundant foliage, the same splendid palaces and magnificent ruins, the same silver river running between its fertile banks. The gay robes of the beautiful people moved hither and thither among the trees. Some were bathing in exactly the place where I had saved Weena, and that suddenly gave me a keen stab of pain. And like blots upon the landscape rose the cupolas above the ways to the Underworld. I understood now what all the beauty of the Over-world people covered. Very pleasant was their day, as pleasant as the day of the cattle in the field. Like the cattle, they knew of no enemies and provided against no needs. And their end was the same.

"I grieved to think how brief the dream of the human intellect had been. It had committed suicide. It had set itself steadfastly towards comfort and ease, a balanced society with security and permanency as its watchword, it had attained its hopes—to come to this at last. Once, life and property must have reached almost absolute safety. The rich had been assured of his wealth and comfort, the toiler assured of his life and work. No doubt in that perfect world there had been no unemployed problem, no social question left unsolved. And a great quiet had followed.

"It is a law of nature we overlook, that intellectual versatility is the compensation for change, danger, and trouble. An animal perfectly in harmony with its environment is a perfect mechanism. Nature never appeals to intelligence until habit and instinct are useless. There is no intelligence where there is no change and no need of change. Only those animals partake of intelligence that have to meet a huge variety of needs and dangers.

"So, as I see it, the Upper-world man had drifted towards his feeble prettiness, and the Underworld to mere mechanical industry. But that perfect state had lacked one thing even for mechanical perfection—absolute permanency. Apparently as time went on, the feeding of the Underworld, however it was effected, had become disjointed. Mother Necessity, who had been staved off for a few thousand years, came back again, and she began below. The Underworld being in contact with machinery, which, however perfect, still needs some little thought outside habit, had probably retained perforce rather more initiative, if less of every other human character, than the upper. And when other meat failed them, they turned to what old habit had hitherto forbidden. So I say I saw it in my last view of the world of Eight Hundred and Two Thousand Seven Hundred and One. It may be as wrong an explanation as mortal wit could invent. It is how the thing shaped itself to me, and as that I give it to you.

"After the fatigues, excitements, and terrors of the past days, and in spite of my grief, this seat and the tranquil view and the warm sunlight were very pleasant. I was very tired and sleepy, and soon my theorising passed into dozing. Catching myself at that, I took my own hint, and spreading myself out upon the turf I had a long refreshing sleep.

"I awoke a little before sunsetting. I now felt safe against being caught napping by the Morlocks, and, stretching myself, I came on down the hill towards the White Sphinx. I had my crowbar in one hand, and the other hand played with the matches in my pocket.

"And now came a most unexpected thing. As I approached the pedestal of the sphinx I found the bronze valves were open. They had slid down into grooves.

"At that I stopped short before them, hesitating to enter.

"Within was a small apartment, and on a raised place in the corner of this was the Time Machine. I had the small levers in my pocket. So here, after all my elaborate preparations for the siege of the White Sphinx, was a meek surrender. I threw my iron bar away, almost sorry not to use it.

"A sudden thought came into my head as I stooped towards the portal. For once, at least, I grasped the mental operations of the Morlocks. Suppressing a strong inclination to laugh, I stepped through the bronze frame and up to the Time Machine. I was surprised to find it had been carefully oiled and cleaned. I have suspected since that the Morlocks had even partially taken it to pieces while trying in their dim way to grasp its purpose.

"Now as I stood and examined it, finding a pleasure in the mere touch of the contrivance, the thing I had expected happened. The bronze panels suddenly slid up and struck the frame with a clang. I was in the dark—trapped. So the Morlocks thought. At that I chuckled gleefully.

"I could already hear their murmuring laughter as they came towards me. Very calmly I tried to strike the match. I had only to fix on the levers and depart then like a ghost. But I had overlooked one little thing. The matches were of the abominable kind that light only on the box.

"You may imagine how all my calm vanished. The little brutes were close upon me. One touched me. I made a sweeping blow in the dark at them with the levers, and began to scramble into the saddle of the machine. Then came one hand upon me and then another. Then I had simply to fight against their persistent fingers for my levers, and at the same time feel for the studs over which these fitted. Once, indeed, they almost got away from me. As it slipped from my hand, I had to butt in the dark with my head—I could hear the Morlock's skull ring—to recover it. It was a nearer thing than the fight in the forest, I think, this last scramble.

"But at last the lever was fixed and pulled over. The clinging hands slipped from me. The darkness presently fell from my eyes. I found myself in the same grey light and tumult I have already described.

§ 11

"I have already told you of the sickness and confusion that comes with time travelling. And this time I was not seated properly in the saddle, but sideways and in an unstable fashion. For an indefinite time I clung to the machine as it swayed and vibrated, quite unheeding how I went, and when I brought myself to look at the dials again I was amazed to find where I had arrived. One dial records days, another thousands of days, another million of days, and another thousands of millions. Now, instead of reversing the levers I had pulled them over so as to go forward with them, and when I came to look at these indicators I found that the thousands hand was sweeping round as fast as the seconds hand of a watch—into futurity.

"As I drove on, a peculiar change crept over the appearance of things. The palpitating greyness grew darker; then—though I was still travelling with prodigious velocity—the blinking succession of day and night, which was usually indicative of a slower pace, returned, and grew more and more marked. This puzzled me very much at first. The alternations of night and day grew slower and slower, and so did the passage of the sun across the sky, until they seemed to stretch through centuries. At last a steady twilight brooded over the earth, a twilight only broken now and then when a comet glared across the darkling sky. The bank of light that had indicated the sun had long since disappeared; for the sun had ceased to set—it simply rose and fell in the west, and grew ever broader and more red. All trace of the moon had vanished. The circling of the stars, growing slower and slower, had given place to creeping points of light. At last, some time before I stopped, the sun, red and very large, halted motionless upon the horizon, a vast dome glowing with a dull heat, and now and then suffering a momentary extinction. At one time it had for a little while glowed more brilliantly again, but it speedily reverted to its sullen red heat. I perceived by this slowing down of its rising and setting that the work of the tidal drag was done. The earth had come to rest with one face to the sun, even as in our own time the moon faces the earth. Very cautiously, for I remembered my former headlong fall, I began to reverse my motion. Slower and slower went the circling hands until the thousands one seemed motionless and the daily one was no longer a mere mist upon its scale. Still slower, until the dim outlines of a desolate beach grew visible.

"I stopped very gently and sat upon the Time Machine, looking round. The sky was no longer blue. North-eastward it was inky black, and out of the blackness shone brightly and steadily the pale white stars. Overhead it was a deep Indian red and starless, and south-eastward it grew brighter to a glowing scarlet where, cut by horizon, lay the huge hull of the sun, red and motionless. The rocks about me were of a harsh reddish colour, and all the trace of life that I could see at first was the intensely green vegetation that covered every projecting point on their south-eastern face. It was the same rich green that one sees on forest moss or on the lichen in caves: plants which like these grow in a perpetual twilight.

"The machine was standing on a sloping beach. The sea stretched away to the south-west, to rise into a sharp bright horizon against the wan sky. There were no breakers and no waves, for not a breath of wind was stirring. Only a slight oily swell rose and fell like a gentle breathing, and showed that the eternal sea was still moving and living. And along the margin where the water sometimes broke was a thick incrustation of salt—pink under the lurid sky. There was a sense of oppression in my head, and I noticed that I was breathing very fast. The sensation reminded me of my only experience of mountaineering, and from that I judged the air to be more rarefied than it is now.

"Far away up the desolate slope I heard a harsh scream, and saw a thing like a huge white butterfly go slanting and fluttering up into the sky and, circling, disappear over some low hillocks beyond. The sound of its voice was so dismal that I shivered and seated myself more firmly upon the machine. Looking round me again, I saw that, quite near, what I had taken to be a reddish mass of rock was moving slowly towards me. Then I saw the thing was really a monstrous crab-like creature. Can you imagine a crab as large as yonder table, with its many legs moving slowly and uncertainly, its big claws swaying, its long antennæ, like carters' whips, waving and feeling, and its stalked eyes gleaming at you on either side of its metallic front? Its back was corrugated and ornamented with ungainly bosses, and a greenish incrustation blotched it here and there.

I could see the many palps of its complicated mouth flickering and feeling as it moved.

"As I stared at this sinister apparition crawling towards me, I felt a tickling on my cheek as though a fly had lighted there. I tried to brush it away with my hand, but in a moment it returned, and almost immediately came another by my ear. I struck at this, and caught something threadlike. It was drawn swiftly out of my hand. With a frightful qualm, I turned, and saw that I had grasped the antenna of another monster crab that stood just behind me. Its evil eyes were wriggling on their stalks, its mouth was all alive with appetite, and its vast ungainly claws, smeared with an algal slime, were descending upon me. In a moment my hand was on the lever, and I had placed a month between myself and these monsters. But I was still on the same beach, and I saw them distinctly now as soon as I stopped. Dozens of them seemed to be crawling here and there, in the sombre light, among the foliated sheets of intense green.

"I cannot convey the sense of abominable desolation that hung over the world. The red eastern sky, the northward blackness, the salt Dead Sea, the stony beach crawling with these foul, slow-stirring monsters, the uniform poisonous-looking green of the lichenous plants, the thin air that hurts one's lungs; all contributed to an appalling effect. I moved on a hundred years, and there was the same red sun—a little larger, a little duller—the same dying sea, the same chill air, and the same crowd of earthy crustacea creeping in and out among the green weed and the red rocks. And in the westward sky I saw a curved pale line like a vast new moon.

"So I travelled, stopping ever and again, in great strides of a thousand years or more, drawn on by the mystery of the earth's fate, watching with a strange fascination the sun grow larger and duller in the westward sky, and the life of the old earth ebb away. At last, more than thirty million years hence, the huge red-hot dome of the sun had come to obscure nearly a tenth part of the darkling heavens. Then I stopped once more, for the crawling multitude of crabs had disappeared, and the red beach, save for its livid green liverworts and lichens, seemed lifeless. And now it was flecked with white. A bitter cold assailed me. Rare white flakes ever and again came eddying down. To the north-eastward, the glare of snow lay under the starlight of the sable sky, and I could see an undulating crest of hillocks pinkish white. There were fringes of ice along the sea margin, with drifting masses further out; but the main expanse of that salt ocean, all bloody under the eternal sunset, was still unfrozen.

"I looked about me to see if any traces of animal life remained. A certain indefinable apprehension still kept me in the saddle of the machine. But I saw nothing moving, in earth or sky or sea. The green slime on the rocks alone testified that life was not extinct. A shallow sandbank had appeared in the sea and the water had receded from the beach. I fancied I saw some black object flopping about upon this bank, but it became motionless as I looked at it, and I judged that my eye had been deceived, and that the black object was merely a rock. The stars in the sky were intensely bright and seemed to me to twinkle very little.

"Suddenly I noticed that the circular westward outline of the sun had changed; that a concavity, a bay, had appeared in the curve. I saw this grow larger. For a minute perhaps I stared aghast at this blackness that was creeping over the day, and then I realised that an eclipse was beginning. Either the moon or the planet Mercury was passing across the sun's disk. Naturally, at first I took it to be the moon, but there is much to incline me to believe that what I really saw was the transit of an inner planet passing very near to the earth.

"The darkness grew apace; a cold wind began to blow in freshening gusts from the east, and the showering white flakes in the air increased in number. From the edge of the sea came a ripple and whisper. Beyond these lifeless sounds the world was silent. Silent? It would be hard to convey the stillness of it. All the sounds of man, the bleating of sheep, the cries of birds, the hum of insects, the stir that makes the background of our lives—all that was over. As the darkness thickened, the eddying flakes grew more abundant, dancing before my eyes; and the cold of the air more intense. At last, one by one, swiftly, one after the other, the white peaks of the distant hills vanished into blackness. The breeze rose to a moaning wind. I saw the black central shadow of the eclipse sweeping towards me. In another moment the pale stars alone were visible. All else was rayless obscurity. The sky was absolutely black.

"A horror of this great darkness came on me. The cold, that smote to my marrow, and the pain I felt in breathing, overcame me. I shivered, and a deadly nausea seized me. Then like a red-hot bow in the sky appeared the edge of the sun. I got off the machine to recover myself. I felt giddy and incapable of facing the return journey. As I stood sick and confused I saw again the moving thing upon the shoal—there was no mistake now that it was a moving thing—against the red water of the sea. It was a round thing, the size of a football perhaps, or, it may be, bigger, and tentacles trailed down from it; it seemed black against the weltering blood-red water, and it was hopping fitfully about. Then I felt I was fainting. But a terrible dread of lying helpless in that remote and awful twilight sustained me while I clambered upon the saddle.

§ 12

"So I came back. For a long time I must have been insensible upon the machine. The blinking succession of the days and nights was resumed, the sun got golden again, the sky blue. I breathed with greater freedom. The fluctuating contours of the land ebbed and flowed. The hands spun backward upon the dials. At last I saw again the dim shadows of houses, the evidences of decadent humanity. These, too, changed and passed, and others came. Presently, when the million dial was at zero, I slackened speed. I began to recognise our own petty and familiar architecture, the thousands hand ran back to the starting-point, the night and day flapped slower and slower. Then the old walls of the laboratory came round me. Very gently, now, I slowed the mechanism down.

"I saw one little thing that seemed odd to me. I think I have told you that when I set out, before my velocity became very high, Mrs. Watchett had walked across the room, travelling, as it seemed to me, like a rocket. As I returned, I passed again across that minute when she traversed the laboratory. But now every motion appeared to be the exact inversion of her previous ones. The door at the lower end opened, and she glided quietly up the laboratory, back foremost, and disappeared behind the door by which she had previously entered. Just before that I seemed to see Hillyer for a moment; but he passed like a flash.

"Then I stopped the machine, and saw about me again the old familiar laboratory, my tools, my appliances just as I had left them. I got off the thing very shakily, and sat down upon my bench. For several minutes I trembled violently. Then I became calmer. Around me was my old work-shop again, exactly as it had been. I might have slept there, and the whole thing have been a dream.

"And yet, not exactly! The thing had started from the south-east corner of the laboratory. It had come to rest again in the north-west, against the wall where you saw it. That gives you the exact distance from my little lawn to the pedestal of the White Sphinx, into which the Mor-locks had carried my machine.

"For a time my brain went stagnant. Presently I got up and came through the passage here, limping, because my heel was still painful, and feeling sorely begrimed. I saw the *Pall Mall Gazette* on the table by the door. I found the date was indeed to-day, and looking at the timepiece, saw the hour was almost eight o'clock. I heard your voices and the clatter of plates. I hesitated—I felt so sick and weak. Then I sniffed good whole-some meat, and opened the door on you. You know the rest. I washed, and dined, and now I am telling you the story."

"I know," he said, after a pause, "that all this will be absolutely incredible to you. To me the one incredible thing is that I am here to-night in this old familiar room, looking into your friendly faces and telling you these strange adventures."

He looked at the Medical Man. "No. I cannot expect you to believe it. Take it as a lie—or a prophecy. Say I dreamed it in the workshop. Consider I have been speculating upon the destinies of our race until I have hatched this fiction. Treat my assertion of its truth as a mere stroke of art to enhance its interest. And taking it as a story, what do you think of it?"

He took up his pipe, and began, in his old accustomed manner, to tap with it nervously upon the bars of the grate. There was a momentary stillness. Then chairs began to creak and shoes to scrape upon the carpet.

I took my eyes off the Time Traveller's face, and looked round at his audience. They were in the dark, and little spots of colour swam before them. The Medical Man seemed absorbed in the contemplation of our host. The Editor was looking hard at the end of his cigar—the sixth. The Journalist fumbled for his watch. The others, as far as I remember, were motionless.

The Editor stood up with a sigh. "What a pity it is you're not a writer of stories!" he said, putting his hand on the Time Traveller's shoulder.

"You don't believe it?"

"Well——"

"I thought not."

The Time Traveller turned to us. "Where are the matches?" he said. He lit one and spoke over his pipe, puffing. "To tell you the truth . . . I hardly believe it myself. . . . And yet . . ."

"His eye fell with a mute inquiry upon the withered white flowers upon the little table. Then he turned over the hand holding his pipe, and I saw he was looking at some half-healed scars on his knuckles.

"The Medical Man rose, came to the lamp, and examined the flowers. "The gynæceum's odd," he said. The Psychologist leant forward to see, holding out his hand for a specimen.

"I'm hanged if it isn't a quarter to one," said the Journalist. "How shall we get home?"

"Plenty of cabs at the station," said the Psychologist.

"It's a curious thing," said the Medical Man; "but I certainly don't know the natural order of these flowers. May I have them?"

The Time Traveller hesitated. Then suddenly: "Certainly not."

"Where did you really get them?" said the Medical Man.

The Time Traveller put his hand to his head. He spoke like one who was trying to keep hold of an idea that eluded him. "They were put into my pocket by Weena, when I travelled into Time." He stared round the room. "I'm damned if it isn't all going. This room and you and the atmosphere of every day is too much for my memory. Did I ever make a Time Machine, or a model of a Time Machine? Or is it all only a dream? They say life is a dream, a precious poor dream at times—but I can't stand another that won't fit. It's madness. And where did the dream come from? . . . I must look at that machine. If there *is* one!"

He caught up the lamp swiftly, and carried it, flaring red, through the door into the corridor. We followed him. There in the flickering light of the lamp was the machine sure enough, squat, ugly, and askew; a thing of brass, ebony, ivory, and translucent glimmering quartz. Solid to the touch—for I put out my hand and felt the rail of it—and with brown spots and smears upon the ivory, and bits of grass and moss upon the lower parts, and one rail bent awry.

The Time Traveller put the lamp down on the bench, and ran his hand along the damaged rail. "It's all right now," he said. "The story I told you was true. I'm sorry to have brought you out here in the cold." He took up the lamp, and, in an absolute silence, we returned to the smoking-room.

He came into the hall with us and helped the Editor on with his coat. The Medical Man looked into his face and, with a certain hesitation, told him he was suffering from overwork, at which he laughed hugely. I remember him standing in the open doorway, bawling good night.

I shared a cab with the Editor. He thought the tale a "gaudy lie." For my own part I was unable to come to a conclusion. The story was so fantastic and incredible, the telling so credible and sober. I lay awake most of the night thinking about it. I determined to go next day and see the Time Traveller again. I was told he was in the laboratory, and being on easy terms in the house, I went up to him. The laboratory, however, was empty. I stared for a minute at the Time Machine and put out my hand and touched the lever. At that the squat substantial-looking mass swayed like a bough shaken by the wind. Its instability startled me extremely, and I had a queer reminiscence of the childish days when I used to be forbidden to meddle. I came back through the corridor. The Time Traveller met me in the smoking-room. He was coming from the house. He had a small camera under one arm and a knapsack under the other. He laughed when he saw me, and gave me an elbow to shake. "I'm frightfully busy," said he, "with that thing in there."

"But is it not some hoax?" I said. "Do you really travel through time?"

"Really and truly I do." And he looked frankly into my eyes. He hesitated. His eye wandered about the room. "I only want half an hour," he said. "I know why you came, and it's awfully good of you. There's some magazines here. If you'll stop to lunch I'll prove you this time travelling up to the hilt, specimens and all. If you'll forgive my leaving you now?"

I consented, hardly comprehending then the full import of his words, and he nodded and went on down the corridor. I heard the door of the laboratory slam, seated myself in a chair, and took up a daily paper. What was he going to do before lunchtime? Then suddenly I was reminded by an advertisement that I had promised to meet Richardson, the publisher, at two. I looked at my watch, and saw that I could barely save that engagement. I got up and went down the passage to tell the Time Traveller.

As I took hold of the handle of the door I heard an exclamation, oddly truncated at the end, and a click and a thud. A gust of air whirled round me as I opened the door, and from within came the sound of broken glass falling on the floor. The Time Traveller was not there. I seemed to see a ghostly, indistinct figure sitting in a whirling mass of black and brass for a moment—a figure so transparent that the bench behind with its sheets of drawings was absolutely distinct; but this phantasm vanished as I rubbed my eyes. The Time Machine had gone. Save for a subsiding stir of dust, the further end of the laboratory was empty. A pane of the skylight had, apparently, just been blown in.

I felt an unreasonable amazement. I knew that something strange had happened, and for the moment could not distinguish what the strange thing might be. As I stood staring, the door into the garden opened, and the man-servant appeared.

We looked at each other. Then ideas began to come. "Has Mr. _____ gone out that way?" said I.

"No, sir. No one has come out this way. I was expecting to find him here."

At that I understood. At the risk of disappointing Richardson I stayed on, waiting for the Time Traveller; waiting for the second, perhaps still stranger story, and the specimens and photographs he would bring with him. But I am beginning now to fear that I must wait a lifetime. The Time Traveller vanished three years ago. And, as everybody knows now, he has never returned.

EPILOGUE

One cannot choose but wonder. Will he ever return? It may be that he swept back into the past, and fell among the blood-drinking, hairy savages of the Age of Unpolished Stone, into the abysses of the Cretaceous Sea; or among the grotesque saurians, the huge reptilian brutes of the Jurassic times. He may even now—if I may use the phrase—be wandering on some plesiosaurus-haunted Oolitic coral reef, or beside the lonely saline lakes of the Triassic Age. Or did he go forward, into one of the nearer ages, in which men are still men, but with the riddles of our own time answered and its wearisome problems solved? Into the manhood of the race: for I, for my own part, cannot think that these latter days of weak experiment, fragmentary theory, and mutual discord are indeed man's culminating time! I say, for my own part. He, I know—for the question had been discussed among us long before the Time Machine was made—thought but cheerlessly of the Advancement of Mankind, and saw in the growing pile of civilisation only a foolish heaping that must inevitably fall back upon and destroy its makers in the end. If that is so, it remains for us to live as though it were not so. But to me the future is still black and blank—is a vast ignorance, lit at a few casual places by the memory of his story. And I have by me, for my comfort, two strange white flowers—shrivelled now, and brown and flat and brittle—to witness that even when mind and strength had gone, gratitude and a mutual tenderness still lived on in the heart of man.

Notes

CHAPTER 1

1. "The Time Traveller ... speak of him." The Time Traveller is Dr. Moses Nebogipfel, Ph.D., F.R.S., N.W.R., PAID [*sic*] in *The Chronic Argonauts* (see Appendix I) and Wells named him Bayliss in a section of a later, rejected draft of *The Time Machine* (see Appendix VII). In *The National Observer Time Machine* (Appendix III) he is not given a name but is variously referred to as "The Philosophical Inventor," "The Inventor," "The Philosophical Investigator," "The Philosopher," and "The Time Traveller." The *New Review* version of *The Time Machine* (Appendix IV) refers to him as "The Inventor" and "The Time Traveller."

As David Ketterer notes: "the name of the Time Traveller remains an enigma. It is tempting to identify him, by analogy at least, with H. G. Wells." (But Ketterer then goes on to explore a more meaningful analogue with Oedipus [1982, 340].) Unfortunately, two Hollywood films—*The Time Machine* (1960) and *Time After Time* (1979)—have already yielded to that temptation and conveyed to millions that Wells and the Time Traveller were/are identical.

Although all fictional characters are autobiographical to some degree, the assumption that the Time Traveller is merely an alter ego of his author is more misleading than helpful. Wells's presence in *The Time Machine* can be discerned not in a simplistic identification with the main character but in an ironic interplay of the two narrative voices.

None of this, of course, helps us identify the Time Traveller. However, several commentators have advanced reasons why the Time Traveller is never named.

Lake asserts that: "he is not a particular individual, he is all of us. We are all time travellers, but as things are, our voyages can seldom stretch further than seventy or eighty years" (1979, 79–80).

Richard Wasson offers a different explanation: "The naming of the Traveller distances him ... from any social class. His name unlike the others does not refer to a profession existing within the contemporary social framework. ... He is thus distanced from the opaque class identity of his peers and consequently his opinions and judgments of the Morlocks, the Eloi, the struggle between them, and his relation to it, seem to come from a representative, if untypical human. His class anonymity is crucial not only to his assumption of the role of Everyman ... but to the audience acceptance of his descriptions, value judgments and actions in this tale of class war" (1980, 116).

A third reason is suggested by Peter Kemp: "Arnold Bennett, always one of the most perceptive commentators on Wells, told him, 'You are not really interested in individual humanity ... you always recur to a variation of the same type of hero, and you always will, because your curiosity about individualities won't lead you any further.' In *The New Machiavelli* Wells attacks Altiora Bailey (a vindictive depiction of Beatrice Webb) on the grounds that it was 'a favourite trick' of hers 'to speak of everybody as a type; she saw men as samples moving.' Yet in his novels, this is what he repeatedly does. In his first published fiction, *The Time Machine*, most of the characters are not even named but are given labels underlining their generalized nature ..." (1982, 2–3).

2. "expounding a recondite matter to us." In this chapter "us" refers to the Time Traveller's six guests: Filby ("an argumentative person with red hair"), the

Psychologist, the Medical Man, Hillyer (the narrator of the framing or outer narrative) who is not identified by name until chapter 12 (see 12, note 3), the Provincial Mayor (called the "Rector" in the *New Review Time Machine* and referred to by both titles in the Holt edition), and the Very Young Man. In chapter 2, which takes place "the next Thursday," the Psychologist, the Medical Man, and Hillyer are the Time Traveller's guests once again, but Blank the Editor, the Journalist, and the Silent Man ("a quiet, shy man with a beard") appear in place of Filby, the Provincial Mayor, and the Very Young Man. Toward the end of the chapter the Time Traveller refers to his three new guests as Blank, Dash, and Chose.

3. "incandescent lights." The Time Traveller's chairs (which Scholes and Rabkin [1977, 202] consider "implausible") are his own patents, but his household lighting is not innovative. Incandescent illumination was in widespread use during the 1880s and 1890s following the patenting (1886) of the perfected incandescent gas mantle by Auer von Welsbach.

4. "lilies of silver." Keith Nettle (1966, 121) interprets this to mean "the silver fittings" shaped like lilies, which held the lights." However, in the nineteenth century lilies were (as they still are) common ornamental *engravings* on silverware.

5. "the trammels of precision." The constraints of being accurate. The Outer Narrator is underscoring the notion that the atmosphere is not conducive to a discussion of serious matters, a view that the Time Traveller is unable to dispel by the end of the chapter when the Medical Man asks him, "Look here . . . are you perfectly serious? Or is this a trick—like that ghost you showed us last Christmas?"

6. "a lean forefinger." The first of the very few physical details Wells gives us of the Time Traveller. The end of chapter 1 refers to his "queer, broad head" and chapter 2 mentions his "white, sincere face." In chapter 5 he himself states: "I am not a young man." The Outer Narrator is more explicit about the Time Traveller's *personality* than about his appearance: see the first paragraph of chapter 2.

7. "The geometry . . . misconception." The Time Traveller is, of course, referring to Euclidean geometry which mathematicians from the nineteenth century onward (see note 13) considered to be too limited rather than founded on a misconception. As recently as 1962 W. T. Fishback corrected the prevailing view of non-mathematicians thus: "It is widely believed that geometry, as contained in Euclid's *Elements* is perfect and complete; there are no flaws in the text, and all of geometry is to be found there. This is not the case. The geometry of Euclid is only one of many possible geometries . . . Euclid's work is not logically perfect . . . many of Euclid's proofs can no longer be accepted as proofs and the sets of axioms and definitions he gave are incomplete." *Projective and Euclidean Geometry* (New York: John Wiley and Sons, 1962), 1.

8. "You know . . . mere abstractions." These comments are supported by typical textbook definitions of a line and a plane: e.g., a line is a continuous extent of length without breadth or thickness. But Wells is echoing Hinton's words (see next note and Appendix X): "A plane and a line are mere abstractions."

9. "Can a cube . . . existence." This question—and the very idea of The Time Machine itself—may have been an extrapolation from the following passage in an essay by Charles H. Hinton (see note 11), "What is the Fourth Dimension?" (1884): "A being existing in four dimensions must then be thought to be as completely bounded in all four directions as we are in three. . . . Such a being would be able to make but a part of himself visible to us, for a cube would be apprehended by a two-dimensional being as the square in which it stood. Thus a four-dimensional being would suddenly appear as a complete and finite body, and as suddenly disappear, leaving no trace of himself, in space, in the same way that anything

lying on a flat surface, would, on being lifted, suddenly vanish out of the cognizance of beings, whose consciousness was confined to the plane. The object would not vanish by moving in any direction, but disappear instantly as a whole. There would be no barrier, no confinement of our devising that would not be perfectly open to him. He could come and go at pleasure; he would be able to perform feats of the most surprising kind" (1980, 17). See further Appendix X.

Hinton's most frequent "practical" demonstrations of the nature of the Fourth Dimension involved the use of a set of 27 colored *cubes* which fitted together into a single large cube. See further Rucker (1977, 127–28).

10. "a natural infirmity of the flesh." Echoing Romans 6:19: "I speak after the manner of men because of the infirmity of your flesh."

11. "the Fourth Dimension." See chapter 3, note 11.

Costa (1967, 32) comments: "For a generation yet to hear of Albert Einstein, the opening pages of *The Time Machine* provided an introduction to the possibilities of the Fourth Dimension which in 1895 was not elsewhere available outside of scientific journals."

The term and concept of a fourth dimension seems to have been first popularized by Hinton (1853–1907) with his essay "What is the Fourth Dimension?" which appeared in his two-volume *Scientific Romances* (London: Swan Sonnenschein & Co., 1884–1885). Hinton conceived of the fourth dimension as another dimension of space, at right angles to the other three dimensions. By contrast, The Time Traveller expresses two different conceptions of the fourth dimension. Early in chapter 1 he talks about it as a dimension of human consciousness, a notion anticipated not by Hinton or Newcomb (see note 14) but by the "Thoughtland" of Edwin Abbott's *Flatland* (London: Seeley, 1884). But later in the same chapter he seems to be following Hinton and Newcomb in asserting that "Time is only a kind of Space." See further: Philmus (1976, 30); also chapter 12, note 1, and Appendix X.

In his "Preface" to *Seven Famous Novels* (1934, ix), Wells himself explains the origins of his interest in the subject without mentioning Hinton: "In my student days we were much exercised by talk about a possible fourth dimension of space; the fairly obvious idea that events could be presented in a rigid four-dimensional space-time framework had occurred to me, and this is used as the magic trick for a glimpse of the future that ran counter to the placid assumption of that time that Evolution was a pro-human force making things better and better for mankind."

Apropos of the narrative function of the theory of four dimensions, Huntington (1981, 240) argues that Wells "is doing more than merely justifying the 'science' of the story, he is invoking a structure that allows our world and the world of 802, 701 to share the same space. That this 'two-world' structure is important to Wells's imagination is shown by the comparatively large number of stories in which he develops no plot or moral, but in which he takes considerable pains simply to establish a juxtaposition of two incongruous worlds."

12. "*There is no difference . . . moves along it.*" Later in this chapter the Time Traveller corrects the Medical Man's misconceptions about movement in Time by making a similar observation: "Our mental existences, which are immaterial and have no dimensions, are passing along the Time-Dimension with a uniform velocity from the cradle to the grave."

Philmus suggests that Wells may have derived the conception of time as a dimension of consciousness from either William James or Henri Bergson. He quotes a passage from James with which Wells was almost certainly familiar: "The unit of composition of our perception of time is *duration*, with a bow and a stern, as it were,—a rearward and forward-looking end," *Principles of Psychology* (New York: Henry Holt, 1890) I, 609.

But was Wells acquainted with this passage *before* writing *The Time Machine*? Philmus notices that Wells's personal copy of *Principles of Psychology* (now in the Wells Archive, University of Illinois), a gift from his wife, Amy, is inscribed with the date November 9, 1898—i.e., more than four years *subsequent* to the publication of *The Time Machine* in the *National Observer* (March-June 1894). Philmus cautiously observes: "Whether Wells had read James's book prior to his writing the first episode of the *National Observer Time Machine* is not clear. But psychologistic ideas of time were "in the air" in the early 1890s. Henri Bergson, for instance, treats time as *La durée* in his *Essai sur les données immediates de la conscience* (1889) and in subsequent works." See further Philmus (1976, 29–30).

Actually psychologistic conceptions of time had been advanced more than half a century before Bergson. For example, in his major treatise, *The World as Will and Representation* (1818), Supplement: Chapter XV, Schopenhauer states: "Our self-consciousness has not space as its form, but only time; therefore our thinking does not, like our perceiving, take place in *three* dimensions, but merely in *one*, that is, in a line, without breadth and depth."

13. "Four-Dimensional Geometry." Geometry of more than three dimensions was not developed until early in the nineteenth century. Aristotle in Book I of his *Heaven* had stated: "The line has magnitude in one way, the plane in two ways, and the solid in three ways, and beyond these there is no other magnitude because three are all." Mathematicians were still echoing this assumption two thousand years later. Thus, in 1685, John Wallis observed: "Length, Breadth and Thickness, take up the whole of Space. Nor can Fansie [sic] imagine how there should be a Fourth Local Dimension beyond these Three."

Nearly a century later, D'Alembert (1717–1783), in an article on "Dimension" published in Diderot's *Encyclopédie*, suggested provocatively that mechanics could be regarded as a geometry of four dimensions with time as the fourth dimension. But serious interest in the fourth dimension remained dormant until 1827, when Moebius began speculation on the mathematics of four-dimensional space. In 1844 Grassman developed systematically the abstract geometry of several dimensions in his *Ausdehnungslehre* (Expansion Theory). The growth of interest in this aspect of mathematics may be ascertained from the fact that a 1911 bibliography on the geometry of n dimensions listed no fewer than 1,832 references. See further Henry Parker Manning, *Geometry of Four Dimensions* (New York: Macmillan, 1914), 1–11.

14. "Professor Simon Newcomb . . . a month or so ago." Simon Newcomb (1835–1909), Professor of Mathematics, U. S. Navy and also at Johns Hopkins, was President of both the American Mathematical Society and the Astronomical and Astrophysical Society of America, and editor of the *American Journal of Mathematics*.

The New York Mathematical Society was instituted in 1888 and became the American Mathematical Society in 1894.

Newcomb "expounded" on the subject of four-dimensional geometry in his Presidential address to the New York Mathematical Society in December 1893. The address provided the basis of his article, "Modern Mathematical Thought," *Nature* 49 (February 1, 1894), 325–29. (A development of his ideas on this topic was published as "The Philosophy of Hyper-Space", *Science*, n.s. 7 (1898), 1–7.) See Appendix X.

15. "For instance . . . thing." Colin Wilson (1981, 15) referring to this passage, claims that the notion that time is no more than an extra dimension of space both anticipates the Einstein-Minkowski notion of space time and *appears* to be a possible explanation for precognition. But then he points out that time travel "has one logical defect. The time traveller could travel back to meet his self of

the previous day . . . [which is exactly what happens to the hero of David Gerrold's intriguing time-travel novel, *The Man Who Folded Himself*, 1973]. In short, the notion of time travel contains the hidden supposition that there are thousands of parallel universes . . . each a fraction of a second ahead or behind this one in time. But then each universe would either have to be 'frozen' or have its *own* past and future—a contradiction of the original assumption of time as an 'extra dimension'." For other objections to time travel, see note 30 below.

16. "There are balloons." See also the remark concerning "gravitation in a balloon," about a page later.

There had been numerous balloon flights since the pioneer ascent by the Montgolfiers in 1783. Wells, of course, was writing nearly a decade before the Wright Brothers made the first successful airplane flight, at Kittyhawk, N.C., December 17, 1903. In *Anticipations* (1900) he predicted that the first airplane flight would have occurred by 1950. His novel, *The War in the Air* (1908) envisaged a global air war involving airplanes and dirigibles.

17. "fifty miles . . . surface." At that period a reference to the unknown. Fifty miles above the earth's surface would be the mesopause, at the top of the mesosphere layer (of the earth's atmosphere), of which little or nothing was known in the 1890s.

18. "why should . . . the Time-Dimension." The comment anticipates the time-travel idea in Wells's short story "The New Accelerator" (1903), which seems to have been anticipated by William James. See further Philmus (1976, 29).

19. "the accepted account of the Battle of Hastings." William of Normandy (later known as William the Conqueror) defeated Harold, King of England. The battle, which took place at Senlac near Hastings on the south coast of England, occurred, as every British schooboy knows, in 1066. The "accepted account" to which the Psychologist refers was mainly derived from the depiction of the battle in the famous Bayeux Tapestry (c. 1090).

20. " 'Our ancestors . . . anachronisms.' " Mark Twain exploits the comic value of such anachronisms in that earlier time-travel story, *A Connecticut Yankee at King Arthur's Court* (1889).

21. "they would . . . the Little-go." To "plough" was British universities' slang for "fail" with particular reference to examinations. The term had been in use among students since the 1850s. The Little-go was the *colloquial* name, at Cambridge, for the first examination for the B.A. degree, officially known as "The Previous Examination." Originally an examination in the classics, by the 1890s it had become mainly an examination in history, literature, and one or more languages. The comparable examination at Oxford was called "Responsions."

22. "The German scholars . . . Greek so much." The speaker is unidentified—presumably it's the Medical Man. His cynical comment is double-edged. It suggests that German scholars would, somewhat arrogantly, have corrected the pronunciation of the ancient Greeks themselves. In so doing it refers (a) to the controversy between the Erasmians and the Modernists over the pronunciation of ancient Greek and (b) to the dominance of Greek studies by German scholars.

From the sixteenth century onward, many scholars, referring to Quintilian's *Institutio Oratoria* and following the work of Erasmus, developed a hypothetical pronunciation of ancient Greek (based on rhyme and other evidence). The strongest proponents of Erasmian pronunciation were German scholars who introduced most of the refinements or "improvements" in Greek pronunciation during the latter half of the nineteenth century. They were opposed by Modernists, who maintained that the Erasmians had based their hypotheses on false assumptions. (For example, despite the evidence of rhyme, no one could really be certain how the ancient Greeks pronounced diphthongs.) The modern Greeks who spearheaded the Modernist position, preferred to use the pronunciation of modern Greek as a model for pronouncing ancient Greek. But by the 1890s, due primarily to the efforts of German scholars, the Erasmian pronunciation was accepted throughout Europe—except for Greece. See further Friedrich Blass, *Pronunciation of Ancient Greek* (Cambridge: At the University Press, 1890), 5–6.

The dominance of Greek studies by German scholars in the nineteenth century is vividly demonstrated in a two-page listing of eminent nineteenth-century classicists drawn up by Sir John Edwin Sandys. One page is devoted to German-speaking scholars; the other to all the rest of Europe! See *A History of Classical Scholarship* (New York: Hafner Publishing Co., 1958), vol. 3, 48–49.

23. "One might invest . . . hurry on ahead." The Very Young Man anticipates the experiences of Graham, the hero of Wells's *When the Sleeper Wakes* (1899).

24. " 'To discover . . . communistic basis.' " Compare, in chapter 4, the Time Traveller's reaction to the absence of private houses in the year 802,701.

McConnell (1977, 18) notes: "There is much speculation about communism in *The Time Machine*, and it is important to realize that in the 1890s communism was not limited to the Marxist variety. In fact, Marxist Communism had come to a temporary standstill in Europe and was under attack from a number of rivals." On nineteenth-century communism see further Edmund Wilson, *To the Finland Station; A Study in the Writing and Acting of History* (New York: Harcourt Brace & Co., 1940).

25. "Burslem." One of the so-called "Five Towns" in the famous pottery-making region of Staffordshire, England. The other four towns are Stoke-on-Trent, Hanley, Tunstall, and Longton. Arnold Bennett was born and raised in Hanley; his novels deal extensively with the Five Towns.

Wells noted rather whimsically: "Arnold Bennett . . . wrote to me first, in September 1897 . . . to ask how I came to know about the Potteries, which I had mentioned in *The Time Machine* . . . and after that we corresponded. In a second letter he says he is "glad to find the Potteries made such an impression" on me, so I suppose I had enlarged upon their scenic interest . . ." *Experiment in Auto-biography* (1934), 533.

26. "sconces." Ornamental brackets fixed to the wall, for holding candles.

27. "This saddle." *Saddle* is a British term for the seat of a bicycle and this together with Hillyer's earlier description of the "glittering metallic framework" of the model Time Machine suggests a design not unlike a bicycle. My impression concurs with the notion of Alfred Jarry in his essay, "How to Construct a Time Machine" (1899): "The machine consists of an ebony frame, similar to the steel frame of a bicycle." (See further Appendix VIII). Marc Le Bot in *Le Macchine Celibi* (New York: Rizzoli, 1975) p. 44 refers to the Time Machine as "Wells's bicycle-clock." Is it mere coincidence that—in his Preface to the 1931 Random House edition of *The Time Machine*—Wells himself actually makes an association between his novella and a bicycle? "So," he writes, "the *Time Machine* has lasted as long as the diamond-framed safety bicycle which came in about the date of its first publication."

28. "We all saw . . . bare." Suvin (1979, 213) notices how "the technique of domesticating the improbable by previews on a smaller scale, employed in the vivid vanishing of the model machine" recurs in many other stories by Wells. An interesting example is found in *The Invisible Man*: Kemp makes a cat invisible before trying his experiment on himself.

29. "a spill." A long, slender strip of wood or twisted paper used in lighting candles, pipes, etc.

30. "Serious objections." Parrinder (1981, 15) notes: "the fundamental objection to [time travel] . . . I believe, is the one put forward by Israel Zangwill in his column in the *Pall Mall Magazine* for September 1895: to travel forward more

than a few years in time is to travel through one's own death. . . . It is also, one might add, to travel through the death of the machine: metal fatigue and corrosion are often swifter processes than the decay of the human body". Parrinder (1981, 15). Parrinder (1972, 40–42) reprints Zangwill's entire column on *The Time Machine*.

But are the objections of Zangwill and Parrinder really valid? Time travel would, surely, take both the Time Traveller and the Time Machine outside the time frame in which they began? Since the Time Traveller ceased existing in the 1890s, he would not have died in the natural course of events in the 19th or 20th centuries; thus he could not have travelled forward through his own death. Presumably his death would occur in the future of whatever period he finally travelled to.

For various other objections to time-travel see above note 15 and also: Stanislaw Lem, "The Time-Travel Story and Related Matters of SF Structuring," *Science-Fiction Studies*, 1, pt. 3 (Spring 1974), 143–54; Hillary Putnam and J. J. C. Smart, "Time Travel," in Peter A. French, *Philosophers in Wonderland* (Saint Paul, Minn.: Llewellyn Publications 1975), 100–105; Rudolf v. B. Rucker, "Time Travel," in his *Geometry, Relativity and the Fourth Dimension* (New York: Dover Publications, Inc., 1977), 92–99; W. B. Pitkin, "Time and Pure Activity," *Journal of Philosophy, Psychology and Scientific Methods* 11 (1914), 521–26; Peter Nicholls, *The Science in Science Fiction* (New York: Knopf, 1983), 88–99; Amit Goswami, *The Cosmic Dancers* (New York: Harper & Row, 1983), 252–60; Richard Heffern, *Time Travel, Myth or Reality?* (New York: Pyramid Books, 1977); Richard Swinburne, *Space and Time* (New York: St. Martin's Press, 1981), 156.

Suvin (1975, 108–109), bypassing the impossibility of time-travel, argues that "the Time Machine itself is validated by an efficient *forestalling of possible objections* [italics mine], put into the mouth of schematic, none-too-bright, and reluctantly persuaded listeners, rather than by the bogus theory of the fourth dimension or any explanations of the gleaming bars glimpsed in the machine."

31. "presentation below the threshold." I.e., below the limen or point at which the least amount of any given stimulus becomes perceptible. McConnell (1977, 21) explains the comment as "below the threshold of consciousness or, as we now say, subliminally." But these need not be the same. We may be *conscious* that something is being presented to us subliminally even though we cannot perceive it. For example, we could have seen in slow motion (and therefore be conscious of) shots of a movie that are subliminal to us when projected at normal speed.

32. "paradox." Note how in chapter 2 the Psychologist persists in viewing time travel as a paradox; but by that time Hillyer (the outer narrator) has become more critical of his attitude: "the Psychologist volunteered a wooden account of the 'ingenious paradox and trick' we had witnessed that day week." The Editor follows up Hillyer's report of the Psychologist's attitude by remarking: "A man couldn't cover himself with dust by rolling in a paradox, could he?"

33. "A larger edition . . . eyes." See also note 27 above. Although the Time Machine is described as a "larger edition" of the model, a few details (such as the nickel parts) are mentioned only in the description of the full-size machine. With both descriptions Wells gives us very specific details of *parts* of the machine (saddle, white lever, crystalline bars, etc.) while cleverly avoiding clear specification of the machine as a whole.

There is some contradiction in the narrator's reactions to the Time Machine. We are told that it is "a larger edition" of the model which the Outer Narrator describes as "very delicately made" and the Medical Man as "beautifully made." These words, together with the descriptive details of the Time Machine itself, convey the impression that Hillyer and the other guest perceive it as an object of beauty. Yet in chapter 12 the Outer Narrator inexplicably refers to it as "squat" and "ugly."

34. "Or is this a trick . . . Christmas?" Trick ghosts were popular pantomime and parlor entertainments throughout the nineteenth century. For an intriguing account of such "Fantasms" (as they were often called), see Erik Barnouw, *The Magician and the Cinema* (New York: Oxford University Press, 1981), 19–33. See chapter 12, note 12.

CHAPTER 2

1. "I think that at the time . . . believed." John Huntington comments: "It is not by accident that the Time Traveller has the reputation of being too ingenious to be believed. [There] . . . inevitably lurks the question of fraud. The extraordinary truth is impossible to prove, and the narrator takes pains to point out supporting evidence, to analyze his sources' motives. . . ." See further the discussion of stories of fraud and their insights into the nature of fiction ("which is, after all, the quintessential confidence trick") in Huntington (1981, 240–53).

2. "egg-shell china." Nettle (1966, 122) explains this as "china made of very fine porcelain, easily breakable."

This is the first of the narrative's several references or images relating to china or porcelain. In chapter 4 the Time Traveller refers to the "Dresden-china type of prettiness" of the Eloi; in chapter 8 he visits the Palace of Green Porcelain. See also chapter 4, note 4 and chapter 6, note 4.

3. "the Linnaean." One of London's distinguished learned societies. It was instituted in 1788 to preserve the scientific specimens of Carl Von Linné, popularly known as Linnaeus (1707–1778), the Swedish naturalist who developed the modern system for classifying and naming living organisms. During the nineteenth century the Society became a center for scientific discussion. It was there, in 1858, that Charles Darwin first revealed his theory of evolution to his fellow scientists.

4. "Tübingen." A venerable German university, established in the fifteenth century. It is near Stuttgart.

5. "The next Thursday." The first specific "time" reference in the narrative and the one that enables us to ascertain the story's time frame. See Structure section of the Introduction.

6. "Richmond." I.e., the somewhat hilly district of London where the Time Traveller's house is located. A residential area situated southwest of London, it is sometimes called Richmond-on-Thames.

Of relevance to the geographical details in *The Time Machine* is the comment in Mackenzie (1973, 28) that Wells "explicitly linked his destructive fantasies with his keen topographical sense—a link that he made repeatedly in his scientific romances."

7. "four or five men . . . drawing-room." See chapter 1, note 2.

8. "that day week." Exactly a week earlier.

9. "his chin . . . half healed." The result of a fall. See the fourth paragraph of chapter 5.

10. "He walked . . . tramps." The Time Traveller explains the cause of this limp in chapter 7: "The heel of one of my shoes was loose, and a nail was working through the sole . . . so that I was lame." (Two pages later his ravenous appetite also reminds the outer narrator [Hillyer] of a tramp.) See further chapter 6, note 12.

11. "I'm starving . . . meat." Because there was none for him to eat while living among the Eloi. See chapter 4: "Fruit, by the bye, was all their diet. These

people of the remote future were strict vegetarians, and while I was with them, in spite of some carnal cravings, I had to be frugivorous also."

Kemp (1982, 63) offers a further reason for the Time Traveller's hunger: "Travel normally gives Wells's characters an appetite. The Time Traveller is hungry when he arrives in 802,701, and ravenous when he gets back to his own day."

12. "the Amateur Cadger." An unskilled sponger. The Journalist suggests, facetiously, that the Time Traveller has deliberately (but unconvincingly) made himself appear dishevelled and impoverished in order to cadge money from someone.

13. "Does . . . phases." Nettle (1966, 123) incorrectly explains "crossing" as "sweeping the road." Wells uses the word in its (now obsolete) slang sense, meaning a *swindle*. See *N.E.D.* entry on "cross" (sig. 29) and Eric Partridge, *A Dictionary of Slang and Unconventional English* (New York: Macmillan, 1961), 193: entry under "cross." Nettle explains "Nebuchadnezzar phases" as "strange dreams," but in its context in *The Time Machine* it appears to mean *a period of degradation*. According to Daniel 4:4–28 the Babylonian King Nebuchadnezzar was transformed into a beast for seven years.

The Editor is enlarging on the Journalist's suggestion (see note 12 above), by questioning (also facetiously) whether the Time Traveller's appearance implies that he has been behaving disreputably or less than respectably.

14. "caricature." Satire or ridicule.

15. "Our Special Correspondent . . . reports." A curious anticipation of one of Wells's least-known tales (it does not appear in most of the collected editions of Wells's short stories), "The Queer Story of Brownlow's Newspaper," originally published in a 1932 issue of *The Strand Magazine*. Brownlow receives a newspaper printed forty years in the future.

16. "little Rosebery." The Editor wants a reliable racing tip. Little Rosebery was the latest champion racehorse of Archibald Philip Primrose, 5th Earl of Rosebery (1847–1929), Prime Minister in 1894 and highly successful owner and breeder of racehorses. Rosebery's horses won the Derby three times.

17. "until . . . arteries." I.e., "Until I've got some protein into my system." Peptone is a biochemical term for the diffusable substance into which protein is converted (by the enzymes pepsin and trypsin) before it enters the blood stream.

18. "a shilling . . . verbatim note." A shilling would then have been worth the equivalent of twenty cents. The Editor is offering two and a half cents a word for a firsthand account.

19. "anecdotes of Hettie Potter." McConnell (1977, 27) suggests that this is perhaps an "oblique reference" to the Fabian Socialist Beatrice (Potter) Webb (1858–1943) or an allusion to a member of "a well-known family of music-hall entertainers named Potter."

This editor inclines to the second possibility—although he has been unable to verify the fact that there was indeed a late Victorian music-hall entertainer named Hettie Potter.

The first possibility seems very dubious. I have not been able to find any early letters or references to Beatrice Potter in which she is nicknamed Hettie. Before her conversion to Socialism in the late 1880s, Beatrice became known first as a debutante and socialite then as a bluestocking (associated with Herbert Spencer and "Radical" Joseph Chamberlain). As McConnell notes, "From the nineties on [she] was a tireless campaigner for socialism and a frequent visitor of the worst London slums." However, there seems to be no evidence that as 'Hettie Potter' Beatrice Webb was so 'notorious' in the mid-nineties as to be the "object of pointless and insensitive jokes, such as the Journalist appears to be telling" (McConnell's words) and which Wells would have expected the average reader of the period to know about. To the contrary, c. 1884–1894 the reputation of the young Beatrice seems to have been not a subject for scurrilous anecdotes but that of a rising celebrity described thus by two of her recent biographers: "The brilliant and beautiful Miss Potter, who was making a name for herself by writing in distinguished monthlies . . ."—Kitty Muggeridge and Ruth Adam, *Beatrice Webb: A Life* (London: Secker and Warburg, 1967), 89. Finally, since Beatrice Potter had married Sidney Webb in 1892, is it likely that Beatrice *Webb* was still 'popularly' (?) known as 'Hettie Potter' at the time when Wells was revising *The Time Machine* for its first book publication?

20. "you must . . . interruptions." He does, however, *interrupt himself* in chapter 7 in order to show his guests the two flowers he had brought back from the future.

21. "I was . . . four o'clock." The time reference is contradicted by the first paragraph of the next chapter, in which the Time Traveller states: "It was at ten o'clock to-day that the first of all Time Machines began its career." Later in the same paragraph he informs his guests that his long journey began at "nearly half-past three."

CHAPTER 3

1. "last Thursday." See time scheme in Structure section of the Introduction.

2. "Mrs. Watchett." The housekeeper of the Time Traveller, who is evidently a bachelor.

3. "I drew a breath . . . on my mind." In this paragraph and the next and in the second paragraph of chapter 12, Wells provides some striking anticipations of certain motion-picture effects. The alternation of light and darkness resembles the effect of a projector's maltese cross movement revealing a movie image projected at less than silent speed (16 frames per second). Mrs. Watchett's movements ("she seemed to shoot across the room like a rocket") are like fast-motion camerawork. Several details read like descriptions of slow fade-outs: "The laboratory got hazy and went dark. . . . The laboratory grew faint and hazy, then fainter and ever fainter." The "eddying murmur" that fills the Time Traveller's ears resembles a sound-mix dubbed onto a movie. In the next paragraph, one sentence ("The dim suggestion . . . marking a day") could almost be describing a dissolve into a new shot. Another sentence in the same paragraph suggests a superimposition culminating in a fade-out: "the palpitation of night and day merged into one continuous greyness." In chapter 12 the impression of Mrs. Watchett's fast-motion is also combined with reverse motion: "Now her every motion appeared to be the exact inversion of her previous ones."

What makes these passages extraordinary vis-à-vis their resemblances to film techniques is that Wells was writing them *before* he could possibly have seen a motion picture. Edison's Kinetoscope (a movie peepshow machine) was first exhibited in England on October 17, 1894, at 70 Oxford Street, London. This exhibition marked the beginnings of cinema in the U.K. The inventor Robert W. Paul was the first to exhibit projected motion pictures in Britain. His first public show appears to have been on February 20, 1896, at the Finsbury Technical College. However, Paul had already been reading *The Time Machine* and in so doing conceived the idea of utilizing his motion-picture projector, the Theatrograph, to create a show conveying the illusion of time travel. He filed a British patent for this idea on October 24, 1895 (pat. no. 19984). See further Appendix VIII.

4. "a switchback." British term for a roller-coaster.

5. "night followed . . . black wing." On the stylistic evolution of this image see Bergonzi (1960, 46).

Cf. (later in this chapter) the symbol of the white sphinx, envisaged as a bird of prey: see note 10 below. The image also recalls two famous fictional birds whose wings darkened the sky: the gigantic roc encountered by Sinbad in *The Arabian Nights* and the monstrous crow who terrified Tweedledum and Tweedledee in chapter 5 of *Through the Looking Glass*.

The image of the flapping wing is reiterated in the account of the return journey: see the first paragraph of chapter 12.

6. "I saw huge buildings rise up." Compare this passage and the description a page later of "great and splendid architecture . . . more massive than any buildings of our own time," with Graham's earliest glimpse of the 23rd century in chapter 5 of *When the Sleeper Wakes* (1899): "His first impression was of overwhelming architecture. The place into which he looked was an aisle of Titanic buildings, curving spaciously in either direction. . . .''

7. "the sun belt . . . solstice." I.e., The sun seemed to be swaying from its highest to its lowest point. The solstices are the two times in each year when the sun is at its greatest distance from the celestial equator. It reaches its most northerly distance (the summer solstice) on June 21st and its most southerly distance (the winter solstice) on December 22nd.

8. "our rudimentary civilisation." The Time Traveller's poor estimate of his own time is shared by Hillyer in the Epilogue: "I, for my own part, cannot think that these latter days of weak experiment, fragmentary theory, and mutual discord, are indeed man's culminating time!"

9. "I saw . . . intermission." The Time Traveller's first awareness of the climatic and environmental changes that had overtaken the planet. When he arrives in 802,701, he learns the extent of these changes: The Thames has shifted its position; the air is warmer; there is no evidence of agriculture yet the earth has become a garden displaying an abundance of delicate, unfamiliar blossoms and hypertrophied fruits and flowers; there are no weeds or fungi, no pestiferous insects, no diseases, and no signs of putrefaction or decay; and aside from the Eloi and the Morlocks the only animate life forms observed by the Time Traveller are sparrows and butterflies. At night he also discovers that all the old constellations have gone from the sky (see chapter 7). He attributes the environmental changes to horticulture and theorizes (in chapter 5) that the climatic change could have been due either to the sun growing hotter or to the earth having drawn nearer to the sun.

10. "the interstices." The spaces or crevices.

11. "a profound . . . dimensions." The Time Traveller's fears are realized by Gottfried Plattner, the hero of Wells's "The Plattner Story" (1897). Plattner, a schoolmaster, performs a scientific experiment which unexpectedly blasts him into "what is called the Fourth Dimension."

12. "a winged sphinx." This, perhaps the most memorable single image in *The Time Machine*, was depicted on the front cover of the first British edition of *The Time Machine* (Heinemann, 1895).

According to Schopenhauer the Sphinx of antiquity expressed "the continuity, indeed the unity of human with animal and all other nature, thus that of the microcosmos with the macrocosmos . . ." (*Essays and Aphorisms* [Baltimore: Penguin Books, 1970], 219).

Casey Fredericks sees the White Sphinx of *The Time Machine* as a figurative embodiment of both the conjunction of the upper world of the Eloi and the subterranean world of the Morlocks and "the conjunction along the time axis of the future and the past as embodied in the time-traveler himself." Fredericks (1982, 71).

Frank Scafella sums up many other interpretations: We do not know what prompted Wells to imagine his Time Traveller face to face with the Sphinx at the very opening of his narrative, but that he did so is significant. For one thing, it means that *The Time Machine* must be read as a variation of Oedipus's encounter with the Sphinx on the road to Thebes. For another, the Sphinx, according to Bacon, is a symbol of Science. For still another, the White Sphinx is alluded to or figures directly in the action on 15 of the 70-odd pages of the narrative. Moreover, in the presence of the White Sphinx, the Time Traveller experiences a variety of psychic states which range from the awe of his initial awareness through dread and despair to a resolve to hold himself in check by the exercise of reason. This sequence of emotions charts a transformation in the mind of the Time Traveller from an essentially contemplative to an intensely practical mode of response to the world." Scafella (1981, 255).

See further Lake (1979, 77–78) and Ketterer (1982, 340).

13. "verdigris." A green or bluish coating that appears on the surface of bronze, copper, or brass when these metals are exposed to the air for a long time.

14. "What might appear . . . powerful?" The first glimpse of the narrative's Huxleyan pessimism, in which, unwittingly, the Time Traveller also anticipates both the Eloi ("What if . . . the race had lost its manliness") and the Morlocks ("What if . . . the race . . . had developed into something inhuman"). In view of what he later discovers about the relationship between the Morlocks and the Eloi, there is also a disturbing irony in his speculation—later in the same paragraph—that in this future world *he* might seem like "a foul creature to be incontinently slain."

15. "I might . . . slain." Anthony West discerns in this paragraph "the seed idea for *The War of the Worlds.* West (1984, 232). Patrick Parrinder offers a very different comment: "The temerity of the prophet is underlined by the Time Traveller's sense of impotence. At one level this will account for his ruthlessness later on, his readiness to turn on the Morlocks armed with a crowbar [sic] and a box of matches. At the same time, we can see that Wells's courage as a prophet does not fail him in the story, but that what he sees in the face of the Sphinx is, simply, the coming universal death." Parrinder (1981, 21).

16. "buskins." A half-boot laced from the ankle to the knee (or just below it).

17. "that hectic beauty . . . much." McConnell (1977, 34) remarks, "The phrase and concept *consumptive . . . hectic beauty* was associated with the 'decadent' writers and artists of the Victorian fin-de-siècle, in particular with Aubrey Beardsley, Oscar Wilde and other contributors to *The Yellow Book.* In their obsessive, unorthodox eroticism and their defense of "pure" (i.e., non-functional, non-mechanical) art, the decadents are an important source for Wells's conception of the Eloi."

CHAPTER 4

1. "The absence . . . at once." A superficial impression that, of course, proves false. Wells develops the theme of fear during chapters 5 through 7.

2. "He came . . . shoulders." Kemp (1982, 27) observes Wells's "fondness for depicting humans recoiling from predatory extremities. Even the mild Eloi are introduced as briefly creepy—as they wonderingly finger the Traveller, he feels 'soft little tentacles upon my back and shoulders'."

3. "I could fancy myself . . . nine-pins." In chapter 9 The Time Traveller does precisely this to the Morlocks.

4. "their Dresden-china type of prettiness." Cf. also such later images as "pagoda-like plants," "little doll of a creature" (the Time Traveller's description of Weena), and the Palace of Green Porcelain, described in chapter 6 as a building whose "facade had an Oriental look: the face of it having the lustre . . . of a certain

type of Chinese porcelain." The decorative "chinoiserie" and "japonisme" which Wells associates with the Eloi and their world was in vogue in the eighteen nineties especially among the "decadents" (Beardsley's designs were strongly influenced by Japanese painting and the pioneers of art nouveau.) See chapter 11, note 19. Wells's linkage of consumptive-like beauty (end of chapter 3) with "Dresden-china type of prettiness" is curiously echoed in chapter 4 of *When the Sleeper Wakes* (1899): " . . . a crop-haired anaemic lad with features of the Chinese type."

5. "the year . . . odd". He gives the precise year four pages later. See note 16 below.

6. "I had always . . . everything." This negative view of human progress was at least two decades ahead of its time. Historian Paul Johnson notices that it was not until the 1914–18 War had run its course that it was widely held that "progress in the sense the Victorians had understood it, as something continuous and almost inexorable, was dead. In 1920, the great classical scholar J. B. Bury published a volume, *The Idea of Progress*, proclaiming its demise." See further Johnson's *Modern Times* (New York: Harper & Row, 1983), 13.

7. "They all withdrew . . . blossom." Cf. at the end of this chapter: "To adorn themselves with flowers . . . no more." Cf. also three similar scenes in chapter 5: (a) "she [Weena] . . . presented me with a big garland of flowers". (b) "They spent all their time in playing gently, in bathing in the river, in making love in a half-playful fashion, in eating fruit and sleeping." (c) "The male pursued the female, flinging flowers at her as he ran."

Could Wells have based such idyllic scenes on early descriptions of life in Polynesia—such as the following passage by the French explorer Bougainville? "If happiness lies in the abundance of every necessity of life, in inhabiting a superb land enjoying the most beautiful climate (the soil producing everything without the need for cultivation), in enjoying perfect health, in respiring always the purest and most salubrious airs, in leading a life of freedom, gentle, calm, divorced from all passions . . . I say that no people could ever be so blessed as the nation whose homeland is New Cythera [Tahiti]" (quoted in Roselene Dousset and Etienne Taillemite, *The Great Book of the Pacific* [Secaucus, N.J.: Chartwell Books, 1979], 152).

8. "old Phoenician decorations." The decorations of the Phoenicians (c. 8th through 6th centuries B.C.) were a synthesis of elements from several sources: Egyptian-like motifs; galloping or flying animals borrowed from the art of Crete and Mycenae; symmetrical groupings of human figures characteristic of Mesopotamian decorations; and sphinxes and griffins that were uniquely Phoenician. Abstract Phoenician decorations (as on glassware) usually consisted of undulating colored lines.

9. "I, dressed . . . speech." The description recalls the scenes in *A Midsummer Night's Dream* III.i and IV.i in which the grotesque-looking Bottom, decked with flowers, is escorted by fairies to the bower of Titania.

10. "very hard white metal." Manufactured, presumably, by the Morlocks. In chapter 6, during his descent to their underground world, the Time Traveller comes upon a table made of the same white metal.

11. "hypertrophied." Abnormally enlarged presumably by horticultural development or mutation.

12. "frugivorous." Dieting on fruits.

13. "Ichthyosaurus." An extinct, marine reptile that flourished during the Mesozoic period, more than 50 million years ago. It had a snout, fins, paddlelike flippers, and a tapering body.

14. "I determined . . . amusement." McConnell (1981, 83) remarks: "it is one of the most brilliant devices of *The Time Machine* that no one, in the Traveller's narrative of the future, *speaks*. . . . Weena gives the Traveller some flowers . . .

that gesture . . . is also a sign that the future is inarticulate, that it has no names except the names we choose."

15. "the Thames . . . position." The Thames, England's main river, rises in the Cotswolds, and in its upper course winds through a broad valley—to which the Time Traveller refers again in the next chapter. The length of the river from its source to the sea is approximately 210 miles.

A shift by only one mile may seem rather insignificant; but the Thames is a river that has not been known to change its course to any appreciable extent since records were kept. See further chapter 8, note 2.

16. "the year . . . A.D." 802,701 is "a numerical series that contains a . . . hint that the machine is running down"—Mackenzie (1973, 124).

In the *National Observer Time Machine* the Time Traveller journeys to 12,203 not to 802,701. In the *New Review* and Holt texts the Eloi and the Morlocks are referred to as "the people of the year Thirty-two thousand odd."

17. "aluminium." The British spelling of *aluminum*. The metal had been known since 1825 when it was first produced by the Danish physicist Hans Christian Oersted. See also note 10 above.

18. "very beautiful pagoda-like plants." See chapter 4, note 4.

19. "It was here . . . proper place." A reference to his first confrontation with a Morlock: in chapter 5.

20. "Communism." See chapter 1, note 24. This is the first of the Time Traveller's theories about the Eloi and their world. His whole range of hypotheses is concisely summarized by Suvin (1979, 230): "(a) Communist classless society; (b) degenerated classless society; (c) degenerated class society; (d) degenerated inverted class society." These theories, he claims, comprise "the whole logical gamut of socio-political SF, or of utopian and antiutopian fiction as the ideal poles of sociological SF from More and Plato to the present day."

21. "this close resemblance of the sexes." Concerning the androgynous character of the Eloi, McConnell (1977, 41) comments: "This is not—or not only—a striking anticipation of the 'unisex' phenomenon of the 1960s and 1970s. Along with other theories of social reform, the late nineteenth century produced many arguments favoring liberation from or abolition of traditional sexual roles, including the unselective eroticism of the *Yellow Book* aesthetes, the defenses of homosexuality of Edward Carpenter (1844–1929), and the origins of the Women's Suffrage movement, espoused by novelists like Grant Allen."

22. "cupola." A roof or ceiling created out of a dome built on a polygonal or circular base.

23. "griffins' heads." The griffin was an ancient mythological beast with the head and wings of an eagle and the body of a lion. It frequently occurs in Phoenician decorations.

24. "obelisk." A familiar form of ancient Egyptian monument or imitation of it. It is a tapering, four-sided stone shaft with a pyramidal apex.

25. "After all . . . human needs." McConnell (1977, 43) notes that the arguments in this paragraph are "a fairly commonplace version of 'social Darwinism' or the extension to the realm of human culture of Darwin's idea of the 'survival of the fittest' in Nature." For a lively onslaught on such arguments see Bernard Shaw's preface to *Back to Methuselah* (1921).

26. "brilliant butterflies . . . thither." Note the survival of the butterfly—or something like it—in the remote future: "I saw a thing like a huge white butterfly go slanting and fluttering up into the sky. . . ." See further chapter 11, note 8.

27. "I shall have to tell you later . . . changes." See chapter 8, note 11.

28. "Under the new . . . decay." Cf. Huxley (1968, 51–52).

McConnell (1977, 45), reads this passage as a covert critique of the aestheticism of the eighteen nineties. George Orwell echoes the passage in chapter XII of *The Road to Wigan Pier* (1937), in the course of a critique of Wells's utopias.

29. "We are kept keen ... necessity." This idea is echoed in chapter 10: "Only those animals partake of intelligence that have to meet a huge variety of needs and dangers."

Cf. also Huxley (1968, 86): "If we may permit ourselves a larger hope of abatement of the essential evil of the world. . . . I deem it an essential condition of the realization of that hope that we cast aside the notion that escape from pain and sorrow is the proper object of life."

CHAPTER 5

1. "gibbous." Illuminated so as to appear convex on both margins. This is likely to be seen when the moon is more than half full but less than full.

2. "white leprous face." Like the pallid, blotchy face of a leper. On Wells's imagery of disease, decay and death, see Lake (1979, 77–84).

3. "the sense ... vanished." This is the first of several sinister anticipations of the Morlocks, building to the climax of the Time Traveller's actual encounter with one later in the chapter (see note 25 below). Note the other disturbing anticipations, playing on the hero's uncertainties and fears: (a) "I remember ... startling some white animal that, in the dim light, I took for a small deer"; (b) "I thought I heard a sound like a chuckle ... but I must have been mistaken"; (c) "something, I knew not what, had taken it [the Time Machine] into the hollow pedestal of the White Sphinx." (d) "I woke ... with an odd fancy that some greyish animal had just rushed out of the chamber."; (e) "I thought I could see ghosts ... Twice I fancied I saw a solitary white ape-like creature running rather quickly up the hill ... and once near the ruins I saw a leash of them carrying some dark body. . . . I doubted my eyes."; (f) "a pair of eyes—was watching me out of the darkness."

4. "malachite." Copper carbonate, a copper ore often used for making ornamental objects.

5. "But they ... matches." But matches existed in 802,701 even before the Time Traveller's arrival: he finds a box of them in the Palace of Green Porcelain (chapter 8).

6. "I am ... vigil." Westernized—as opposed to oriental. Here, more specifically, the Time Traveller is saying that he is too much of a European to do nothing but keep watch in one place for a long time.

Nettle (1966, 125) explains this passage as follows: "The Time Traveller is saying that Eastern peoples are more contemplative and patient than Western peoples and that he is therefore being typically Western in his impatience."

7. "That way lies monomania." Cf. *King Lear* III.iv.21–22: "O! that way madness lies; let me shun that; No more of that."

8. "their language ... propositions." McConnell (1981, 83) describes this as "an ideally Edenic language, but one emptied of the powers of abstraction or a sense of history."

9. "peering down into the shafted darkness." I.e., into the underworld of the Morlocks. Wells here invokes a key image of class confrontation: that of the "social explorer" gazing down into "the abyss" into which he later descends to encounter the brutish masses. See further Peter Keating, *Into Unknown England, 1866–1913: Selections from the Social Explorers* (1976).

10. "sanitary apparatus." Nettle (1966, 51) defines this as "the drains for disposing of sewage."

11. "visions of Utopias." The Greek word for "nowhere" was the name Sir

Thomas More (1478–1535) gave to the island where he located his ideal, imaginary society described in *Utopia* (1516). L. S. Mercier's *Memoirs of the Year 2500* (1772) established the tradition of Utopian romances dedicated to the idea of progress and the perfectibility of man, and most nineteenth-century Utopian fiction either followed this tradition or reacted strongly against it. Edward Bellamy's *Looking Backward* (1888) became the most popular and influential work of the progressive "school." The most notable anti-progressive reactions of the late nineteenth century were Richard Jefferies' *After London* (1885), W. H. Hudson's *A Crystal Age* (1887), and William Morris's *News from Nowhere* (1890) all of which picture societies that have repudiated industry and technology. Wells's vision of the indolent and "decadent" Eloi was, in turn, a reaction against the anti-progressive Utopians.

12. "But while such details . . . found here." McConnell (1981, 83) comments: "Other utopias always involve excessively detailed description of the scenery and architecture of the ideal state . . . Wells in a single stroke lets himself out of the boring burden of describing fully the future world in which his hero finds himself, and at the same time . . . makes that world more believable. . . ."

13. "postal orders." The British term for *money orders*.

14. "Conceive the tale . . . and the like?" Cf. Edgar Allan Poe's satirical "Thousand-and-Second Tale of Scheherazade" (1845) in which the King (Shahriyah) rejects Scheherazade's account of the technological wonders of the nineteenth century as a pack of lies.

15. "The Golden Age." In Greek and Roman mythology the Golden Age was the earliest and finest age of the world when the human race existed in total freedom from strife and misery. See Hesiod, *Works and Days*, 108 and Ovid, *Metamorphoses*, I, 89.

In its original British edition (1895), *The Time Machine* was divided into sixteen chapters each with its own title. Chapter 5 in that edition (comprising about half of the present chapter 4) was called "In the Golden Age," an obviously ironic title in reference to the Eloi and the Morlocks.

16. "sepulture." The act or custom of interment; burial.

17. "she kissed . . . hers." V. S. Pritchett, noting that where love is born, Wells is Walt Disney at his worst, cites as notable examples "faint squirms of idyllic petting in *The Time Machine*" (quoted in Bergonzi [1976], 32).

18. "her name was Weena." Anthony West (1984, 369–70) tells us that Wells's "more refined admirers often complained of the tiny flaw that allowed him to give his females such awful names—poor Weena of *The Time Machine* being a favoured case in point."

Suvin (1974, 222) suggests that Wells derived the name from Eveena, the tiny child-bride in Percy Greg's *Across the Zodiac: The Story of a Wrecked Record* (1880). However, the name could simply have been a variation on "weenie" (a contraction of "teenie-weenie"), a British children's slang term for "tiny." "Tweeny" was a nineteenth-century slang term for a maidservant. One of Barrie's characters in *The Admirable Crichton* is little Tweeny, the "between maid," so-called because she is not anything in particular as a servant.

19. "sea anemones." Marine polyps found in tide pools and rocky crevices beside the seashore.

20. "palps." Feelers or tendrils.

21. "a leash of them." Three of them in a group. The term is generally used of a trio of greyhounds.

22. "Grant Allen." A novelist and writer (1848–1899) on biological subjects. In *Pen Portraits and Reviews* (London: Constable & Co. Ltd., 1949), 55, Bernard Shaw referred to him as "one of the most amiably helpful men that ever lived."

23. "or the earth nearer the sun." See chapter 11, note 16.

24. "such speculations . . . parent body." The reference to "the younger Darwin" is not to Charles Darwin (1809–1882)—as several commentators have stated—but to the astronomer and mathematician Sir George Howard Darwin (1845–1912), Charles's second son. George Darwin's "speculations" are to be found in his publications for the period 1883–1894, collected in his *Scientific Papers* (Cambridge: At the University Press, 1907), four volumes.

Wells could also have found similar speculations in Camille Flammarion's *La Fin du Monde* (1893–1894), translated as *Omega: the Last Days of the World* (1894, 275): "If the earth should fall into the sun, it would make good for ninety-five years the actual loss of solar energy. Venus would make good this loss for eighty-four years; Mercury for seven; Mars for thirteen; Jupiter for 32,254; Saturn for 9652; Uranus for 1610; and Neptune for 1890 years. That is to say, the fall of all the planets into the sun would produce heat enough to maintain the present rate of expenditure for about 46,000 years."

25. "some inner planet." Inner planets are those whose orbits lie between the earth and the sun: i.e., Venus and Mercury. See also chapter 11, note 22.

26. "I turned . . . ape-like figure." This is the Time Traveller's first real sight of a Morlock— see above note 3.

27. "a queer . . . peculiar manner." Lake (1979, 81) comments thus on the Morlocks' avoidance of daylight: "The Morlocks are the ghostly harbingers of the End [the ultimate doom of mankind]. And because the End is brought on by blind, sub-human forces, the Morlocks have to be blind (in daylight) and sub-human too—in defiance of extrapolative logic. For if the Eloi are made decadent by a too easy life, why should the subterranean workers be made decadent by a hard one? Would not their grim conditions in fact lead to selection for intelligence, for survival of the cunningest? And their blindness in daylight could only have arisen after a breakdown of their former electric lighting—but no such breakdown could have occurred if they had remained intelligent." At this point, somewhat inconsistently, Lake lets Wells off the hook by adding: "But none of this matters much, because Wells is motivated not by scientific but poetic logic."

28. "It was so like a human spider." From here onward most of the Time Traveller's references to the Morlocks are expressions of revulsion, often emphasizing their resemblance to non-human life forms: e.g. "the little monster," "this bleached, obscene nocturnal Thing," "this new vermin," "They were just the half-bleached colour of . . . worms . . . they were filthily cold to the touch," "nauseatingly inhuman," "ant-like," "human rats," "helpless abominations," "damned souls." At the start of chapter 7 he says: "Instinctively I loathed them"; in chapter 8 he states: "it was impossible, somehow to feel any humanity in the things". Significantly, some of these reactions actually *precede* the 'explanation' (at the start of chapter 6) of his feelings about them: "Probably my shrinking was largely due to the sympathetic influence of the Eloi, whose disgust of the Morlocks I now began to appreciate."

Caudwell (1938, 94) comments from a Marxian perspective: "Wells could never see his 'Morlocks' as Wasserman sees them as 'poor, wretched, driven, desperate, half-mad creatures'. He could never burn with indignation and be restless at the thought of the proletariat 'Under Fire', exploited, transported to Siberia, always and everywhere the most suffering class."

Compare and contrast the terms in which Wells describes the Eloi: e.g., "very beautiful and graceful," "Dresden-china type of prettiness," "hectic beauty," "fragile thing." It is evident from his language that the Time Traveller's responses to both 'races' are, first and foremost, determined by aesthetic preferences. The Time Traveller underscores his rationale in chapter 7: "However great their intellectual degradation, the Eloi had kept too much of the human form not to claim my sympathy."

29. "Man had not . . . animals." Suvin (1979, 239–40) refers to "Chris\ pher Caudwell's critique [in *Studies in a Dying Culture*] implying that the Time Traveller occupies an intermediate position between the two new species, a position isotopic with the position of the petty bourgeois Wells disdainful of a decadent upper class but horrified and repelled by a crude lower class." This critique, he comments, "seems to me, for all the nuances and elaborations it needs, to remain a key for interpreting the topographic and color symbolism of that episode."

30. "But, gradually . . . ages." The passage lends support to Parrinder's view (1981, 19) that *The Time Machine* "may be read as a response to a particular Utopia, William Morris's *News from Nowhere* . . . the classic example of the kind of book in which the narrator travels forward into the world of his remote descendants to find consolation for the political defeats of his own lifetime."

31. "Lemur." A small, furry, arboreal and nocturnal mammal with a face like a fox. Originating in Madagascar, the animal is related to the monkey family. The word *lemures* is an old religious term for *ghosts*.

32. "the white fish of the Kentucky caves." The reference is to one of the famous sights of Mammoth Cave in Edmonson County, Kentucky, 85 miles SSW of Louisville. The fish, which belong to the carp family, are one to six inches long, blind, colorless, and viviparous.

33. "those large eyes . . . light". This is reiterated in the next chapter: "Their eyes were abnormally large and sensitive, just as are the pupils of the abysmal fishes, and they reflected the light in the same way."

34. "Beneath my feet . . . enormously." According to Charles Knight (London, 1871) there were some 1300 miles of tunnels under London in 1865. These would have included railroad tunnels, subways, drains and sewers, gas and water supply conduits, electric telegraph cables, and pneumatic despatch tubes. See further Edward Walford, *Old and New London* (London: Cassell & Company Ltd., 1880), vol. 5, 224–42.

35. "and these tunnellings . . . new race." Kemp (1982, 14), following Eisenstein (1972, 119–121), explains the probable creative origin of the subterranean world of the Morlocks thus: "it seems fabricated from [Wells's] memories of the underground servant-tunnels at Up Park (there are similar ventilation shafts) and the underground kitchen in Atlas House where he spent much of his childhood." See also the early chapter of *Experiment in Autobiography* (1934).

36. "At first . . . point that way." Philmus (1969, 532–33) notes: "The Time Traveller himself says that he arrived at his explanation by extrapolating (to appropriate a useful word from the jargon of science fiction) from tendencies existing in the present." Then, citing this specific paragraph from chapter 5, he continues: "What this passage implies is that the procedure for interpreting the vision of *The Time Machine* recapitulates the process by which the fiction was 'hatched'; so that the science-fictional method of prophecy is itself 'the key to the whole position.' "

37. "the Metropolitan Railway in London." Originally the North Metropolitan Railway, it opened in 1853 with a 3.5 mile line between Paddington and Farringdon Street. The Metropolitan ran through a number of tunnels which had been excavated by a rather primitive cut-and-cover method. The railway was London's busiest line in the 1890s, carrying approximately 300 trains a day. It was not electrified until 1905.

38. "there are new electric railways." If this is taken as a reference to electric railways *in London*, it can refer only to the City and South London line which opened December 18, 1890. The Central Line, generally considered to be the first section of London's "Tube," was begun in 1891 and officially opened in 1900. If Wells's reference extends to electric railways *outside London*, he might also have

been thinking of the Bessbrook and Newry electric line in Ireland, the first such line in the United Kingdom, which opened in 1885.

39. "there are subways." In British parlance this refers not to underground railroads but to pedestrian underpasses.

40. "lost its birthright in the sky." Nettle (1966, 127) defines this phrase as: "lost its natural right to be situated above ground."

41. "an East-end worker." The horrendous slums of London's East End also housed some of the most appalling sweatshops in Victorian England, many of which were located in basements. There are vivid description of such East End basement sweatshops in Jack London's *People of the Abyss* (New York & London: Macmillan, 1903).

42. "etiolated." Whitened or bleached through lack of sunlight.

43. "Its triumph . . . fellow-man." The Time Traveller's speculation recalls Huxley (1968, 35–36): "I have endeavored to show that, when the ethical process has advanced so far as to secure every member of the society in the possession of the means of existence, the struggle for existence as between man and man, within that society is, *ipso facto*, at an end. And, as it is undeniable that the most highly civilized societies have substantially reached this position, it follows that, so far as they are concerned, the struggle for existence can play no important part within them. In other words, the kind of evolution which is brought about in the state of nature cannot take place."

44. "cicerone." A guide. The Italians used the name in reference to guides who showed tourists Roman antiquities. The name is derived from Cicero (106–43 B.C.), the Roman orator.

45. "I had no . . . books." McConnell (1981, 62) comments: "Wells refers contemptuously to the convention, in Utopian fiction, of having the character explain the workings of the ideal society in all its complexity to the wondering visitor from our world."

46. "The too-perfect . . . degeneration." The idea is derived from Huxley: "It is an error to imagine that evolution signifies a constant tendency to increased perfection. That process undoubtedly involves a constant remodelling of the organism in adaptation to new conditions; but it depends on the nature of those conditions whether the direction of the modifications effected shall be upward or downward. Retrogressive is as practicable as progressive metamorphosis." See Huxley (1968, 199) and Themes section of Introduction.

In the 1890s the subject of cultural and biological degeneration was hotly debated in the wake of Max Nordau's controversial *Degeneration* [originally in German as *Entartung*, Berlin, 1892], New York: D. Appleton & Co., 1895.

Wells himself had already enlarged on the theme of evolutionary degeneration in his article "Zoological Retrogression," *Gentleman's Magazine* 271 (September 1891): "There is almost always associated with the suggestion of advance in biological phenomena an opposite idea, which is its essential complement . . . evolutionary antithesis—degradation." Cf. also: (a) "the purely 'animal' about . . . [man] is being and must be, beyond all question, suppressed in his ultimate development"—Wells, "The Man of the Year Million," *Pall Mall Gazette* 57 (6 November 1893), 3; (b) "The phenomena of degeneration rob one of any confidence that . . . [life's] new forms . . . will be . . . 'higher' . . . than the old." —Wells, "Biooptimism," *Nature* 52 (29 August 1895), 411.

47. "Morlocks . . . called." The reader need search no further than the end of Part II of *The Chronic Argonauts* to discover that Wells adapted the name from *warlock* (a wizard or magician), the term Old Pritchard uses to denounce Dr. Nebogipfel (see Appendix I). However, other, more fanciful derivations have been suggested. Thus Lake (1979, 78–79) associates the first syllable of "Morlock" with

the Latin word *mors*, and goes on to state: "One important meaning of the Morlocks . . . is simply Death itself." Nettle (1966, xi) offers an amusingly far-fetched explanation: "It is appropriate that the name of the apparently subservient race below ground should suggest a prison or dungeon with 'more locks'."

Additional "derivations" have connected the name with *Moloch* (the god to whom the Canaanites and Phoenicians sacrificed children) and *Mohock* (eighteenth-century ruffians, often aristocrats in disguise, who revelled in attacking people at night on the London streets).

48. "the 'Eloi'." Several derivations of the name are possible. Bergonzi (1961, 48) suggests associations not only with their *elfin* looks but also from the French *eloigné = distant* (i.e., the Eloi are people of the distant future) and "their apparent status as an *elite*: there may also be a suggestion of *eld* meaning old age and decrepitude." St. Eligius (7th century) was called 'Eloi' or 'Loy' by medieval French and English writers. Chaucer, describing his Prioress, tells us that "hire gretteste ooth was but by Seinte Loy." St. Eligius was a courtier and artist and founder of a school of enamel-work centered at Limoges. The possible link with the beautiful Eloi of *The Time Machine* is suggested by the fact that "Eligius was apparently a man of great physical beauty . . . and a lover of personal adornment" (Muriel Bowden, *A Commentary on the General Prologue to the Canterbury Tales* [New York: Macmillan, 1948], 103). *Elohim* is the Hebrew word for God—suggesting that the Eloi have luminous or radiant qualities. Eloi might also be a contrived variation on the word *alloy*—i.e., an alloy is a debasement of pure metal, and the Eloi are, despite their beauty, a degenerate offshoot of the human species.

Note that the name 'Eloi' is not mentioned in the *National Observer* serialization of *The Time Machine*.

CHAPTER 6

1. "Things one sees . . . museum." Bleaching is one consequence of preserving specimens in formaldehyde. The allusion to a zoological museum anticipates the Time Traveller's visit to the Palace of Green Porcelain (chapter 8).

2. "Going to the south-westward . . . Combe Wood." A misspelling of Coombe Wood, located just to the south of Richmond Park, at the base of Kingston Hill. In the 1890s, this was a rural area with a farm that belonged to Lord Archibald Campbell. It is now mainly a golf course. Topographical maps of the late Victorian period show that the "rising country" beside Coombe Wood reached an elevation of 400 feet above sea level.

3. "I observed . . . structure." Banstead is located about 4 miles southeast of Coombe Wood. The first paragraph of chapter 8 indicates that the Palace of Green Porcelain, the "vast green structure" mentioned in the sentence under consideration, "lay very high upon a turfy down." Banstead has an elevation of 800 feet above sea level and is actually the highest point visible to the southeast of Coombe Wood.

4. "the facade . . . porcelain." The reference is probably to a kind of porcelain with celadon glaze produced c. A.D. 900 through 1100 in the Chinese province of Chekiang. See chapter 2, note 2.

Was this image inspired by Wells's observation of model pagodas in the Victoria and Albert Museum or the Royal Albert Hall? At the start of the tenth chapter of *Love and Mr. Lewisham* (1900) he reminisces over his visits to the galleries of the V&A which was located just across the road from the Normal School of Science where he studied in the 1880's. In 1884 (the year in which Wells entered the Normal School) four green soapstone pagodas from Foochow were exhibited in an upper gallery of the Albert Hall (just a few yards from the Normal School) as part of the International Health Exhibition. See *China Imperial Maritime Customs* III Miscellaneous Series no. 12 (London: William Clowes, 1884). These pagodas, which might easily have been mistaken for porcelain, were later shifted temporarily to the Victoria and Albert Museum prior to their return to China.

London's most famous Oriental-looking structure was (and still is) the ten-story 163-foot high Pagoda in the Royal Botanical Gardens at Kew, northwest of Richmond. but that was/is neither green nor a palace. The Crystal Palace in Sydenham was located in the right direction but was neither green nor Oriental in appearance. The celebrated Porcelain Pagoda at Nanking (completed A.D. 1430) was constructed of heavy tile bricks with colored green glazes decorated with incised pictures of dragons. Wells might have been been familiar with its frequent depiction in books about China.

5. "I began to feel over the parapet . . . proceed." Peter N. Stearns, *Be a Man! Males in Modern Society* (1979) p.39, exemplifies the descent into a mineshaft as "one of the real tests of nineteenth-century masculinity." See also chapter 5, note 9.

6. "they did not . . . incontinently." Another instance of 'cultural' degeneration. Note that the Eloi are also unfamiliar with fire: in chapter 9 Weena has to be restrained from playing with flames.

7. "halitus." A vapor or exhalation.

8. "Presently the walls . . . blackness." Anthony West, Wells's son, is one of several commentators who have noted the relation of this description to Wells's psycho-biography. "When my father had first seen Uppark it had been an ogre's castle—the hated other place to which his mother had withdrawn when she broke up the family household. . . . Soon after he first saw it he had discovered the Housekeeper's Room, the seat of empire for which she had forsaken him and his father. The room was buried deeply in the ground . . . [It] was a sombre, almost lightless, and heavily airless space . . . [like] the huge underground kitchen buried beneath a shrubbery at some distance from the main building, and connected with it by a tunnel—a long passage dimly lit in the daytime by light from overhead skylights made secure by prison-like metal gratings. My father's initial response to his discovery of this nether world of underprivilege below Uppark had been one of blind rage. . . . His bottled-up feelings . . . finally burst out into the open in his descriptions of the loathly caverns inhabited by the light-fearing Morlocks in *The Time Machine*." West (1984, 226–27).

9. "a Kodak." In the 1890s, the arbitrary name devised by George Eastman (1854–1932) as a trademark for his portable camera using roll film became widely used as a synonym for a camera. The Time Traveller has equipped himself with "a small camera" when Hillyer last sees him (chapter 12).

10. "four safety-matches . . . remained to me." Cf. his problem with matches at the end of chapter 10. See also chapter 9, note 3, and chapter 10, note 3.

11. "lank fingers . . . face." A variation on his nightmare in chapter V: "I had been restless, dreaming . . . that sea-anemones were feeling over my face with their soft palps." Or was he really dreaming then? See also chapter 11, note 12.

12. "I will confess . . . narrow tunnel." Kemp (1982, 167) observes that many of Wells's novels "are studies in escape, either from immediate danger or from the more insidious menace of stultifying circumstances. *The Time Machine*, with its hero constantly on the move from physical attack, is a good example of the first. . . ."

13. "my feet were grasped . . . backward." L. Thomas Williams glosses both this detail and the Time Traveller's lameness with Claude Lévi-Strauss's observation in "The Structural Study of Myth": "In mythology it is a universal character of men born from the earth that the moment they emerge from the depth, they either cannot walk or do it clumsily." Williams (1983, 304).

CHAPTER 7

1. "mechanical servants". I.e. ignorant domestics. Cf. "rude mechanicals", *Midsummer Night's Dream* III.ii.9.

2. "the Carlovingian kings." Three Frankish rulers named Carloman, descendants of Charles Martel. The last Carloman (d. A.D. 884) became King of Burgundy. His degeneracy cost him the throne.

3. "Nemesis." The inevitable punishment. Nemesis was the Greek goddess of retribution and vengeance.

4. "Ages ago . . . changed!" The idea is anticipated in Bulwer-Lytton's *The Coming Race* (1871). Aldiss (1975, 84) without making a connection with *The Time Machine*, quotes from Bulwer-Lytton's novel the following passage in which the anonymous hero (cf. the nameless Time Traveller) reflects on the future menace to upper-world man of a "submerged nation" of super-beings: "The more I think of a people calmly developing, in regions excluded from our sight and deemed uninhabitable by our sages, powers surpassing our most disciplined modes of force . . . the more deeply I pray that ages may yet elapse before there emerges into sunlight our inevitable destroyers." Bernard Shaw, a diligent reader of Bulwer-Lytton seems to have echoed the same passage when he warns us, in *Man and Superman* (1905) that the Superman may come "like a thief in the night."

5. "a fastness." A stronghold.

6. "mallows." Herbaceous plants with round-toothed leaves and white, purple or rose-colored flowers.

7. "The Time Traveller paused . . . narrative." His second interruption of the story. He had momentarily interrupted his narrative near the start of chapter 5 to comment on the attachment of the Time Machine's levers.

8. "towards Wimbledon" Wimbledon is a south London suburb located about one mile southeast of Richmond Park and one mile east of Kingston-Upon-Thames. The Time Traveller proceeds over the "hill crest" of Kingston Hill and heads southwest across Wimbledon Common in the general direction of Merton and Carshalton.

9. "the Morlocks . . . ant-hill." Two pages later the Morlocks are described as "ant-like." See also chapter 5, note 28.

10. "a Faun." A rural demi-god of the Romans. It had horns, pointed ears and goat's feet. As in Mallarmé's poem, the inspiration for Debussy's famous ballet, *Prelude à l'aprés-midi d'un faune*, the faun is a symbol of sensuality, eroticism, and sometimes languor. McConnell (1977, 72) notes: "the fact that here he has lost his head may well represent the author's judgement on the unintelligent eroticism of this future society."

11. "the tree-boles." The stems or trunks of trees.

12. "All the old constellations . . . sky." On the face of it this seems incredible. Eight hundred thousand years is, after all, a brief period in astronomical terms. So is it likely that the night sky would have changed so drastically? The answer is 'yes'. The bright star system *Alpha Centauri* would probably not have been visible from Earth a mere 500,000 years ago. It may therefore be assumed that most—if not all—of the old constellations will be gone from the sky 800,000 years hence.

13. "Sirius." The so-called Dog Star in the constellation *Canis Major*. It is the most brilliant star in the sky although it is 8.8 light years distant from our planet.

14. "one bright planet . . . old friend." Venus, often called the Evening Star, is the second planet from the sun and the sixth largest in the solar system.

15. "the great precessional cycle . . . describes." The earth's motion is not

uniform. As a result of the moon's gravitational pull, it wobbles on its axis. This wobble is know as *precession*.

McConnell (1977, 73) states: "The Time Traveller, doubtless under the pressure of the moment, miscalculates: from the late nineteenth century to 802,701 the precessional cycle would have been completed only thirty times." However, McConnell is correcting the Time Traveller on the assumption that the precessional cycle is consistently 26,000 years when, in fact, it fluctuates between 24,000 and 26,000 years. Forty precessional cycles would thus take a period of between 960,000 and 1,004,000 years. The earlier figure looks reasonably close to 802,701. It seems obvious to this editor that the Time Traveller is not miscalculating but merely making a rough estimate.

16. "rill." A small stream or rivulet.

17. "His prejudice . . . instinct." Kemp (1982, 34) remarks: "The cannibalism and carnivorous preying in . . . [Wells's] books are designed to frighten man into a full awareness of his biological condition. The flesh is made to creep by reminders that it is flesh, and, as such edible, valuable to others in the struggle for survival."

18. "a Carlyle-like scorn . . . decay." Thomas Carlyle (1795–1881) denounced the "Aristocracy of the Moneybag" in *The French Revolution*, Book VII, chapter viii.

CHAPTER 8

1. "the Palace of Green Porcelain." Located at or near Banstead: see chapter 6, note 3 and map.

On the symbol of the Palace of Green Porcelain, Hennelly (1979, 162) notes: "The Palace, 'this ancient monument of an intellectual age' . . . is complex. Its fossilized treasures not only warn against the vanity of human wishes and the 'futility of all ambition' . . . such as the Time Traveller's and the Morlocks' emphases on future glory, but it also admonishes hedonists like the Dinner Guests and Eloi who live only for the present and thus court no great expectations."

2. "estuary." The mouth of a river where the river current meets the tides. The Time Traveller's discovery of an estuary where populous south London districts had existed in the 19th century is another striking indication that the course of the Thames had shifted. (See chapter 4, note 15).

3. "Wandsworth and Battersea." Two south London boroughs about five and six miles, respectively, north and northeast of Banstead.

4. "I only learned . . . so human." The Time Traveller rather narrowly equates being human with being literate.

5. "valves." The separate leaves of a double-door.

6. "At the first glance . . . museum." See chapter 6, note 1.

7. "Megatherium." The huge ground sloth (a giant mammal) of the Pleistocene period, c. 70 million years ago.

8. "Brontosaurus." A gigantic, herbivorous dinosaur that roamed the American continent during the Jurassic period, c. 150 million years ago. The largest of all land animals, it attained a height of 12 feet and a length of 70 feet.

9. "South Kensington." Kensington is a London borough north of the Thames, bounded by Chelsea to the southeast and Willesden to the northwest. South Kensington is famed as the location of many of London's great museums as well as the Royal Albert Hall and the Albert Memorial.

The locale also has an important Wellsian association. In 1884, at the age of eighteen, Wells was awarded a government scholarship enabling him to become a student at the Normal School of Science in Exhibition Road, South Kensington.

(The School was part of the University of London.) It was there that he studied biology under Thomas Henry Huxley.

In the text, however, the Time Traveller is thinking specifically of two of South Kensington's museums: the Natural History Museum in Cromwell Road and the Science Museum just around the corner in Exhibition Road. The Natural History Museum has a "Gallery of Palaeontology" and the Science Museum exhibits many "big machines" illustrating the history of technology (see allusions in the next paragraph).

10. "The Palaeontological Section." Palaeontology is the branch of biological science concerned with the study of fossil remains.

11. "the inevitable process . . . treasures." The Time Traveller had said, in chapter 4, that he would subsequently explain what had happened to the "processes of putrefaction and decay." See chapter 4, note 27.

12. "sea-urchin." A marine animal with a round body covered with prickles or spines.

13. "this ancient monument . . . age". Contrast this museum of the future with the museum of the past in Chris Marker's film, *La Jetée* (1964), which is also visited by a time traveller and a woman he encounters during his journey through time.

14. "it might be, even a library!" Jorge Luis Borges describes the antithesis to this in his "Library of Babel," *Labyrinths* (1962).

15. "saltpetre." British spelling of saltpeter, a name given to potassium nitrate in its natural state. The name means *salt of rock*—Latin "sal petrae"—referring to the fact that the chemical is sometimes found encrusted on rocks. The Time Traveller associates saltpeter, like sulphur, with the manufacture of explosives.

16. "nitrates." Nitrates (salts of nitric acid) can be used to make spectacular fireworks. Nitric acid is basic to the manufacture of T.N.T., nitroglycerine, and guncotton.

17. "deliquesced." Melted or dissolved away as a result of attracting and absorbing moisture from the air.

18. "I am no specialist in mineralogy." Possibly a private joke. Wells failed his final examination in geology while he was a student at the Normal School of Science.

19. "desiccated." Dehydrated; dried out.

20. "It may be . . . hill." The note—by Wells—contributes to the narrative's semblance of authenticity.

21. "area." A very small garden space sunk slightly below the general level of a house, located just outside the front windows of the basement.

22. "signal-box." A railroad control-room. It contains rows of levers that work the signals and enable the signalman to switch trains to the required lines. The levers often have break-clips resembling those found on the handles of bicycles.

23. "mace." A medieval war weapon, which, typically, had the appearance of a club with a spiked metal head. A lever with a break-clip would vaguely resemble such a weapon.

24. "Very inhuman . . . things." Cf. the end of the next chapter where he has to restrain himself from a "massacre" of the Morlocks.

25. "the *Philosophical Transactions*." The journal of the Royal Society, Britain's foremost scientific association. Its full title is *Philosophical Transactions of the Royal Society*. The journal was originally established by H. Oldenburg in 1665. From 1887 onward it was issued in the form of two separate journals, one focusing on biology, and the other on physics and mathematics. The Time Traveller's seventeen papers on physical optics would obviously have appeared in the latter.

26. *"The Land of the Leal."* A Scots dialect ballad by Carolina, Baroness Nairne (1766–1846). It was written in 1798 for the Baroness's friend Mrs. Campbell Colquhoun when she lost her first-born child. *Leal* is Scots dialect for loyal, true, or honest. The term *Land of the Leal* means the realm of the blessed departed— i.e., Heaven.

There is a long and informative note on the ballad by 'M.P.' in *Notes and Queries* 6th Series vol.IV (November 19, 1881), 409–12. The tune that traditionally accompanied the poem—and which the Time Traveller presumably whistled— was an arrangement by Finly Dun of an ancient air known as "Hey Tutti Taiti." (See *Notes and Queries* 6th Series I, 139).

27. *"cancan."* The famous Parisian dance to the tempo of a galop (²/₄ time). It made its first appearance c. 1830 in French public ballrooms and over the next half century developed into a suggestive dance in which female performers wore frilly skirts and gave high kicks.

28. "camphor." A whitish, translucent, crystalline substance used in certain medications; the Time Traveller is interested in it because it is highly flammable: see the final paragraph of this chapter.

29. "hermetically sealed." Airtight.

30. "a sepia painting." A picture with predominantly brown tints. Sepia is a brown pigment derived from the secretions of cuttlefish.

31. "Belemnite." A fossil bone of an extinct cuttlefish; it is usually cylindrical, straight and smooth.

32. "steatite." Soapstone, usually of a suet-grey or greyish-green color.

33. "lignite." A brownish-black coal with a wood-like texture.

34. "dynamite cartridges." Containers filled with a mixture of nitroglycerin and kieselguhr (a fine, silica-rich earth): In the late nineteenth century one of the few safe forms in which such explosives could be transported.

CHAPTER 9

1. "my little one." I.e., Weena.

2. "carbuncles." Deep red—like garnets (semi-precious stones that are cut without facets).

3. "I hastily felt . . . gone!" He doesn't lose all the matches, but the loss of the *match-box* almost proves disastrous. See the end of chapter 10; also chapter 6, note 9.

4. "I could feel . . . blows." Kemp (1982, 39) comments: " 'Succulent' is a word more likely to be used by a Morlock to describe flesh."

5. "I stood . . . my feet". The Time Traveller had originally imagined doing this to the Eloi. See the second paragraph of chapter 4.

6. "tumulus." A barrow or burial mound.

CHAPTER 10

1. "Very pleasant . . . the same." Nettle (1966, 129) notes that "the language in this passage is similar to that found in the Authorized Version of the Bible."

2. "It is a law . . . dangers ". See chapter 4, note 28.

3. "The matches . . . box." I.e., safety matches which light only on the prepared striking surface of a matchbox. The Time Traveller would have preferred "lucifers," the strike-anywhere matches. See chapter 6, note 10.

CHAPTER 11

1. "One dial . . . thousands of millions." As McConnell (1977, 93) notes, there seems to be an inconsistency between the indication here that the dials

measured time in days and the implication in chapter 4 that they measured time in years ("the year Eight Hundred and Two Thousand Seven Hundred and One A.D.").

2. "the tidal drag." Nettle (1966, 129) explains this as "the influence of the moon, causing the tides." But Wells is here referring to the Sun. Again, as with the comment discussed in chapter 7, note 11, this *looks* like an inaccuracy. It is widely believed that the earth's tides are affected only by the moon. But the sun also plays its part. The tidal drag is actually caused one-third by the sun and two-thirds by the moon.

3. "the huge hull of the sun." Nettle (1966, 129) notes: "The sun is here likened to a ship partly out of sight on the horizon".

4. "lichen." Plants belonging to a compound group of fungi and algae living in symbiotic union.

5. "It was the same . . . twilight." Kemp (1982, 142) comments: "This touch of sharp scientific precision, pinning the fantasy to fact, is typical of Wells."

6. "There were no breakers . . . stirring." Also, since there is no indication in this chapter that the moon still orbited the earth, there would be no lunar attraction to create tides.

7. "I noticed . . . than it is now." The experience is reiterated later in the chapter: "the thin air that hurts one's lungs"; "the pain I felt in breathing."

8. "a thing like a huge white butterfly." Perhaps a descendant of the butterflies of 802,701 (see chapter 4, note 26). However, Eisenstein (1976, 162) speculates that this "thing" is "what has survived the English sparrow."

Wells quotes President Theodore Roosevelt's irrepressibly optimistic reaction to this section of the book: " 'Suppose, after all,' he said slowly, 'that should prove to be right, and it all ends in your butterflies and morlocks [sic]. *That doesn't matter now.* The effort's real. It's worth going on with. It's worth it. It's worth it—even so' . . ." *Experiment in Autobiography* (1934), 648–49.

9. "carters' whips." Long, thin leather horsewhips used by haulage drivers.

10. "bosses." Decorative knobs or protuberances.

11. "palps." Sense organs in the form of feelers.

12. "I felt . . . by my ear." A repeat of his experience with the Morlocks. See chapter 6, note 11.

13. "algal slime." A viscous secretion found on algae and kelp.

14. "As I stared . . . these monsters". Suvin (1979, 235) comments: "In the last episode, the tentacled 'thing' does not attack the Time Traveller because he flees in time, but it is clearly the master of that situation. It is reinforced by the additional presence of liverwort and lichen, the only land survivors; of the desolate inorganic landscape; and of the blood-red Sun in eclipse, which sugggests the nearing end of Earth and the whole solar system. The episode . . . telescopes the taxonomic progression of land animal/sea animal, animals/plants, organic/inorganic, existence of the Earth and the solar system/destruction of same—the last being left to the . . . extrapolative mechanism of the reader."

15. "foliated." Separated into leaf-like layers.

16. "crustacea." Arthropods such as lobsters, crabs, and wood lice, whose bodies are covered with a crust or hard shell.

17. "At last . . . darkling heavens." Actually the sun's physical size would not have appeared to have increased significantly in thirty million years. A change of the magnitude indicated would take *billions* of years! When and if that condition is realized, the vastly increased level of radiation will have eliminated *all* life-forms from the Earth's surface, and, I regret to say, a Time Traveller would not survive the experience of stepping out of his Time Machine.

18. "liverworts." A kind of moss that grows on damp surfaces and on trees.

19. "The green slime on the rocks . . . beach." An image strongly associated

with late nineteenth century avant-garde painting and "japonisme" (see chapter 4, note 4).

Siegfried Wichmann observes: "Towards 1900 the motif of the rock in the sea became a major theme in European landscape painting. Japanese woodcuts of course played their part in this. Jagged rocks in the sea, cliffs eaten into by the water, sharp reefs and rearing outcrops of rock encircled by spray became themes in their own right. . . . Impressionism, Symbolism, and Art Nouveau all made this theme a characteristic motif. . . . Rocks in the sea appear in countless versions in Chinese and above all Japanese painting." Wichmann (1985, 146).

In this chapter the image seems appropriate as a symbol of the outcome of the "decadence" represented in the "japonisme" of the Eloi.

20. "I fancied . . . this bank." Eisenstein (1976, 161–65) makes a good case for regarding this black object as a descendant of the Morlocks. Lake (1979, 84) comments thus on Eisenstein's argument: "If we can accept this, then there is another symbolic linkage between the parts of the story. The Morlock line is still the enemy, but with a color change from white to the more final death color, black."

21. "The stars . . . very little." Stars appear to twinkle because of atmospheric disturbances (air currents) that distort their light as it reaches the Earth. The unsteady air also breaks up starlight into the colors which seem to emanate from the stars. The Time Traveller is perceiving the stars with little distortion because 30 million years hence the Earth's atmosphere has become much thinner. This also accounts for the pain he feels in breathing (see final paragraph of this chapter).

22. "Either the moon . . . very near to the earth." Cf. the following passage from Wells's short story "The Star" in *Tales of Space and Time* (1899): "Men, looking up, near blinded, at the star, saw that a black disc was creeping across the light. It was the moon, coming between the star and the earth."

The Time Traveller is, presumably, observing a transit of the moon or Venus. The planet Mercury would not be visible to the naked eye. On "inner planet" see chapter 5, note 25.

23. "All the sounds . . . over." Here Wells may have been echoing either or both of the following passages (a) Huxley (1968, 199): "If what the practical philosophers tell us, that our globe has been in a state of fusion, and, like the sun, is gradually cooling down, is true; then the time must come when evolution will mean adaptation to an universal winter, and all forms of life will die out, except such low and simple organisms as the Diatom of the Arctic and Antarctic ice and the Protococcus of the red snow." (b) Grant Allen (1881, 224–25): "Life, indeed, viewed cosmically, is but a superficial phenomenon produced by arrested solar radiation on the outer crust of a cooling nebula, and it will disappear some day, from this earth at least, amid the universal chilling of an exhausted world."

See also Wells's own articles, "On Extinction," *Chambers's Journal* 10 (September 3, 1893), 623–24 and "The Extinction of Man," *Pall Mall Gazette* 59 (September 25, 1894), 3.

24. "The darkness . . . absolutely black." Cf. the description in this paragraph and the previous one with Camille Flammarion's vision of Earth's last days, in *Omega*: "One thing is certain, that the sun will finally lose its heat. . . . The radiation of heat and light will then diminish. . . . The sun will become a dark red ball, then a black one, and night will be perpetual. The moon, which shines only by reflection, will no longer illumine the lonely nights. Our planet will receive no light but that of the stars. The solar heat having vanished, the atmosphere will remain undisturbed, and an absolute calm, unbroken by any breath of air, will reign. If the oceans still exist they will be frozen ones, no evaporation will form clouds, no rain will fall, no stream will flow . . . . and the earth, a dark ball, a frozen tomb, will continue to revolve about the black sun, travelling

through an endless night and hurrying away with all the solar system into the abyss of space. *It is to the extinction of the sun that the earth will owe its death, twenty, perhaps forty million years hence.*" [Italics in the original]. Flammarion (1894, 109–10). Cf. also the visions of *fin du globe* in Gabriel De Tarde, *Fragment d'Histoire Future* (1884) and Jules Verne, *Hier et Demain* (1905).

25. "the size of a football." I.e., the size (and shape) of a soccer ball. In British English "football" means *soccer*. (The British use an oval ball—like an American football—in playing rugby). Eisenstein (1976, 76) viewing this "round thing" as the ultimate offspring of man, advises us to "Note particularly the size of the creature; it is about 'the size of a football'—which is to say, about the size of a human head."

CHAPTER 12

1. "So I came back." Nicholls (1983, 90) notes that "Wells in *The Time Machine* seems to have used the simplest of all models of time, in which it is seen as a river. The time traveller goes further and further downstream into the future, almost to the end of the world, and then returns (with almost no lapse of contemporary time) to his late-Victorian present. None of his actions changes the course of time and it is as if the time-river has just one, permanent and unchanging course." Along similar lines, Paul Valéry comments: "Even Wells, in his famous story *The Time Machine*, employs and explores time *as it was*, old time, the time which was believed in *before* him . . . " Paul Valéry, "Literature and Our Destiny" in *Remarks on the Modern World* (Paris, 1962), 252.

2. "Mrs. Watchett . . . previous ones." See chapter 3, note 3.

3. "Hillyer." The narrator of the framing or outer narrative: this is the first mention of his name. As McConnell (1977, 98) states, most commentaries on *The Time Machine* incorrectly assume that Hillyer is the Time Traveller's manservant. ". . . At the end of . . . chapter [12], the narrator tells how he breaks into the Time Traveller's laboratory, on the day *after* the narrative, to see the Traveller disappearing on his last voyage into the future. Naturally, then, on his journey *back* to the day of his narrative, the Time Traveller might glimpse the narrator briefly—on the day, that is, after he tells his tale."

4. "the *Pall Mall Gazette*." A London evening paper to which Wells was a frequent contributor. Established in 1865, its most distinguished editors were John Morley and W. T. Stead. In the 1890s it was edited by Harry Cust.

5. " ' I know', he said . . . incredible to you." Philmus (1969, 534) observes: "Perhaps no one in the audience takes this vision seriously because, as Wells speculated elsewhere [in his article on "The Extinction of Man", see chapter 11, note 23], 'It is part of the excessive egotism of the human animal that the bare idea of its extinction seems incredible to it.' "

6. "His eye . . . little table." In *Other Inquisitions*, Jorge Luis Borges reflects thus on this episode of the story: [The Time Traveller] "returns with his hair grown gray and brings with him a wilted flower from the future. . . . More incredible than a celestial flower or the flower of a dream is the flower of the future, the unlikely flower whose atoms now occupy other spaces and have not yet been assembled." See further Philmus (1974, 242).

7. "gynaeceum." Now obsolete spelling of *gynoecium* = the pistil or pistils (collectively) of a flower.

8. "the natural order." A division of botanical (or zoological) classification ranking below a *class*.

9. " 'The story I told you was true." Philmus (1969, 534–35) comments: "His insistence that 'The story I told you was true' . . . implies that he takes his prophecy literally, that he allows it the same ontological status that he himself

has. Thus to dramatize the assertion that his tale is literally true, he must go back into the world of the future since he cannot accept it as fiction, as an invented metaphor, he must disappear into the dimension where his vision 'exists'. The demand that his vision be literally true, in other words, requires that the Traveller be no more real than it is; and his return to that world fulfills this demand."

10. "next day." I.e., Friday. See time scheme in Structure section of Introduction.

11. " 'I'm frightfully busy . . . thing in there.' " This somewhat bitter reference to the Time Machine is perhaps an echo of the Medical Man's contemptuous comment on the demonstration of the model Time Machine: "He said he had seen a similar thing at Tübingen" (chapter 2).

12. "phantasm." Common nineteenth-century term for an apparition, ghost, or creation of the imagination. See chapter 1, note 34.

13. "as everybody knows." What "everybody knows"—mentioned almost parenthetically—is a Macaulayan device to support the 'veracity' of the Time Traveller's story.

14. "he has never returned." I fail to locate in the text any evidence to support the following assumptions of Scholes and Rabkin (1977, 203–204): (1) "The Time Traveller, sympathetic towards the victimized Eloi, determines to set off again with the equipment and skills to help them. He promises to return, if he lives and thus succeeds. . . ." (2) "the undoubted fact of the Time Traveller's death." The Time Traveller's stated purpose is not to help the Eloi but to collect unassailable proof of his time travelling, and the Epilogue leaves us quite *uncertain* of his destination or whether he is alive or dead.

Hennelly (1979, 165–66) *speculates* more cautiously about what might have happened if the Time Traveller returned to 802,701: "Has he failed and been killed by the Morlocks, whom by now he should certainly *know* how to handle? Has he escaped to settle down with the pretty Eloi, perhaps returning prior to the death of Weena to save her again, before the fact [a variation on this notion occurs at the finale of George Pal's 1960 film adaption] . . .? There is obviously no textual evidence for this reading. Is the future merely a *possible* future, a potential schizophrenia which will only be realized if the current wasteland mentality is not cured . . .? Or, following the conditions of the Romance . . . has he simply returned to the allegorical present to save both the Eloi and the Morlocks and thereby redeem the realistic present of Victorian England? The Traveller's symbolic identification with Prometheus throughout the tale supports this last hypothesis. . . ." See also Epilogue, note 10.

EPILOGUE

1. "It may be . . . savages." Kemp (1982, 19) notes: "when the Traveller fails to come back from his second time-jaunt, the narrator's mind immediately turns to dangers arising from the man's edibility . . ."

2. "the Age of Unpolished Stone." The earlier part of the Stone Age (c. One Million B.C. to c. 8000 B.C.) during which man used primitive ("unpolished") stone implements. Around 8000 B.C. man began using polished stone tools, and this marks the beginning of the Neolithic or New Stone Age. Note also Well's comment: "Man has undergone . . . but an infinitesimal alteration in his intrinsic nature since the age of unpolished stone" ("Human Evolution, an Artificial Process," *Fortnightly Review* 60 [October 1896], 590).

3. "Cretaceous." 135 million to 70 million years ago. The geologic period following the Jurassic and preceding the Tertiary, during which the dinosaurs became extinct and the earliest mammals evolved. Much of what is now land was covered by seas in which most of the world's chalk deposits were formed.

4. "the grotesque saurians." Dinosaurs.

5. "the Jurassic times." 180 million to 135 million years ago. Often called the Age of Dinosaurs.

6. "if I may use the phrase." Donald Williams cites this phrase in context as evidence of Wells's uneasiness about the consistency of the notion of time travel in his story (*Journal of Philosophy* 48, 15 [19 July 1951], 457–72).

See further Hillary Putnam and J. J. C. Smart, "Time Travel," in Peter A. French, ed., *Philosophers in Wonderland* (Saint Paul, Minn.: Llewellyn Publications, 1975), 104.

7. "plesiosaurus." A marine dinosaur that flourished c. 150 million years ago. It had a small head, a long neck, and four limbs rather like seal's flippers.

8. "Oolitic coral reef." Sea reefs formed from deposits of limestone (calcium carbonate) that appear like rounded or granular concretions cemented together.

9. "Triassic Age." 225 million to 180 million years ago. An era known to geologists particularly for its fossil ammonites (extinct mollusks) which once flourished in the saline waters that covered much of the land surface.

10. "Or did he go forward . . . ages." Note that the Outer Narrator does *not* mention the possibility that the Time Traveller may have returned to 802,701.

11. "And I have by me . . . heart of man." The story's ultimate commingling of compassion and despair with a profound sense of the mutability and evanescence of our species is exquisitely symbolized in the image of the two faded flowers.

Scholes and Rabkin (1977, 204) offer the following summation of the Outer Narrator's closing words: "This strange narrative optimism . . . leaves the reader with an ambivalence not merely about science and the putative benefits of technology, but about the essential meaning of humanity."

Philmus (1974, 242), disagreeing with Borges's remarks on the Time Traveller's flowers (see chapter 12, note 7), states: "The future is real, possibly catastrophic, but not beyond redemption; this is the testimony the flower of the future mutely offers. Borges, on the contrary, seems to regard that flower as a hieroglyphic of despair: the future is already inexorably configured in the particulate structure of present time, what will happen is already destiny."

Probable Route of the Time Traveller

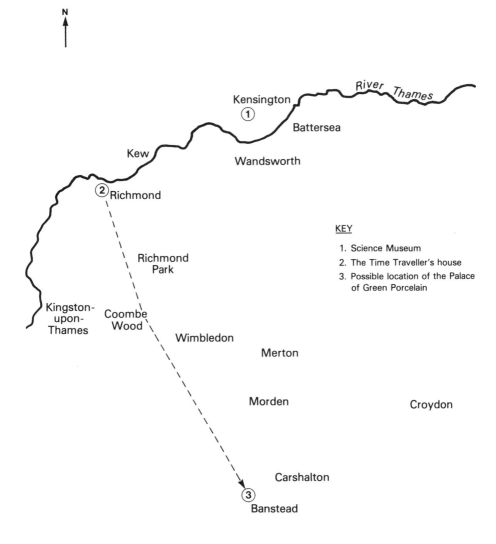

N

Kensington
①

River Thames

Battersea

Wandsworth

Kew

②Richmond

Richmond
Park

KEY

1. Science Museum
2. The Time Traveller's house
3. Possible location of the Palace
   of Green Porcelain

Kingston-
upon-
Thames

Coombe
Wood

Wimbledon

Merton

Morden

Croydon

Carshalton

③

Banstead

Select Bibliography

Aldiss, Brian W. *Billion Year Spree: The True History of Science Fiction*. New York: Schocken Books, 1974. A critical history of science fiction. Lively and provocative.

Amis, Kingsley. *New Maps of Hell: A Survey of Science Fiction*. New York: Harcourt Brace, 1960. A pioneering critical commentary mainly on social aspects of science fiction.

Asimov, Isaac. *Asimov on Science Fiction*. Garden City, N.Y.: Doubleday, 1981. Introductory.

———. "When It Comes to Time Travel, There's No Time Like the Present," *New York Times* (5 October 1986), section 2, pp. 1, 32. Considers current interest in time travel in the wake of Coppola's film, *Peggy Sue Got Married*.

Bailey, J. O. *Pilgrims through Space and Time*. Westport, Connecticut: Greenwood Press, 1972. Reprint of a pioneer survey of science-fiction plots and themes.

Batchelor, John. *H. G. Wells*. Cambridge: At the University Press, 1985. Perceptive survey with half-a-dozen worthwhile pages on *TM*.

Bergonzi, Bernard. *The Early H. G. Wells: A Study of the Scientific Romances*. Manchester: At the University Press, 1961. Basic. Includes the complete text of *The Chronic Argonauts*.

———, ed. *H. G. Wells: A Collection of Critical Essays*. Englewood Cliffs, New Jersey: Prentice-Hall, 1976. Includes several key articles: V. S. Pritchett's "The Scientific Romances," Bergonzi's "*The Time Machine*: An Ironic Myth," and Philmus's "The Logic of Prophecy in *The Time Machine*."

———. "The Publication of *The Time Machine*, 1894–5," *Review of English Studies* New Series 11 (1960), 42–51. Basic.

Borges, Jorge Luis. "The First Wells," in *Other Inquisitions: 1937–1952*. New York: Washington Square Press, 1966. A brief but intriguing essay. See further Philmus (1974).

Borello, Alfred. *H. G. Wells: Author in Agony*. Carbondale and Edwardsville: Southern Illinois University Press, 1972. Brief discussion of *TM*.

Caudwell, Christopher. *Studies in a Dying Culture*. London: John Lane, 1938. Contains a controversial, Marxian essay on Wells.

Costa, Richard Hauer. *H. G. Wells*. New York: Twayne Publishers, Inc., 1967. General survey of HGW with a brief critique of *TM*.

Eisenstein, Alex. "Very Early Wells: Origins of Some Major Physical Motifs in *The Time Machine* and *The War of the Worlds*," *Extrapolation* 13 (1972), 119–26. Key article.

———. "*The Time Machine* and the End of Man," *Science Fiction Studies* 3 (July 1976), 161–65. Key article.

Fredericks, Casey. *The Future of Eternity*. Bloomington: Indiana University Press, 1982. Some good insights into *TM*.

Gill, Stephen. *The Scientific Romances of H. G. Wells (A Critical Study)*. Cornwall, Ontario: Vesta Publications, 1975. Slight chapter on *TM*.

Gottesman, Ronald and Harry M. Geduld. *The Girl in the Hairy Paw*. New York: Avon Books, 1976. The Introduction summarizes the mythology of apes and gorillas.

Haight, Gordon S. "H. G. Wells's 'The Man of the Year Million'," *Nineteenth Century Fiction* 12 (1958), 325. Perceptive.

Haining, Peter, ed. *The H. G. Wells Scrapbook.* New York: Clarkson N. Potter, Inc., 1978. Includes a photograph of 23 Eardley Road, Sevenoaks, where the *New Review Time Machine* was written, and several illustrations of *TM* from books and pulps.

Haynes, Roslynn D. *H. G. Wells: Discoverer of the Future.* London: Macmillan Press, Ltd., 1980. Useful discussion of various critiques of time travel.

Heffern, Richard. *Time Travel: Myth or Reality?* New York: Pyramid Books, 1977. "In this book, I have attempted to compile some of what is known about the subject of time travel." Useful bibliography.

Hennelly, Mark M., Jr. "*The Time Machine*: A Romance of 'The Human Heart'," *Extrapolation* 20, no.2 (Summer 1979), 154–67. Key article.

Hillegas, Mark R. "Cosmic Pessimism in H. G. Wells's Scientific Romances," *Papers of the Michigan Academy of Science, Arts, and Letters* 46 (1961), 655–63. Pioneering article on Huxley's influence on Wells.

———. *The Future as Nightmare: H. G. Wells and the Anti-Utopians.* New York: Oxford University Press, 1967. Basic.

Hinton, Charles H. *Speculations on the Fourth Dimension.* ed. Rudolf v. B. Rucker. New York: Dover Publications, Inc., 1980. Key source for *TM*. See Appendix X.

Hughes, David Y. and Robert M. Philmus. "The Early Science Journalism of H. G. Wells: A Chronological Survey," *Science Fiction Studies* 1, pt. 2 (Fall 1973), 98–114.

Hughes, David Y. "Bergonzi and After in the Criticism of Wells's Science Fiction," *Science Fiction Studies* 3 (1976), 165–74.

———. "The Garden in Wells's Early Science Fiction," in Suvin and Philmus, *H. G. Wells and Modern Science Fiction.*

———. "Criticism in English of H. G. Wells's Science Fiction: A Select Annotated Bibliography," *Science Fiction Studies* 6, pt. 3 (November 1979), 309–19.

Huntington, John. "Thinking by Opposition: The 'Two-World' Structure in H. G. Wells's Short Fiction," *Science Fiction Studies* 25, vol. 8 (1981), 240–53. Key article.

———. *The Logic of Fantasy: H. G. Wells and Science Fiction.* New York: Columbia University Press, 1982. Excellent chapter on *TM*.

Huxley, Thomas Henry. *Evolution and Ethics and Other Essays.* New York: Greenwood Press, 1968. Reprint of a major source for *TM*.

Jackson, Holbrook. *The Eighteen Nineties; A Review of Art and Ideas at the Close of the 19th Century.* New York: Capricorn Books, 1966. Useful background.

Jarry, Alfred. *Oeuvres Complètes.* Textes établis, préséntes et annotés par Michel Arrive. Paris: Gallimard, 1972. See Appendix VIII.

Jarry, Alfred. *Selected Works of Alfred Jarry.* Edited by Roger Shattuck and Simon Watson Taylor. New York: Grove Press, 1965.

Jensen, Paul. "H. G. Wells on the Screen," *Films in Review* 18:9 (November 1967), 521–27.

Keen, Stephen. *The Culture of Time and Space 1880–1918.* Cambridge, Mass.: Harvard University Press, 1986. A searching overview of the changes in technology and culture that created new modes of understanding and experiencing time and space in the years before World War I. Highly recommended as background reading.

Kemp, Peter. *H. G. Wells and the Culminating Ape.* New York: St. Martin's Press, 1982. Sporadic insights into *TM*.

Ketterer, David. "Oedipus as Time Traveller," *Science Fiction Studies* 9 (1982),

340–41. Glosses two passages in the final chapter of *TM*.

Lake, David J. "The White Sphinx and the Whitened Lemur: Images of Death in *The Time Machine*," *Science Fiction Studies* 6, pt. 1 (March 1979), 77–84. Excellent on Wells's imagery.

Le Bot, Marc. *Le Macchine Celibi*. New York: Rizzoli, 1975. Provocative treatments of machine imagery.

Lem, Stanislaw. "The Time-Travel Story and Related Matters of SF Structuring," *Science Fiction Studies* 1, pt. 3 (Spring 1974), 143–54. Key article.

LeMire, Eugene D. "H. G. Wells and the World of Science Fiction," *University of Windsor Review* (Windsor, Ontario) 2, no. 1 (Fall 1966), 59–66. Brief but useful comments on *TM*.

Levin, Martin. *Whatever Happened to Lady Chatterley's Lover!* Kansas City & New York: Andrews, McMeel & Parker, 1985. Contains (p. 19) an amusing spoof of *TM*.

Mackenzie, Norman and Jeanne. *H. G. Wells: A Biography*. New York: Simon & Schuster, 1973. Basic.

McConnell, Frank D., ed. *H. G. Wells, The Time Machine The War of the Worlds: A Critical Edition*. New York: Oxford University Press, 1977. McConnell's Introduction claims: "This is the first annotated critical edition of *The Time Machine* and *The War of the Worlds*," but *TM*, at least, had been annotated earlier by Keith Nettle (see below). McConnell's notes, like Nettle's, are brief but often useful. The text he uses is unreliable.

Nettle, Keith, ed. *The Time Machine with an Introduction and Notes*. London: Heinemann Educational Books, Ltd., 1966. As far as I know, this was the first attempt to edit *TM*. The edition was intended for foreigners learning English. Nettle's notes are occasionally useful, often idiosyncratic or inaccurate.

Nicholls, Peter. *The Science in Science Fiction*. New York: Knopf, 1983. Scientific perspectives on the idea of time travel.

O'Neill, Gerard K. *2081: A Hopeful View of the Human Future*. New York: Simon & Schuster, 1981. In general, a good ego-boost for any descendants of the Time Traveller's guests. Notes (p. 254): "It would not violate causality . . . to devise a machine capable of viewing any event in history in complete three dimensional color with stereophonic sound."

Parrinder, Patrick. *H. G. Wells*. Edinburgh: Oliver & Boyd, 1970.

——. *H. G. Wells: The Critical Heritage*. London & Boston: Routledge & Kegan Paul, 1972. Reprints the original reviews of the Heinemann *TM*.

——. "*News from Nowhere, The Time Machine*, and the Breakup of Classical Realism," *Science Fiction Studies* 3 (1976), 265–74. Key article.

—— and Robert M. Philmus. *H. G. Wells's Literary Criticism*. Brighton, Sussex & Totowa, New Jersey: Spiers & Boden and Barnes & Noble, 1980. Pages 222–51 contain a selection of Wells's writings on science fiction, Utopian fiction, and fantasy. Basic.

——. "*The Time Machine*: H. G. Wells's Journey through Death," *The Wellsian* (London) 4 (Summer 1981), 15–23. "*The Time Machine* survives first and foremost as an unrivalled extrapolation of the Darwinian vision of man. . . . Death and extinction are . . . at the centre of the evolutionary vision."

Philmus, Robert M. "*The Time Machine*: or, The Fourth Dimension as Prophecy," *PMLA* 84 (1969), 530–35. Key article.

——. *Into the Unknown: the Evolution of Science Fiction from Francis Godwin to H. G. Wells*. Berkeley: University of California Press, 1970.

——. "Wells and Borges and the Labyrinths of Time," *Science Fiction Studies* 1, pt. 4 (Fall 1974), 237–48. Provocative insights into both writers. See entry on Borges above.

————. "*Futurological Congress* as Metageneric Text," *Science Fiction Studies* 13 (1986), 313–28. Comparative readings of a work by Stanislaw Lem and *TM*.

———— and David Y. Hughes, eds. *H. G. Wells: Early Writings in Science and Science Fiction.* Berkeley: University of California Press, 1975. Basic. Includes the whole of the *National Observer Time Machine*, excerpts from the *New Review Time Machine*, and a selection of Wells's early journalism of direct relevance to *TM*.

————. "The Logic of Prophecy in *The Time Machine*" in Bergonzi (1976).

————. "Revisions of the Future: *The Time Machine*," *Journal of General Education* 28 (1976), 23–30. Expanded version of pages 47–56 of Philmus and Hughes (1975).

Priestley, J. B. *Man and Time.* Garden City, New York: Doubleday & Company, Inc., 1964. Chapter 4 deals with "Time in Fiction and Drama," but is quite superficial.

Pritchett, V. S. *The Living Novel.* London: Chatto and Windus, 1946. Contains an oft-quoted chapter on Wells's scientific romances that has been reprinted in Bergonzi (1976).

Ramsaye, Terry. *A Million and One Nights.* New York: Simon and Schuster, 1964. Reprint of work originally published in 1926. See Appendix IX.

Rifkin, Jeremy and Ted Howard. *Entropy: A New World View.* New York: Bantam Books, Inc., 1981. Implications of the second law of thermodynamics for our current world situation. A valuable follow-up to reading *TM*.

Rothman, Tony. "The Seven Arrows of Time," *Discover*, February 1987, 63–77. Discusses the mystery of why "physicists can't find a single arrow of time that points in any direction but ahead"—even though "time flows backward into the past as readily as it does into the future" in both the Newtonian and Einsteinian universes.

Rucker, Rudolf v. B. *Geometry, Relativity and the Fourth Dimension.* New York: Dover, 1977. An intriguing follow-up to chapter 1 of *TM*.

Scafella, Frank. "The White Sphinx and *The Time Machine*," *Science Fiction Studies* 8 (1981), 255–65. Key article: useful to read it in conjunction with Lake (1979).

Scholes, Robert and Eric S. Rabkin. *Science Fiction: History Science Vision.* London, Oxford, New York: Oxford University Press, 1977. Provocative pages on *TM*.

Shipman, Pat. "The Myths and Perturbing Realities of Cannibalism," *Discover*, March 1987, 70–76. Intriguing reading in connection with the Morlock-Eloi relationship: "A few thousand years ago our species couldn't or wouldn't recognize the humanity of others. . . ."

Smith, David C. *H. G. Wells: Desperately Mortal.* New Haven and London: Yale University Press, 1986. The most authoritative biography of Wells. Contains new material on *TM*.

Sussman, Herbert L. *Victorians and the Machine: The Literary Response to Technology.* Cambridge: Harvard University Press, 1968. Useful background.

Suvin, Darko. "A Grammar of Form and a Criticism of Fact: *The Time Machine* as a Structural Model of Science Fiction," *Comparative Literature Studies* 10 (1973), 334–52. Basic—like all of Suvin's writings on Wells and science fiction.

————. "H. G. Wells and Earlier Science Fiction," *Science Fiction Studies* 1 (1974), 221–22.

————. "Wells as the Turning Point of the SF Tradition," *Minnesota Review* 4 (Spring 1975), 106–15.

———— and Robert M. Philmus, eds. *H. G. Wells and Modern Science Fiction.*

Lewisburg: Bucknell University Press, 1977. Includes Suvin's "A Grammar of Form and a Criticism of Fact: The Time Machine as a Structural Model for Science Fiction," Philmus's "Borges and Wells and the Labyrinths of Time," and Hughes's "The Garden in Wells's Early Science Fiction." Invaluable.

———. *Metamorphoses of Science Fiction: On the Poetics and History of a Literary Genre.* New Haven: Yale University Press, 1979. The most searching analysis of *TM.* Indispensable.

Tarde, Gabriel de. *Underground Man.* Preface by H. G. Wells. Westport, Connecticut: Hyperion Press, Inc., 1974. Reissue of a work originally published in 1905. Wells's Preface to de Tarde's story of mankind driven underground as a consequence of the extinction of the sun contains a passage that strikingly recalls chapter 11 of *The Time Machine*: "The conception of the sun seized in a mysterious, chill grip and flickering from hue to hue in the skies of a darkened, amazed and terrified world, could be presented in images of stupendous majesty and splendour. There arise visions of . . . the abrupt sight of the countless stars made visible by this great abdication, the thickening of the sky to stormy masses of cloud so that these are hidden again, the soughing of a world-wide wind, and then first little flakes and then the drift and driving of the multiplying snow . . . the shiver of the cold. . . ."

Verne, Jules. *Yesterday and Tomorrow.* New York: Ace Books, Inc., 1965. Verne's vision of *fin du globe.* His final work, written in 1905.

Wagar, W. Warren. *Terminal Visions; The Literature of Last Things.* Bloomington: Indiana University Press, 1982. Useful for comparative background, but less perceptive on Wells than on other writers.

Wasson, Richard. "Myth and the Ex-Nomination of Class in *The Time Machine,*" *Minnesota Review* 15 (Fall 1980), 112–22. Key article.

Wells, H. G. "Preface" to *Seven Famous Novels.* New York: Knopf, 1934.

———. *Experiment in Autobiography.* New York: Macmillan, 1934.

———. "The New Accelerator," in H. G. Wells, *Twelve Stories and a Dream.* London: Macmillan, 1903. A short story about the speeding up of the human metabolism by the use of a drug. A notable variation on the subject of time travel. Originally published in the *Strand,* December 1901.

———. "The Plattner Story," in H. G. Wells, *The Plattner Story and Others.* A short story about a chemistry teacher who blows himself into the Fourth Dimension. Originally published in the *New Review,* April 1896.

———. "The Star," in H. G. Wells, *Tales of Space and Time* (1899). New York: Harper, 1899. Remarkable account of a virtual *fin du globe* resulting from the intrusion of an alien star into the solar system. The story was originally published in the *Graphic,* Christmas 1897.

———. *The Time Machine, The Wonderful Visit, and Other Stories.* New York: Charles Scribner's Sons, 1924. Vol.1 of the Atlantic Edition of the Works of H. G. Wells. Important "Preface" by HGW.

———. *The Time Machine and The War of the Worlds.* Edited by Frank D. McConnell. See McConnell above.

———. *The Time Machine.* Edited by Keith Nettle. See Nettle above.

West, Anthony. *H. G. Wells: Aspects of a Life.* New York: Random House, 1984. Biographical revelations by a son of HGW.

West, Geoffrey. *H. G. Wells; A Sketch for a Portrait.* London: Gerald Howe, 1930. Contains important appendix: "A Note on Student Writings and *The Time Machine.*" See Appendix II to this edition.

Wichmann, Siegfried. *Japonisme: The Japanese Influence on Western Art in the 19th and 20th Centuries.* New York: Park Lane, 1985. Valuable for throwing light on some of the imagery of *TM.*

Williams, L. Thomas. *Journeys to the Center of the Earth: Descent and Initiation in Selected Science Fiction*. Ph.D. dissertation, Indiana University-Bloomington, 1983.

Wilson, Colin and John Grant, eds. *The Directory of Possibilities*. New York: The Rutledge Press, 1981. Includes a discussion of problems of time travel and time paradoxes.

Wykes, Alan. *H. G. Wells in the Cinema*. London: Jupiter Books, 1977. Some good stills, but meager on facts and of no critical value.

After The Time Machine:

A SELECT CHRONOLOGICAL LIST OF FICTION AND DRAMA ABOUT
TIME TRAVEL AND RELATED THEMES

Allen, Grant. *The British Barbarians* (1895)
Pawlowski, Gaston de. *Voyage to the Land of the Fourth Dimension* (1912)
Dunsany, Lord. *If* (1922)
Lindsay, David. *The Haunted Woman* (1922)
Wallace, Edgar. *Planetoid 127* (1924)
Cummings, Ray. *The Man Who Mastered Time* (1924)
Hamilton, Edmond. *The Time Raider* (1927)
Wright, Sidney Fowler. *The World Below* (1929)
Stapledon, W. Olaf. *Last and First Men* (1930)
Taine, John (Eric Temple Bell). *Seeds of Life* (1931)
————. *The Time Stream* (1931)
Fearn, John Russell. *The Intelligence Gigantic* (1933)
Taine, John (Eric Temple Bell). *Before the Dawn* (1934)
Fearn, John Russell. *Liners of Time* (1935)
Williamson, Jack. *The Legion of Time* (1938)
Sprague de Camp, L. *Lest Darkness Fall* (1939)
Weinbaum, Stanley G. *The New Adam* (1939)
Van Vogt, A.E. *The Weapons Shops of Ishar* (1942)
Priestley, J.B. *Three Time Plays* (1947)
Bradbury, Ray. "A Sound of Thunder" (1953). Perhaps the most frequently an-
    thologized short story about time travel. It is included in Bradbury's col-
    lection, *The Golden Apples of the Sun* (1953)
Asimov, Isaac. *The End of Eternity* (1955)
Maine, Charles Eric (David McIlwain). *Timeliner* (1955)
Silverberg, Robert. *The Time Hoppers* (1956)
Leiber, Fritz. *The Big Time* (1958)
Brunner, John. *Times Without Number* (1962)
Laumer, Keith. *A Trace of Memory* (1962)
Anderson, Poul. *The Corridors of Time* (1965)
Ballard, J. G. *Crystal World* (1966)
Hoyle, Fred. *October the First Is Too Late* (1966)
Moorcock, Michael. *Behold the Man* (1966)
Aldiss, Brian W. *An Age* (1967)
Brunner, John. *Quicksand* (1967)
Dick, Philip K. *Counter-Clock World* (1967)
Harrison, Harry. *The Time-Machined Saga* (1967)
Dick, Philip K. *Ubik* (1969)
Silverberg, Robert. *Up the Line* (1969)
Finney, Jack. *Time and Again* (1970)
Maddock, Larry. *The Time-Trap Gambit* (1970)
Laumer, Keith. *Dinosaur Beach* (1971)

Anderson, Poul. *There Will Be Time* (1972)
Aldiss, Brian W. *Frankenstein Unbound* (1973)
Gerrold, David. *The Man Who Folded Himself* (1973)
Simak, Clifford W. *Our Children's Children* (1973)
Matheson, Richard. *Bid Time Return* (1975)
Dickson, Gordon R. *Time Storm* (1977)
Brunner, John. *The Tides of Time* (1983)
Silverberg, Robert and Martin H. Greenberg, eds. *The Time Travelers* (1985). Key anthology of four novellas by Isaac Asimov, Murray Leinster, John Wyndham, and Henry Kuttner & C. L. Moore.

Adaptations and Spin-offs

The Time Machine has been adapted for film, television, radio, sound recording (phonograph records and cassettes), and comic books. There have also been numerous spin-offs: movies, television programs, books, and stories about time travel directly or indirectly inspired by Wells's novella.

FILM AND TELEVISION

Most adaptations of *The Time Machine* are of little or no interest to students of Wells. The only one that has come close to being a faithful adaptation was a version presented on British television (January 25, 1949) in which Russell Napier appeared as the Time Traveller and Mary Donn played Weena. Regrettably, this adaptation is not at present available for viewing in the U.S.A. Neither is the 1973 Canadian movie adaptation directed by Terence McCarthy.

The two film versions that *are* available are travesties of Wells, interesting primarily to movie buffs whose tastes run to special effects and *schlock*. George Pal's 1960 adaptation distorts and trivializes the original plot and themes, transforming *The Time Machine* into a mindless Hollywood melodrama about an intrepid scientist named George Wells (Rod Taylor) who becomes romantically involved with Weena (Yvette Mimieux), then arouses the apathetic Eloi and leads them to victory over a horde of shaggy, gorilla-like Morlocks. Shortly before Pal's death I asked him why his version did not include the *fin du globe* finale; he told me he was thinking of saving that episode for a sequel.

Even worse than Pal's version is Henning Schellerup's 1979 adaptation, putatively based on the "Classics Illustrated" comic book version. Actually the comic book treatment is far closer to Wells and in every way superior to Schellerup's movie! The film's hero, inexplicably named Neil Perry (John Beck), campaigns against bureaucratic villainy and takes side-trips to the Old West and one or two other places before heading into the future for his encounters with sexy young Weena (Priscilla Barnes) and a bunch of glowing-eyed Morlocks. The sets for this movie are among the crudest I've ever seen.

Only three of the countless spin-offs deserve mention here. The most significant one is the German silent film *Metropolis* (directed by Fritz Lang, 1926). Wells, in *The Way the World Is Going* (1929), imperceptively dismissed Lang's epic, the cinema's first great science-fiction movie, as the "silliest film," adding, guardedly: "I dislike this soupy whirlpool none the less because I find decaying fragments of my own juvenile work of thirty years ago, *The Sleeper Awakes*, floating about in it." An extremely curious comment—since the two-world structure of *Metropolis* (oppressed Workers toiling in the depths and a pleasure garden for the Capitalists on the sunlit surface) as well as a key episode of the plot (the hero exploring the dark underworld to discover the Workers' secret) are obviously taken from *The Time Machine*.

Planet of the Apes (directed by Franklin J. Schaffner, 1968) draws heavily upon the fourth book of *Gulliver's Travels* (the Apes, like Swift's Houyhnhnms, are the masters of Men) and upon *The Time Machine* (the hero travels through time to a distant future in which inarticulate humans, reduced to savagery, are preyed upon by intelligent apes.) The film is based on Pierre Boulle's 1963 novel of the same title.

In *Time After Time* (directed by Nicholas Meyer, 1979) young H. G. Wells (Malcolm MacDowell) pursues Jack the Ripper (David Warner)—via the time machine—from Victorian London to 1970s California. The initial situation is ingenious but it soon gives way to an absurd love affair between an impossibly naive Wells and an infuriatingly lethargic Amy Robbins (Mary Steenburgen). Regrettably, the hero and heroine do *not* turn out to be victims of the Ripper.

BOOKS

Friedell, Egon. *The Return of the Time Machine*. New York: Daw Books, Inc., 1972. Originally published as *Die Riese mit der Zeitmaschine*. Munich: R. Piper & Co., Verlag, 1946. A sequel to *The Time Machine* "by an admirer and correspondent of Wells."

Pal, George and Joe Morhaim. *Time Machine II*. New York: Dell Publishing Co., Inc., 1981. A sequel to *The Time Machine*: "Somewhere far in the future an eccentric inventor readied his craft to travel back to his own country and time—back to a gaslit Victorian England. With him was Weena, his gentle wife, about to give birth at any moment."

Priest, Christopher. *The Space Machine*. New York: Popular Library, 1978. "Mars was invading the earth! . . . Now at last we can learn the story . . . of a man and a woman from Victorian England who travelled through time and space to a startling rendezvous with destiny. . . ."

PICTORIAL VERSIONS AND COMIC BOOKS

Wells, H. G. *The Time Machine*. Classics Illustrated Comic Book 133. New York: Gilberton Company, Inc., 1956. Excludes the "further vision" of the end of the world.

———. West Haven, Ct.: Pendulum Press, Inc, 1973. Pictorial book version with test questions.

PHONOGRAPH RECORDINGS AND CASSETTES

Great Science Fiction Film Music. POO LP104. Contains Russ Garcia's music to George Pal's 1960 film of *TM*.

Wells, H. G. *The Time Machine*. New York: Caedmon Records [n.d.]. Caedmon TC 1678. LP record of James Mason reading an abridged version. Liner note by Isaac Asimov.

———. Dayton, Ohio: T.o.T. Productions, Inc., [n.d.]. Record 1807. LP record of Adventure Hour dramatization for children by Professor Margaret C. Tyler.

———. New York: A.A. Records, Inc. [n.d.]. Record 288. LP of Golden Records adaptation for children.

———. Downsville, Ontario: Listen for Pleasure recording 7044. Reading by Robert Hardy. 2 cassettes.

APPENDIXES

APPENDIX I

The Chronic Argonauts

I. THE STORY FROM AN EXOTERIC POINT OF VIEW

Being the Account of Dr Nebogipfel's sojourn in Llyddwdd

About half-a-mile outside the village of Llyddwdd by the road that goes up over the eastern flank of the mountain called Pen-y-pwll to Rwstog is a large farm-building known as the Manse. It derives this title from the fact that it was at one time the residence of the minister of the Calvinistic Methodists. It is a quaint, low, irregular erection, lying back some hundred yards from the roadway, and now fast passing into a ruinous state.

Since its construction in the latter half of the last century this house has undergone many changes of fortune, having been abandoned long since by the farmer of the surrounding acres for less pretentious and more commodious headquarters. Among others Miss Carnot, 'the Gallic Sappho' at one time made it her home, and later on an old man named Williams became its occupier. The foul murder of this tenant by his two sons was the cause of its remaining for some considerable period uninhabited; with the inevitable consequence of its undergoing very extensive dilapidation.

The house had got a bad name, and adolescent man and Nature combined to bring swift desolation upon it. The fear of the Williamses which kept the Llyddwdd lads from gratifying their propensity to invade its deserted interior, manifested itself in unusually destructive resentment against its external breakables. The missiles with which they at once confessed and defied their spiritual dread, left scarcely a splinter of glass, and only battered relics of the old-fashioned leaden frames, in its narrow windows; while numberless shattered tiles about the house, and four or five black apertures yawning behind naked rafters in the roof, also witnessed vividly to the energy of their trajection. Rain and wind thus had free way to enter the empty rooms and work their will there, old Time aiding and abetting. Alternately soaked and desiccated, the planks of floor-

The Chronic Argonauts by H. G. Wells was first published in *The Science Schools Journal* (London), April, May, June 1888. It appears here together with the *National Observer Time Machine* and excerpts from the *New Review Time Machine* by kind permission of A. P. Watt Ltd. and the Literary Executors of the Estate of H. G. Wells.

ing and wainscot warped apart strangely, split here and there, and tore themselves away in paroxysms of rheumatic pain from the rust-devoured nails that had once held them firm. The plaster of walls and ceiling, growing green-black with a rain-fed crust of lowly life, parted slowly from the fermenting laths; and large fragments thereof falling down inexplicably in tranquil hours, with loud concussion and clatter, gave strength to the popular superstition that old Williams and his sons were fated to re-enact their fearful tragedy until the final judgment. White roses and daedal creepers, that Miss Carnot had first adorned the walls with, spread now luxuriantly over the lichen-filmed tiles of the roof, and in slender graceful sprays timidly invaded the ghostly cobweb-draped apartments. Fungi, sickly pale, began to displace and uplift the bricks in the cellar floor; while on the rotting wood everywhere they clustered, in all the glory of purple and mottled crimson, yellow-brown and hepatite. Woodlice and ants, beetles and moths, winged and creeping things innumerable, found each day a more congenial home among the ruins; and after them in ever-increasing multitudes swarmed the blotchy toads. Swallows and martins built every year more thickly in the silent, airy, upper chambers. Bats and owls struggled for the crepuscular corners of the lower rooms. Thus, in the Spring of the year eighteen hundred and eighty-seven, was Nature taking over, gradually but certainly, the tenancy of the old Manse. 'The house was falling into decay,' as men who do not appreciate the application of human derelicts to other beings' use would say, 'surely and swiftly.' But it was destined nevertheless to shelter another human tenant before its final dissolution.

There was no intelligence of the advent of a new inhabitant in quiet Llyddwdd. He came without a solitary premonition out of the vast unknown into the sphere of minute village observation and gossip. He fell into the Llyddwdd world, as it were, like a thunderbolt falling in the daytime. Suddenly, and out of nothingness, he *was*. Rumour, indeed, vaguely averred that he was seen to arrive by a certain train from London, and to walk straight without hesitation to the old Manse, giving neither explanatory word nor sign to mortal as to his purpose there: but then the same fertile source of information also hinted that he was first beheld skimming down the slopes of steep Pen-y-pwll with exceeding swiftness, riding, as it appeared to the intelligent observer, upon an instrument not unlike a sieve and that he entered the house by the chimney. Of these conflicting reports, the former was the first to be generally circulated, but the latter, in view of the bizarre presence and eccentric ways of the newest inhabitant, obtained wider credence. By whatever means he arrived, there can be no doubt that he was in, and in possession of the Manse, on the first of May; because on the morning of that day he was inspected by Mrs Morgan ap Lloyd Jones, and subsequently by the numerous persons her report brought up the mountain slope, engaged in the curious occupation of nailing sheet-tin across the void window sockets of his new domicile—'blinding his house', as Mrs Morgan ap Lloyd Jones not inaptly termed it.

He was a small-bodied, sallow faced little man, clad in a close-fitting garment of some stiff, dark material, which Mr Parry Davies, the Llyddwdd shoemaker, opined was leather. His aquiline nose, thin lips, high cheek-ridges, and pointed chin, were all small and mutually well proportioned; but the bones and muscles of his face were rendered excessively prominent and distinct by his extreme leanness. The same cause contributed to the sunken appearance of the large eager-looking grey eyes, that gazed forth from under his phenomenally wide and high forehead. It was this latter feature that most powerfully attracted the attention of an observer. It seemed to be great beyond all preconceived ratio to the rest of his countenance. Dimensions, corrugations, wrinkles, venation, were alike abnormally exaggerated. Below it his eyes glowed like lights in some cave at a cliff's foot. It so over-powered and suppressed the rest of his face as to give an *unhuman* appearance almost, to what would otherwise have been an unquestionably handsome profile. The lank black hair that hung unkempt before his eyes served to increase rather than conceal this effect, by adding to unnatural altitude a suggestion of hydrocephalic projection: and the idea of something ultra human was furthermore accentuated by the temporal arteries that pulsated visibly through his transparent yellow skin. No wonder, in view even of these things, that among the highly and over-poetical Cymric of Llyddwdd the sieve theory of arrival found considerable favour.

It was his bearing and actions, however, much more than his personality, that won overbelievers to the warlock notion of matters. In almost every circumstance of life the observant villagers soon found his ways were not only not *their* ways, but altogether inexplicable upon any theory of motives they could conceive. Thus, in a small matter at the beginning, when Arthur Price Williams, eminent and famous in every tavern in Caernarvonshire for his social gifts, endeavoured, in choicest Welsh and even choicer English, to inveigle the stranger into conversation over the sheet-tin performance, he failed utterly. Inquisitional supposition, straightforward enquiry, offer of assistance, suggestion of method, sarcasm, irony, abuse, and at last, gage of battle, though shouted with much effort from the road hedge, went unanswered and apparently unheard. Missile weapons, Arthur Price Williams found, were equally unavailing for the purpose of introduction, and the gathered crowd dispersed with unappeased curiosity and suspicion. Later in the day, the swarth apparition was seen striding down the mountain road towards the village, hatless, and with such swift width of step and set resolution of countenance, that Arthur Price Williams, beholding him from afar from the 'Pig and Whistle' doorway was seized with dire consternation, and hid behind the Dutch oven in the kitchen till he was past. Wild panic also smote the school-house as the children were coming out, and drove them indoors like leaves before a gale. He was merely seeking the provision shop, however, and erupted thencefrom after a prolonged stay, loaded with a various armful of blue parcels, a loaf, herrings, pigs' trotters, salt pork, and a black bottle, with which he returned in the same swift projectile gate to the Manse. His way of shopping was to name, and to name simply, without solitary other word of explanation, civility or request, the article he required.

The shopkeeper's crude meteorological superstitions and inquisitive commonplaces, he seemed not to hear, and he might have been esteemed deaf if he had not evinced the promptest attention to the faintest relevant remark. Consequently it was speedily rumoured that he was determined to avoid all but the most necessary human intercourse. He lived altogether mysteriously, in the decaying manse, without mortal service or companionship, presumably sleeping on planks or litter, and either preparing his own food or eating it raw. This, coupled with the popular conception of the haunting partricides, did much to strengthen the popular supposition of some vast gulf between the newcomer and common humanity. The only thing that was inharmonious with this idea of severance from mankind was a constant flux of crates filled with grotesquely contorted glassware, cases of brazen and steel instruments, huge coils of wire, vast iron and fire-clay implements, of inconceivable purpose, jars and phials labelled in black and scarlet—POISON, huge packages of books, and gargantuan rolls of cartridge paper, which set in towards his Llyddwdd quarters from the outer world. The apparently hieroglyphic inscriptions on these various consignments revealed at the profound scrutiny of Pugh Jones that the style and title of the new inhabitant was Dr Moses Nebogipfel, Ph.D., F.R.S., N.W.R., PAID; at which discovery much edification was felt, especially among the purely Welsh-speaking community. Further than this, these arrivals, by the evident unfitness for any allowable mortal use, and inferential diabolicalness, filled the neighbourhood with a vague horror and lively curiosity, which were greatly augmented by the extraordinary phenomena, and still more extraordinary accounts thereof, that followed their reception in the Manse.

The first of these was on Wednesday, the fifteenth of May, when the Calvinistic Methodists of Llyddwdd had their annual commemoration festival; on which occasion, in accordance with custom, dwellers in the surrounding parishes of Rwstog, Peu-y-garn, Caergyllwdd, Llanrdd, and even distant Llanrwst flocked into the village. Popular thanks to Providence were materialized in the usual way, by means of plumb-bread and butter, mixed tea, *terza*, consecrated flirtations, kiss-in-the-ring, rough-and-tumble football, and vituperative political speechmaking. About half-past eight the fun began to tarnish, and the assembly to break up; and by nine numerous couples and occasional groups were wending their way in the darkling along the hilly Llyddwdd and Rwstog road. It was a calm warm night; one of these nights when lamps, gas and heavy sleep seem stupid ingratitude to the Creator. The zenith sky was an ineffable deep lucent blue, and the evening star hung golden in the liquid darkness of the west. In the north-north-west, a faint phosphorescence marked the sunken day. The moon was just rising, pallid and gibbous over the huge haze-dimmed shoulder of Pen-y-pwll. Against the wan eastern sky, from the vague outline of the mountain slope, the Manse stood out black, clear, and solitary. The stillness of the twilight had hushed the myriad murmurs of the day. Only the sounds of footsteps and voices and laughter, that came fitfully rising and falling from the roadway, and an intermittent hammering in the darkened dwelling, broke the silence. Suddenly a strange whizzing, buzzing whirr filled the night air, and a bright flicker glanced across the dim path of the wayfarers. All eyes were turned in astonishment to the old Manse. The house no longer loomed a black featureless block but was filled to overflowing with light. From the gaping holes in the roof, from chinks and fissures amid tiles and brickwork, from every gap which Nature or man had pierced in the crumbling old shell, a blinding blue-white glare was streaming, beside which the rising moon seemed a disc of opaque sulphur. The thin mist of the dewy night had caught the violet glow and hung, unearthly smoke, over the colourless blaze. A strange turmoil and outcrying in the old Manse now began, and grew ever more audible to the clustering spectators, and therewith came clanging loud impacts agains the window-guarding tin. Then from the gleaming roof-gaps of the house suddenly vomited forth a wondrous swarm of heteromerous living things—swallows, sparrows, martins, owls, bats, insects in visible multitudes, to hang for many minutes a noisy, gyring, spreading cloud over the black gables and chimneys, . . . and then slowly to thin out and vanish away in the night.

As this tumult died away the throbbing humming that had first arrested attention grew once more in the listener's hearing, until at last it was the only sound in the long stillness. Presently, however, the road gradually awoke again to the beating and shuffling of feet, as the knots of Rwstog people, one by one, turned their blinking eyes from the dazzling whiteness and, pondering deeply, continued their homeward way.

The cultivated reader will have already discerned that this phenomenon, which sowed a whole crop of uncanny thoughts in the minds of these worthy folk, was simply the installation of the electric light in the Manse. Truly, this last vicissitude of the old house was its strangest one. Its revival to mortal life was like the raising of Lazarus. From that hour forth, by night and day, behind the tin-blinded windows, the tamed lightning illuminated every corner of its quickly changing interior. The almost frenzied energy of the lank-haired, leather-clad little doctor swept away into obscure holes and corners and common destruction, creeper sprays, toadstools, rose leaves, birds' nests, birds' eggs, cobwebs, and all the coatings and lovingly fanciful trimmings with which that maternal old dotard, Dame Nature, had tricked out the decaying house for its lying in state. The magneto-electric apparatus whirred incessantly amid the vestiges and the wainscoted dining-room, where once the eighteenth century tenant had piously read morning prayer and eaten his Sunday dinner; and in the place of his sacred symbolical sideboard was a nasty heap of coke. The oven of the bakehouse supplied substratum and material for a forge, whose snorting, panting bellows, and intermittent, ruddy, spark-laden blast made the benighted, but Bible-lit Welsh women murmur in liquid Cymric, as they hurried by: 'Whose breath kindleth coals, and out of his mouth is a flame of fire.' For the idea these good people formed of it was that a tame, but occasionally restive, leviathan had been added to the terrors of the haunted house. The constantly increasing accumulation of pieces of machinery, big brass castings, block tin, casks, crates, and packages of innumerable articles, by their demands for space, necessitated the sacrifice of most of the slighter partitions of the house; and the beams and flooring of the upper chambers were also mercilessly sawn away by the tireless scientist in such a way as to convert them into mere shelves and corner brackets of the atrial space between cellars and rafters. Some of the sounder planking was utilized in the making of a rude broad table, upon which files and heaps of geometrical diagrams speedily accumulated. The production of these latter seemed to be the object upon which the mind of Dr Nebogipfel was so inflexibly set. All other circumstances of his life were made entirely subsidiary to this one occupation. Strangely complicated traceries of lines they were—plans, elevations, sections by surfaces and solids, that, with the help of logarithmic mechanical apparatus and involved curvigraphical machines, spread swiftly under his expert hands over yard after yard of paper. Some of these symbolized shapes he despatched to London, and they presently returned, *realized*, in forms of brass and ivory, and nickel and mahogany. Some of them he himself translated into solid models of metal and wood; occasionally casting the metallic ones in moulds of sand, but often laboriously hewing them out of the block for greater precision of dimension. In this second process, among other appliances, he employed a steel circular saw set with diamond powder and made to rotate with extraordinary swiftness, by means of steam and multiplying gear. It was this latter thing, more than all else, that filled Llyddwdd with a sickly loathing of the Doctor as a man of blood and darkness. Often in the silence of midnight—for the newest inhabitant heeded the sun but little in his incessant research—the awakened dwellers around Pen-y-pwll would hear, what was at first a complaining murmur, like the groaning of a wounded man, '*gurr*-urr-urr-URR', rising by slow gradations in pitch and intensity to the likeness of a voice in despairing passionate protest, and at last ending abruptly in a sharp piercing shriek that rang in the ears for hours afterwards and begot numberless grewsome dreams.

The mystery of all these unearthly noises and inexplicable phenomena, the Doctor's inhumanly brusque bearing and evident uneasiness when away from his absorbing occupation, his entire and jealous seclusion, and his terrifying behaviour to certain officious intruders, roused popular resentment and curiosity to the highest, and a plot was already on foot to make some sort of popular inquisition (probably accompanied by an experimental ducking) into his proceedings, when the sudden death of the hunchback Hughes in a fit, brought matters to an unexpected crisis. It happened in broad daylight, in the roadway just opposite the Manse. Half a dozen people witnessed it. The unfortunate creature was seen to fall suddenly and roll about on the pathway, struggling violently, as it appeared to the spectators, with some invisible assailant. When assistance reached him he was purple in the face and his blue lips were covered with a glairy foam. He died almost as soon as they laid hands on him.

Owen Thomas, the general practitioner, vainly assured the excited crowd which speedily gathered outside the 'Pig and Whistle', whither the body had been carried, that death was unquestionably natural. A horrible zymotic suspicion had gone forth that deceased was the victim of Dr Nebogipfel's imputed aerial powers. The contagion was with the news that passed like a flash though the village and set all Llyddwdd seething with a fierce desire for action against the worker of this iniquity. Downright superstition, which had previously walked somewhat modestly about the village, in the fear of ridicule and the Doctor, now appeared boldly before the sight of all men, clad in the terrible majesty of truth. People who had hitherto kept entire silence as to their fears of the imp-like philosopher suddenly discovered a fearsome pleasure in whispering dread possibilities to kindred souls, and from whispers of possibilities their sympathy-fostered utterances soon developed into unhesitating asserverations in loud and even high-pitch tones. The fancy of a captive leviathan, already alluded to, which had up to now been the horrid but secret joy of a certain conclave of ignorant old women, was published to all the world as indisputable fact; it being stated, on her own authority, that the animal had, on one occasion, chased Mrs Morgan ap Lloyd Jones almost into Rwstog. The story that Nebogipfel had been heard within the Manse chanting, in conjunction with the Williamses, horrible blasphemy, and that a 'black flapping thing, of the size of a young calf', had thereupon entered the gap in the roof, was universally believed in. A grisly anecdote, that owed its origination to a stumble in the churchyard, was circulated, to that effect that the Doctor had been caught ghoulishly tearing with his long white fingers at a new-made grave. The numerously attested declarations that Nebogipfel and the murdered Williams had been seen hanging the sons on a ghostly gibbet, at the back of the house, was due to the electric illumination of a fitfully wind-shaken tree. A hundred like stories hurtled thickly about the village and darkened the moral atmosphere. The Reverend Elijah Ulysses Cook, hearing of the tumult, sallied forth to allay it, and narrowly escaped drawing on himself the gathering lightning.

By eight o'clock (it was Monday the twenty-second of July) a grand demonstration had organized itself against the 'necromancer'. A number of bolder hearts among the men formed the nucleus of the gathering, and at nightfall Arthur Price Williams, John Peters, and others brought torches and raised their spark-raining flames aloft with curt ominous suggestions. The less adventurous village manhood came straggling late to the rendezvous, and with them the married women came in groups of four or five, greatly increasing the excitement of the assembly with their shrill hysterical talk and active imaginations. After these the children and young girls, overcome by undefinable dread, crept quietly out of the too silent and shadowy houses into the yellow glare of pine knots, and the tumultuary noise of the thickening people. By nine, nearly half the Llyddwdd population was massed before the 'Pig and Whistle'. There was a confused murmur of many tongues, but above all the stir and chatter of the growing crowd could be heard the coarse, cracked voice of the blood-thirsty old fanatic, Pritchard, drawing a congenial lesson from the fate of the four hundred and fifty idolators of Carmel.

Just as the church clock was beating out the hour, an occultly originated movement up hill began, and soon the whole assembly, men, women, and children, was moving in a fear-compacted mass, towards the ill-fated doctor's abode. As they left the brightly-lit public house behind them, a quavering female voice began singing one of those grim-sounding canticles that so satisfy the Calvinistic ear. In a wonderfully short time, the tune had been caught up, first by two or three, and then by the whole procession, and the manifold shuffling of heavy shoon grew swiftly into rhythm with the beats of the hymn. When, however, their goal rose, like a blazing star, over the undulation of the road, the volume of the chanting suddenly died away, leaving only the voices of the ringleaders, shouting indeed now somewhat out of tune, but, if anything, more vigorously than before. Their persistence and example nevertheless failed to prevent a perceptible breaking and slackening of the pace, as the Manse was neared, and when the gate was reached, the whole crowd came to a dead halt. Vague fear for the future had begotten the courage that had brought the villagers thus far: fear for the present now smothered its kindred birth. The intense blaze from the gaps in the deathlike silent pile lit up rows of livid, hesitating faces: and a smothered, frightened sobbing broke out among the children. 'Well,' said Arthur Price Williams, addressing Jack Peters, with an expert assumption of modest discipleship, 'what do we do *now*, Jack?' But Peters was regarding the Manse with manifest dubiety, and ignored the question. The Llyddwdd witch-find seemed to be suddenly aborting.

At this juncture old Pritchard suddenly pushed his way forward, gesticulatng weirdly with his bony hands and long arms. '*What!*' he shouted, in broken notes, 'fear ye to smite when the Lord hateth? *Burn* the warlock!' And seizing a flambeau from Peters, he flung open the rickety gate and strode on down the drive, his torch leaving a coiling trail of scintillant sparks on the night wind. 'Burn the warlock,' screamed a shrill voice from the wavering crowd, and in a moment the gregarious human instinct had prevailed. With an outburse of incoherent, threatening voice, the mob poured after the fanatic.

Woe betide the Philosopher now! They expected barricaded doors; but with a groan of conscious insufficiency, the hinge-rusted portals swung wide at the push of Pritchard. Blinded by the light, he hesitated for a second on the threshold, while his followers came crowding up behind him.

Those who were there say that they saw Dr Nebogipfel, standing in the toneless electric glare, on a peculiar erection of brass and ebony and ivory; and that he seemed to be smiling at them, half pityingly and half scornfully, as it is said martyrs are wont to smile. Some assert, moreover, that by his side was sitting a tall man, clad in ravenswing, and some even aver that this second man—whom others deny—bore on his face the likeness of the Reverend Elijah Ulysses Cook, while others declare that he resembled the description of the murdered Williams. Be that as it may, it must now go unproven for ever, for suddenly a wondrous thing smote the crowd as it swarmed in through the entrance. Pritchard pitched headlong on the floor senseless. Wild shouts and shrieks of anger, changed in mid utterance to yells of agonizing fear, or to the mute gasp of heart-stopping horror: and then a frantic rush was made for the doorway.

For the calm, smiling doctor, and his quiet, black-clad companion, and the polished platform which upbore them, had vanished before their eyes!

How an Esoteric Story became Possible

A silvery-foliaged willow by the side of a mere. Out of the cress-spangled waters below, rise clumps of sedge-blades, and among them glows the purple fleur-de-lys, and sapphire vapour of forget-me-nots. Beyond is a sluggish stream of water reflecting the intense blue of the moist Fenland sky; and beyond that a low osier-fringed eyot. This limits all the visible universe, save some scattered pollards and spear-like poplars showing against the violet distance. At the foot of the willow reclines the Author watching a copper butterfly fluttering from iris to iris.

Who can fix the colours of the sunset? Who can take a cast of flame? Let him essay to register the mutations of mortal thought as it wanders from a copper butterfly to the disembodied soul, and thence passes to spiritual motions and the vanishing of Dr Moses Nebogipfel and the Rev. Elijah Ulysses Cook from the world of sense.

As the author lay basking there and speculating, as another once did under the Budh tree, on mystic transmutations, a presence became apparent. There was a somewhat on the eyot between him and the purple horizon—an opaque reflecting entity, making itself dimly perceptible by reflection in the water to his averted eyes. He raised them in curious surprise.

What was it?

He stared in stupefied astonishment at the apparition, doubted, blinked, rubbed his eyes, stared again, and believed. It was solid, it cast a shadow, and it upbore two men. There was white metal in it that blazed in the noontide sun like incandescent magnesium, ebony bars that drank in the light, and white parts that gleamed like polished ivory. Yet withal it seemed unreal. The thing was not square as a machine ought to be, but all awry: it was twisted and seemed falling over, hanging in two directions, as those queer crystals called triclinic hang; it seemed like a machine that had been crushed or warped; it was suggestive and not confirmatory, like the machine of a disordered dream. The men, too, were dreamlike. One was short, intensely sallow, with a strangely-shaped head, and clad in a garment of dark olive green; the other was, grotesquely out of place, evidently a clergyman of the Established Church, a fair-haired, pale-faced respectable-looking man.

Once more doubt came rushing in on the author. He sprawled back and stared at the sky, rubbed his eyes, stared at the willow wands that hung between him and the blue, closely examined his hands to see if his eyes had any new things to relate about them, and then sat up again and stared at the eyot. A gentle breeze stirred the osiers; a white bird was flapping its way through the lower sky. The machine of the vision had vanished! It was an illusion—a projection of the subjective—an assertion of the immateriality of mind. 'Yes,' interpolated the sceptic faculty, 'but *how comes it that the clergyman is still there?*'

The clergyman had not vanished. In intense perplexity the author examined this black-coated phenomenon as he stood regarding the world with hand-shaded eyes. The author knew the periphery of that eyot by heart, and the question that troubled him was, 'Whence?' The clergyman looked as Frenchmen look when they land at Newhaven—intensely travel-worn; his clothes showed rubbed and seamy in the bright day. When he came to the edge of the island and shouted a question to the author, his voice was broken and trembled. 'Yes,' answered the author, 'it is an island. *How did you get there?*'

But the clergyman, instead of replying to this asked a very strange question.

He said 'Are you in the nineteenth century?' The author made him repeat that question before he replied. 'Thank heaven,' cried the clergyman rapturously. Then he asked very eagerly for the exact date.

'August the ninth, eighteen hundred and eighty-seven,' he repeated after the author. 'Heaven be praised!' and sinking down on the eyot so that the sedges hid him, he audibly burst into tears.

Now the author was mightily surprised at all this, and going a certain distance along the mere, he obtained a punt, and getting into it he hastily poled to the eyot where he had last seen the clergyman. He found him lying insensible among the reeds, and carried him in his punt to the house where he lived, and the clergyman lay there insensible for ten days.

Meanwhile, it became known that he was the Rev. Elijah Cook, who had disappeared from Llyddwdd with Dr Moses Nebogipfel three weeks before.

On August 19th, the nurse called the author out of his study to speak to the invalid. He found him perfectly sensible, but his eyes were strangely bright, and his face was deadly pale. 'Have you found out who I am?' he asked.

'You are the Rev. Elijah Ulysses Cook, Master of Arts, of Pembroke College, Oxford, and Rector of Llyddwdd, near Rwstog, in Caernarvon.'

He bowed his head. 'Have you been told anything of how I came here?'

'I found you among the reeds,' I said. He was silent and thoughtful for a while. 'I have a deposition to make. Will you take it? It concerns the murder of an old man named Williams, which occurred in 1862, this disappearance of Dr Moses Nebogipfel, the abduction of a ward in the year 4003——'

The author stared.

'The year of our Lord 4003,' he corrected. 'She would come. Also several assaults on public officials in the years 17,901 and 2.'

The author coughed.

'The years 17,901 and 2, and valuable medical, social, and physiographical data for all time.'

After a consultation with the doctor, it was decided to have the deposition taken down, and this is what constitutes the remainder of the story of the Chronic Argonauts.

On August 29th 1887, the Rev. Elijah Cook died. His body was conveyed to Llyddwdd, and buried in the churchyard there.

II. THE ESOTERIC STORY BASED ON THE CLERGYMAN'S DEPOSITIONS

The Anachronic Man

Incidentally it has been remarked in the first part, how the Reverend Elijah Ulysses Cook attempted and failed to quiet the superstitious excitement of the villagers on the afternoon of the memorable twenty-second of July. His next proceeding was to try and warn the unsocial philosopher of the dangers which impended. With this intent he made his way from the rumour-pelted village, through the silent, slumbrous heat of the July afternoon, up the slopes of Pen-y-pwll, to the old Manse. His loud knocking at the heavy door called forth dull resonance from the interior, and produced a shower of lumps of plaster and fragments of decaying touchwood from the rickety porch, but beyond this the dreamy stillness of the summer mid-day remained unbroken. Everything was so quiet as he stood there expectant, that the occasional speech of the hay-makers a mile away in the fields, over towards Rwstog, could be distinctly heard. The reverend gentleman waited long, then knocked again, and waited again, and listened, until the echoes and the patter of rubbish had melted away into the deep silence, and the creeping in the blood-vessels of his ears had become oppressively audible, swelling and sinking with sounds like the confused murmuring of a distant crowd, and causing a suggestion of anxious discomfort to spread slowly over his mind.

Again he knocked, this time loud, quick blows with his stick, and almost immediately afterwards, leaning his hand against the door, he kicked its panels vigorously. There was a shouting of echoes, a protesting jarring of hinges, and then the oaken door yawned and displayed, in the blue blaze of the electric light, vestiges of partitions, piles of planking and straw, masses of metal, heaps of papers and overthrown apparatus, to the rector's astonished eyes. 'Doctor Nebogipfel, excuse my intruding,' he called out, but the only response was a reverberation among the black beams and shadows that hung dimly above. For almost a minute he stood there, leaning forward over the threshold, staring at the glittering mecha-nisms, diagrams, books, scattered indiscriminately with broken food, packing cases, heaps of coke, hay, and microcosmic lumber, about the undivided house cavity; and then, removing his hat and treading stealthi-ly, as if the silence were a sacred thing, he stepped into the apparently deserted shelter of the Doctor.

His eyes sought everywhere, as he cautiously made his way through the confusion, with a strange anticipation of finding Nebogipfel hidden somewhere in the sharp black shadows among the litter, so strong in him was an indescribable sense of a perceiving presence. This feeling was so vivid that, when, after an abortive exploration, he seated himself upon Nebogipfel's diagram-covered bench, it made him explain in a forced hoarse voice to the stillness—'He is not here. I have something to say to him. I must wait for him.' It was so vivid, too, that the trickling of some grit down the wall in the vacant corner behind him made him start round in a sudden perspiration. There was nothing visible there, but turning his head back, he was stricken rigid with horror by the swift, noiseless ap-parition of Nebogipfel, ghastly pale, and with red stained hands, crouching upon a strange-looking metallic platform, and with his deep grey eyes looking intently into the visitor's face.

Cook's first impulse was to yell out his fear, but his throat was paralysed, and he could only stare fascinated at the bizarre countenance that had thus clashed suddenly into visibility. The lips were quivering and the breath came in short convulsive sobs. The un-human forehead was wet with perspiration, while the veins were swollen, knotted and purple. The Doctor's red hands, too, he noticed, were trembling, as the hands of slight people tremble after intense muscular exertion, and his lips closed and opened as if he, too, had a difficulty in speaking as he gasped, 'Who—what do you do here?'

Cook answered not a word, but stared with hair erect, open mouth, and dilated eyes, at the dark red unmistakeable smear that streaked the pure ivory and gleaming nickel and shining ebony of the platform.

'What are you doing here?' repeated the doctor, raising himself. 'What do you want?'

Cook gave a convulsive effort. 'In Heaven's name, *what* are you?' he gasped; and then black curtains came closing in from every side, sweeping the squatting, dwarfish phantasm that reeled before him into rayless, voiceless night.

The Reverend Elijah Ulysses Cook recovered his perceptions to find himself lying on the floor of the old Manse, and Doctor Nebogipfel, no longer blood-stained and with all trace of his agitation gone, kneeling by his side and bending over him with a glass of brandy in his hand. 'Do not be alarmed, sir,' said the philosopher with a faint smile, as the clergyman opened his eyes. 'I have not treated you to a disembodied spirit, or anything nearly so extraordinary . . . May I offer you this?'

The clergyman submitted quietly to the brandy, and then stared perplexed into Nebogipfel's face, vainly searching his memory for what occurrences had preceded his insensibility. Raising himself at last into a sitting posture, he saw the oblique mass of metals that had appeared with the doctor, and immediately all that happened flashed back upon his mind. He looked from this structure to the recluse, and from the recluse to the structure.

'There is absolutely no deception, sir,' said Nebogipfel with the slightest trace of mockery in his voice. 'I lay no claim to work in matters spiritual. It is a *bona fide* mechanical contrivance, a thing emphatically of this sordid world. Excuse me—just one minute.' He rose from his knees, stepped upon the mahogany platform, took a curiously curved lever in his hand and pulled it over. Cook rubbed his eyes. *There* certainly was no deception. The doctor and the machine had vanished.

The reverend gentleman felt no horror this time, only a slight nervous shock, to see the doctor presently re-appear 'in the twinkling of an eye' and get down from the machine. From that he walked in a straight line with his hands behind his back and his face downcast, until his progress was stopped by the intervention of a circular saw; then, turning round sharply on his heel, he said:

'I was thinking while I was . . . away . . . Would you like to come? I should greatly value a companion.'

The clergyman was still sitting, hatless, on the floor. 'I am afraid,' he said slowly, 'you will think me stupid——'

'Not at all,' interrupted the doctor. 'The stupidity is mine. You desire

to have all this explained . . . wish to know where I am going first. I have
spoken so little with men of this age for the last ten years or more that
I have ceased to make due allowances and concessions for other minds.
I will do my best, but that I fear will be very unsatisfactory. It is a long
story . . . Do you find that floor comfortable to sit on? If not, there is a
nice packing case over there, or some straw behind you, or this bench—
the diagrams are done with now, but I am afraid of the drawing pins. You
may sit on the Chronic Argo!'

'*No*, thank you,' slowly replied the clergyman, eyeing that deformed
structure thus indicated, suspiciously; 'I am *quite* comfortable here.'

'Then I will begin. Do you read fables? Modern ones?'

'I am afraid I must confess to a good deal of fiction,' said the clergyman depreciatingly. 'In Wales the ordained ministers of the sacraments
of the Church have perhaps *too* large a share of leisure——'

'Have you read the Ugly Duckling?'

'Hans Christian Andersen's—yes—in my childhood.'

'A wonderful story—a story that has even been full of tears and heart
swelling hopes for me, since first it came to me in my lonely boyhood
and saved me from unspeakable things. That story, if you understand it
well, will tell you almost all that you should know of me to comprehend
how that machine came to be thought of in a mortal brain . . . Even when
I read that simple narrative for the first time, a thousand bitter experiences
had begun the teaching of my isolation among the people of my birth—
I knew the story was for me. The ugly duckling that proved to be a swan,
that lived through all contempt and bitterness, to float at last sublime.
From that hour forth, I dreamt of meeting with my kind, dreamt of en-
countering that sympathy I knew was my profoundest need. Twenty years
I lived in that hope, lived and worked, lived and wandered, loved even,
and, at last, despaired. Only once among all those millions of wondering,
astonished, indifferent, contemptuous, and insidious faces that I met with
in that passionate wandering, looked *one* upon me as I desired . . .
looked——'

He paused. The Reverend Cook glanced up into his face, expecting
some indication of the deep feeling that had sounded in his last words.
It was downcast, clouded, and thoughtful, but the mouth was rigidly firm.

'In short, Mr Cook, I discovered that I was one of those superior
Cagots called a genius—a man born out of my time—a man thinking the
thoughts of a wiser age, doing things and believing things that men now
cannot understand, and that in the years ordained to me there was nothing
but silence and suffering for my soul—unbroken solitude, man's bitterest
pain. I knew I was an Anachronic Man; my age was still to come. One
filmy hope alone held me to life, a hope to which I clung until it had
become a certain thing. Thirty years of unremitting toil and deepest
thought among the hidden things of matter and form and life, and then

that, the Chronic Argo, *the ship that sails through time*, and now I go to join my generation, to journey through the ages till my time has come.'

The Chronic Argo

Dr Nebogipfel paused, looking in sudden doubt at the clergyman's perplexed face. 'You think that sounds mad,' he said, 'to travel through time?'

'It certainly jars with accepted opinions,' said the clergyman, allowing the faintest suggestion of controversy to appear in his intonation, and speaking apparently to the Chronic Argo. Even clergymen of the Church of England you see can have a suspicion of illusions at times.

'It certainly *does* jar with accepted opinions,' agreed the philosopher cordially. 'It does more than that—it defies accepted opinions to mortal combat. Opinions of all sorts, Mr Cook,—Scientific Theories, Laws, Articles of Belief, or, to come to elements, Logical Premises, Ideas, or whatever you like to call them,—all are, from the infinite nature of things, so many diagrammatic caricatures of the ineffable,—caricatures altogether to be avoided save where they are necessary in the shaping of results— as chalk outlines are necessary to the painter and plans and sections to the engineer. Men, from the exigencies of their being, find this hard to believe.'

The Rev. Elijah Ulysses Cook nodded his head with the quiet smile of one whose opponent has unwittingly given a point.

'It is as easy to come to regard ideas as complete reproductions of entities as it is to roll off a log. Hence it is that almost all civilized men believe in the *reality* of the Greek geometrical conceptions.'

'Oh! pardon me, sir,' interrupted Cook. 'Most men know that a geometrical point has no existence in matter, and the same with a geometrical line. I think you underrate . . .'

'Yes, yes, *those* things are recognized,' said Nebogipfel calmly; 'but now . . . a cube. Does that exist in the material universe?'

'Certainly.'

'An instantaneous cube?'

'I don't know what you intend by that expression.'

'Without any other sort of extension; a body having length, breadth, and thickness, exists?'

'What other sort of extension *can* there be?' asked Cook, with raised eyebrows.

'Has it never occurred to you that no form can exist in the material universe that has no extension in time? . . . Has it never glimmered upon your consciousness that nothing stood between men and a geometry of four dimensions—length, breadth, thickness, and *duration*—but the inertia of opinion, the impulse from the Levantine philosophers of the bronze age?'

'Putting it that way,' said the clergyman, 'it does look as though there was a flaw somewhere in the notion of tridimensional being; *but* . . .' He became silent, leaving that sufficiently eloquent 'but' to convey all the prejudice and distrust that filled his mind.

'When we take up this new light of a fourth dimension and re-examine our physical science in its illumination,' continued Nebogipfel, after a pause, 'we find ourselves no longer limited by hopeless restriction to a certain beat of time—to our own generation. Locomotion along lines of duration—chronic navigation comes within the range, first, of geometrical theory, and then of practical mechanics. There *was* a time when men could only move horizontally and in their appointed country. The clouds floated above them unattainable things, mysterious chariots of those fearful gods who dwelt among the mountain summits. Speaking practically, man in those days was restricted to motion in two dimensions; and even there circumambient ocean and hypoborean fear bound him in. But those times were to pass away. First, the keel of Jason cut its way between the Symplegades, and then in the fulness of time, Columbus dropped anchor in a bay of Atlantis. Then man burst his bidimensional limits, and invaded the third dimension, soaring with Montgolfier into the clouds, and sinking with the diving bell into the purple treasure-caves of the waters. And now another step, and the hidden past and unknown future are before us. We stand upon a mountain summit with the plains of the ages spread below.'

Nebogipfel paused and looked down at his hearer.

The Reverend Elijah Cook was sitting with an expression of strong distrust on his face. Preaching much had brought home certain truths to him very vividly, and he always suspected rhetoric. 'Are those things figures of speech,' he asked; 'or am I to take them as precise statements? Do you speak of travelling through time in the same way as one might speak of Omnipotence making His pathway in the storm, or do you—a—mean what you say?'

Dr Nebogipfel smiled quietly. 'Come and look at these diagrams,' he said, and then with elaborate simplicity he commenced to explain again to the clergyman the new quadridimensional geometry. Insensibly Cook's aversion passed away, and seeming impossibility grew possible, now that such tangible things as diagrams and models could be brought forward in evidence. Presently he found himself asking questions, and his interest grew deeper and deeper as Nebogipfel slowly and with precise clearness unfolded the beautiful order of his strange invention. The moments slipped away unchecked, as the Doctor passed on to the narrative of his research, and it was with a start of surprise that the clergyman noticed the deep blue of the dying twilight through the open doorway.

'The voyage,' said Nebogipfel concluding his history, 'will be full of un-dreamt of dangers—already in one brief essay I have stood in the very jaws of death—but it is also full of the divinest promise of undreamt-of joy. Will you come? Will you walk among the people of the Golden Years? . . .'

But the mention of death by the philosopher had brought flooding back to the mind of Cook, all the horrible sensations of that first apparition.

'Dr Nebogipfel . . . one question?' He hesitated. 'On your hands . . . *Was it blood?*'

Nebogipfel's countenance fell. He spoke slowly.

'When I had stopped my machine, I found myself in this room as it used to be. *Hark!*'

'It is the wind in the trees towards Rwstog.'

'It sounded like the voices of a multitude of people singing . . . When I had stopped I found myself in this room as it used to be. An old man, a young man, and a lad were sitting at a table—reading some book together. I stood behind them unsuspected. "Evil spirits assailed him," read the old man; "but it is written, 'to him that overcometh shall be given life eternal.' They came as entreating friends, but he endured through all their snares. They came as principalities and powers, but he defied them in the name of the King of Kings. Once even it is told that in his study, while he was translating the New Testament into German, the Evil One himself appeared before him . . ." Just then the lad glanced timorously round, and with a fearful wail fainted away . . .'

'The others sprang at me . . . It was a fearful grapple . . . The old man clung to my throat, screaming "Man or Devil, I defy thee . . ." '

'I could not help it. We rolled together on the floor . . . the knife his trembling son had dropped came to my hand . . . *Hark!*'

He paused and listened, but Cook remained staring at him in the same horror-stricken attitude he had assumed when the memory of the blood-stained hands had rushed back over his mind.

'Do you hear what they are crying? *Hark!*'

Burn the warlock! Burn the murderer!

'Do you hear? There is no time to be lost.'

Slay the murderer of cripples. Kill the devil's claw!

'Come! Come!'

Cook, with a convulsive effort, made a gesture of repugnance and strode to the doorway. A crowd of black figures roaring towards him in the red torchlight made him recoil. He shut the door and faced Nebogipfel.

The thin lips of the Doctor curled with a contemptuous sneer. 'They will kill you if you stay,' he said; and seizing the unresisting visitor by the wrist, he forced him towards the glittering machine. Cook sat down and covered his face with his hands.

In another moment the door was flung open, and old Pritchard stood blinking on the threshold.

A pause. A hoarse shout changing suddenly into a sharp shrill shriek.

A thunderous roar like the bursting forth of a great fountain of water.

The voyage of the Chronic Argonauts had begun.

End of Part II of the Chronic Argonauts

How did it end? How came it that Cook wept with joy to return once more to this nineteenth century of ours? Why did not Nebogipfel remain with him? All that, and more also, has been written, and will or will never be read, according as Fate may have decreed to the Curious Reader.

APPENDIX II

The Second and Third Versions

In the first rewriting Dr Nebogipfel and the Rev Elijah Ulysses Cook still appear, but the scene shifts to a village on the South Downs. They arrive in a future much less changed from our time than that portrayed in *The Time Machine*. The upper and lower worlds exist, but their inhabitants are not yet two distinct species. A scientific aristocracy still survives in a decadent form as a red-robed priesthood, and art and literature are cultivated in a very dilettante manner. The Chronic Argonauts stir up these weary idlers, and even make it fashionable to read books. The priests take their visitors to see a vast museum, but themselves grow bored and leave the pair to explore alone, warning them against the passages which lead "down". They go "down", and discover an underworld working to support the upper world. Eventually some compunction is aroused among the aristocracy, and some kindly disposed persons descend to sing and play to the workers. At this the underworld explodes into revolution, kills them, and rushes up in a mob to carry out a general massacre. In the ensuing panic the Argonauts make for their machine. Cook has become fascinated by a certain Lady Dis, and tries to take her with him, but in the excitement of the escape he discovers . . . that all her beauty is artificial, and flings her off as he climbs into the machine. They travel back to our own time, but overshoot the mark and are nearly killed by a party of Palaeolithic men. At last they hit the nineteenth century, when Nebogipfel drops Cook and then vanishes with the machine.

In the third version . . .

Nebogipfel and Cook are cut out. There is no such underworld as in the earlier version and *The Time Machine*, the future being one in which a ruling class governs by hypnotism, but the end of the story is somewhat similar to that given above. One of the priests determines to put an end to the hypnotism and calls to the people to awake. They awake and kill him, and march with his head on a pole to slay his fellows. In the panic the same revelation is made of the artificial means by which the ruling class has hidden the physical degeneration resulting from their idle life.

The recollections of Professor A. Morley Davies are quoted in Geoffrey West, *H. G. Wells: A Sketch for a Portrait* (London: Gerald Howe, 1930), 291–92.

APPENDIX III

The *National Observer Time Machine*

TIME TRAVELLING

Possibility or Paradox
The Philosophical Inventor was expounding a recondite matter to his friends. The fire burnt brightly, and the soft radiance of the incandescent lights in the lilies of silver, caught the bubbles that flashed and passed in our glasses of amber fluid. Our chairs, being his patents, embraced and caressed us rather than submitted to be sat upon, and there was that luxurious after-dinner atmosphere, when thought runs gracefully free of the trammels of precision. And he put it to us in this way, as we sat and lazily admired him and his fecundity.

'You must follow me carefully here. For I shall have to controvert one or two ideas that are almost universally accepted. The geometry, for instance, they taught you at school is founded on a misconception.'

'Is not that rather a large thing to expect us to begin upon?' said the argumentative person with the red hair.

'I do not mean to ask you to accept anything without reasonable ground for it. But you know of course that a mathematical line, a line of thickness *nil*, has no real existence. They taught you that. Neither has a mathematical plane. These things are mere abstractions.'

'That is all right,' said the man with the red hair.

'Nor can a cube, having only length, breadth, and thickness, have a real existence.'

'There I object,' said the red-haired man. 'Of course a solid body may exist. All real things—'

'So most people think. But wait a moment. Can an *instantaneous* cube exist?'

'Don't follow you,' said the red-haired man.

'Can a cube that does not last for any time at all, have a real existence?'

The red-haired man became pensive.

'Clearly,' the Philosophical Inventor proceeded; 'any real body must have extension in *four* directions: it must have length, breadth, thickness, and—duration. But through a natural infirmity of the flesh, which I will explain to you in a moment, we incline to overlook the fact. There are really four dimensions, three which we call the three planes of space, and a fourth, time. There is, however, a tendency to draw an unreal difference between the former three and the latter, because it happens that our consciousness moves intermittently in one direction along the latter from the beginning to the end of our lives.

'That,' said the very young man, making spasmodic efforts to relight his cigar over the lamp; 'that [is] very clear, indeed.'

'Now it is very remarkable that this is so extensively overlooked,' continued the Philosophical Inventor with a slight accession of cheerfulness. 'Really this is what is meant by the fourth dimension, though some people who talk about the fourth dimension do not know they mean it. It is only another way of looking at time. *There is no difference between time and any of the three dimensions of space except that our consciousness moves along it.* But some foolish people have got hold of the wrong side of that idea. You have all heard what they have to say about this fourth dimension.'

'*I* have not,' said the provincial mayor.

'It is simply this. That space, as our mathematicians have it, is spoken of as having three dimensions, which one may call length, breadth, and thickness, and is always definable by reference to three planes, each at right angles to the others. But some philosophical people have been asking why *three* dimensions particularly—why not another direction at right angles to the other three?—and have even tried to construct a four-dimensional geometry. Professor Simon Newcombe [*sic*] was expounding this to the New York Mathematical Society only a month or so ago. You know how on a flat surface which has only two dimensions we can represent a figure of a three-dimensional solid, and similarly they think that by models of three dimensions they could represent one of four—if they could master the perspective of the thing. See?'

'I think so,' murmured the provincial mayor, and knitting his brows he lapsed into an introspective state, his lips moving as one who repeats mystic words. 'Yes, I think I see it now,' he said after some time, brightening in a quite transitory manner.

'Well, I do not mind telling you I have been at work upon this geometry of four dimensions for some time, assuming that the fourth dimension is time. Some of my results are curious. For instance, here is a portrait of a man at eight years old, another at the age of fifteen, another seventeen, another of twenty-three, and so on. All these are evidently sections, as it were, three-dimensional representations of his four-dimensioned being, which is a fixed and unalterable thing.'

'Scientific people,' proceeded the philosopher after the pause required for the proper assimilation of this, 'know very well that time is only a kind of space. Here is a popular scientific diagram, a weather record. This line I trace with my finger shows the movement of the barometer. Yesterday it was so high, yesterday night it fell, then this morning it rose again, and so gently upward to here. Surely the mercury did not trace this line in any of the dimensions of space generally recognised? But certainly it traced such a line, and that line, therefore, we must conclude was along the time-dimension.'

'But,' said the red-haired man, staring hard at a coal in the fire; 'if time is really only a fourth dimension of space, why is it, and why has it always been, regarded as something different? And why cannot we move about in time as we move about in the other dimensions of space?'

The philosophical person smiled with great sweetness. 'Are you so sure we can move freely in space? Right and left we can go, backward and forward freely enough, and men have always done so. I admit we move freely in two dimensions. But how about up and down? Gravitation limits us there.'

'Not exactly,' said the red-haired man. 'There are balloons.'

'But before the balloons, man, save for spasmodic jumping and the inequalities of the surface, had no freedom of vertical movement.'

'Still they could move a little up and down,' said the red-haired man.

'Easier, far easier, down than up.'

'And you cannot move at all in time, you cannot get away from the present moment.'

'My dear sir, that is just where you are wrong. That is just where the whole world has gone wrong. We are always getting away from the present moment. Our consciousnesses, which are immaterial and have no dimensions, are passing along the time-dimension with a uniform velocity from the cradle to the grave. Just as we should travel *down* if we began our existence fifty miles above the earth's surface.'

'But the great difficulty is this,' interrupted the red-haired man. 'You *can* move about in all directions of space, but you cannot move about in time.'

'That is the germ of my great discovery. But you are wrong to say that we cannot move about in time. For instance, if I am recalling an incident very vividly I go back to the instant of its occurrence, I become absentminded as you say. I jump back for a moment. Of course we have no means of staying back for any length of time any more than a savage or an animal has of staying six feet above the ground. But a civilised man knows better. He can go up against gravitation in a balloon, and why should he not be able to stop or accelerate his drift along the time-dimension; or even turn about and travel the other way?'

'Oh, *this*,' began the common-sense person 'is all—'

'Why not?' said the Philosophical Inventor.

'It's against reason,' said the common-sense person.

'What reason?' said the Philosophical Inventor.

'You can show black is white by argument,' said the common-sense person; 'but you will never convince me.'

'Possibly not,' said the Philosophical Inventor. 'But now you begin to see the object of my investigations into the geometry of four dimensions. I have a vague inkling of a machine—'

'To travel through time!' exclaimed the very young man.

'That shall travel indifferently in any direction of space and time as the driver determines.'

The red-haired man contented himself with laughter.

'It would be remarkably convenient. One might travel back, and witness the Battle of Hastings!'

'Don't you think you would attract attention?' said the red-haired man. 'Our ancestors had no great tolerance for anachronisms.'

'One might get one's Greek from the very lips of Homer and Plato!'

'In which case they would certainly plough you for the little-go. The German scholars have improved Greek so much.'

'Then there is the future,' said the very young man. 'Just think! one might invest all one's money, leave it to accumulate at interest, and hurry on ahead!'

'To discover a society,' said the red-haired man, 'erected on a strictly communist basis.'

'It will be very confusing, I am afraid,' said the common-sense person. 'But I suppose your machine is hardly complete yet?'

'Science,' said the philosopher, 'moves apace.'

THE TIME MACHINE

'The last time I saw you, you were talking about a machine to travel through time,' said the red-haired man.

The common-sense person groaned audibly. 'Don't remind him of *that*,' he said.

'My dear Didymus, it is finished,' said the Philosophical Inventor.

With violence, the red-haired man wanted to see it, and at once.

'There is no fire in the workshop,' said the Philosophical Inventor, becoming luxuriously lazy in his pose, 'and besides, I am in my slippers. No; I had rather be doubted.'

'You are,' said the red-haired man. 'But tell us: Have you used it at all?'

'To confess the simple truth, even at my own expense, I have been horribly afraid. But I tried it, nevertheless. The sensations are atrocious—atrocious.'

His eye rested for a moment on the very young man, who with a moist white face was gallantly relighting the cigar the German officer had offered him.

'You see, when you move forward in time with a low velocity of (say) thirty in one, you get through a full day of twenty-four hours in about forty-eight minutes. This means dawn, morning, noon, evening, twilight, night, at about ordinary stage pace. After a few days are traversed, the

alternations of light and gloom give one the sensations of London on a
dismal day of drifting fog. Matters get very much worse as the speed is
increased. The maximum of inconvenience is about two thousand in one;
day and night in less than a minute. The sun rushes up the sky at a
sickening pace, and the moon with its changing phases makes one's brain
reel. And you get a momentary glimmer of the swift stars swinging in
circles round the pole. After that, the faster you go the less you seem to
feel it. The sun goes hop, hop, each day; the night is like the flapping of
a black wing; the moon opens and shuts—full to new and new to full;
the stars trace at last faint circles of silver in the sky. Then the sun,
through the retention of impressions by the eye, becomes a fiery band in
the heavens, with which the ghostly fluctuating belt of the moon inter-
laces, and the tint of the sky becomes a flickering deep blue. At last even
the flickering ceases, and the only visible motion in all the universe is
the swaying of the sun-belt as it dips towards the winter solstice and rises
again to the summer. The transitory sickness is over. So under the burning
triumphal arch of the sun, you sweep through the ages. One has all the
glorious sensations of a swooping hawk or a falling man—for one of those
trapeze fellows told me the sense of falling is very delicious—and much
the same personal concern about the end of it.'

The Philosophical Inventor stopped abruptly, and began to knock the
ashes out of the filthy pipe he smokes.

'Not a bad description of the Cosmic Clock with the pendulum taken
off,' said the very young man after an interval.

'Plausible so far,' said the red-haired man; 'but we have to come to
earth now. Or were you entirely engaged by the heavenly bodies?'

'No,' said the Inventor; 'I noticed a few things. For instance, when I
was going at a comparatively slow pace, Mrs. Watchet[t] came into the
workshop by the door nex[t] to the house and out by the one into the
yard. Really she took a minute or so, I suppose, to traverse the room, but
to me she appeared to shoot across like a rocket. And so soon as the pace
became considerable, the apparent velocity of people became so excessively great that I could no more see them than a man can see a cannon-
ball flying through the air.'

The common-sense person shivered and drew the air in sharply
through his teeth.

'Then it is odd to see a tree grow up, flash its fan of green at you for
a few score of summers, and vanish—all in the space of half an hour.
Houses too shot up like stage buildings, stayed a while, and disappeared,
and I noticed the hills grow visibly lower through the years with the wear
of the gust and rain.'

'It is odd,' said the red-haired man, pursuing a train of thought, 'that
you were not interfered with by people. You see, you have been, I understand, through some hundred thousand years or so'—the Philosopher nodded—'and all that time you have been on one spot. People must have

noticed you, even if you did not notice them. A gentlemen in a easy attitude, dressed in anachronisms, and meditating fixedly upon the celestial sphere, must in the course of ages, have palled upon the species. I wonder they did not try to remove you to a museum or make you . . .'

This amused the German officer very much. Without warning he filled the room with laughter, and some of it went upstairs and woke the children. '*Sehr gut*! Ha, ha! You are axplodet, mein friendt!'

'The same difficulty puzzled me—for a minute or so,' said the Philosopher, as the air cleared. 'But it is easily explained.'

'Gott in Himmel!' said the German officer.

'I don't know if you have heard the expression of "presentation below the threshold." It is a psychological technicality. Suppose, for instance, you put some red pigment on a sheet of paper, it excites a certain visual sensation, does it not? Now halve the amount of pigment, the sensation diminishes. Halve it again, the impression of red is still weaker. Continue the process. Clearly there will always be *some* pigment left, but a time will speedily arrive when the eye will refuse to follow the dilution, when the stimulus will be insufficient to excite the sensation of red. The presentation of red pigment to the senses is then said to be "below the threshold." Similarly my rapid passage through time, traversing a day in a minute fraction of a second, diluted the stimulus I offered to the perception of these excellent people of futurity far below . . .'

'Yes,' said the red-haired man, interrupting after his wont. 'You have parried that. And now another difficulty. I suppose while you were slipping thus invisibly through the ages, people walked about in the space you occupied. They may have pulled down your house about your head and built a brick wall in your substance. And yet, you know, it is generally believed that two bodies cannot occupy the same space.'

'What an old-fashioned person you are!' said the Philosophical Inventor. 'Have you never heard of the Atomic Theory? Don't you know that every body, solid, liquid, or gaseous, is made up of molecules with empty spaces between them? That leaves plenty of room to slip through a brick wall, if you only have momentum enough. A slight rise of temperature would be all one would notice and of course if the wall lasted too long and the warmth became uncomfortable one could shift the apparatus a little in space and get out of the inconvenience.' He paused.

'But pulling up is a different matter. That is where the danger comes in. Suppose yourself to stop while there is another body in the same space. Clearly all your atoms will be jammed in with unparalleled nearness to the atoms of the foreign body. Violent chemical reactions would ensue. There would be a tremendous explosion. Hades! how it would puzzle posterity! I thought of this as I was sailing away thousands of years ahead. I lost my nerve. I brought my machine round in a whirling curve and started back full pelt. And so I pulled up again in the very moment and place of my start, in my workshop, and this afternoon. And ended my first time journey. Valuable, you see, chiefly as a lesson in the method of such navigation.'

'Will you go again?' said the common-sense person.

'Just at present,' said the Philosophical Inventor; 'I scarcely know.'

A.D. 12,203

A Glimpse of the Future

He rose from his easy chair and took the little bronze lamp in his hand, when we reverted to the topic of his Time Machine. He smiled, 'I know you will never believe me,' he said, 'until you see it with your own eyes.' So speaking he led us down the staircase and along the narrow passage to his workshop. 'I have had another little excursion since I saw you last,' he remarked over his shoulder.

'It is an ill thing if one stop it too suddenly,' said he as he stood holding the lamp for us to see; 'though my life was happily spared.'

'What happened?' said the sceptical man, staring suspiciously at the squat framework of aluminium, brass and ebony, that stood in the laboratory. It was an incomprehensible interlacing of bars and tubes, oddly awry, heeling over into the black shadows of the corner as if to elude our scrutiny. By the side of the leather saddle it bore, were two dials and three small levers curiously curved.

'You see how this rail is bent?' said the philosopher.

'I see you have bent it.'

'And that rod of ivory is cracked.'

'It is.'

'The thing fell over as I stopped and flung me headlong.'

He paused but no one spoke. He seemed to take it as acceptance, and proceeded to narrative.

'There was the sound of a clap of thunder in my ears. I may have been stunned for a moment. A pitiless hail was hissing around me, and I was sitting on soft turf beside the overturned Time Machine. I was on what seemed to be a little lawn in a garden, surrounded by rhododendron bushes, and I noticed that their mauve and purple blossoms were dropping in a shower under the beating of the hailstones. Over the machine, the rebounding dancing hail hung in a little cloud, and it drove along the ground like smoke. In a moment I was wet to the skin. "Fine hospitality," said I, "to a man who has travelled innumerable years to see you." I stood up and looked round me. A colossal figure, carved apparently of some white stone, loomed indistinctly beyond the bushes through the hazy downpour. But all else of the world was invisible.'

'H'm,' said the sceptic, 'this is interesting. May I ask the date?'

Our host pointed silently to the little dials.

'*Years*, ten—these divisions are thousands? I see now. Ten thousand, three hundred and nine,' said the common-sense person, reading. '*Days*, two hundred and forty-one. That is counting from now?'

'From now,' said the Inventor. The common-sense person seemed satisfied by these figures, and the flavour of intelligent incredulity that had survived even the Inventor's exhibition of the machine, began to fade from his expression.

'Go on,' said the doubter, looking hard into the machine.

'My sensations would be hard to describe. As the columns of hail grew thinner I saw the white figure more distinctly. It was very large, for a silver birch tree touched its shoulder. It was of white marble in shape something like a winged sphinx, but the wings instead of being carried vertically over the back were spread on either side. It chanced that the face was towards me, the sightless eyes seemed to watch me. There was the faint shadow of a smile on the lips. I stood looking into this enigmatical countenance for a little space, half a minute, perhaps, or half an hour. As the hail drove before it, denser or thinner, it seemed to advance and recede. At last I tore my eyes far away from it for a moment, and saw that the hail curtain had worn threadbare, and that the sky was lightening with the promise of the sun. I looked up again at the crouching white shape, and suddenly the full temerity of my voyage came upon me. What might appear when that hazy curtain was altogether withdrawn? What might not have happened to men? What if cruelty had grown into a common passion? What if in this interval the race had lost its manliness, and had grown into something inhuman, unsympathetic and overwhelmingly powerful? To them I might seem some old-world savage animal only the more dreadful and disgusting for my likeness to themselves, a foul creature to be incontinently slain. I was seized with a panic fear. Already I saw other vast shapes, huge buildings with intricate parapets, and a wooded hillside dimly creeping in upon me through the lessening storm. I turned in frantic mood to the Time Machine, and strove hard to readjust it.

'As I did so the shafts of the sun smote through the thunder-storm. The grey downpour was swept aside, and vanished like the trailing garments of a ghost. Above me was the intense blue of the summer sky with some faint brown shreds of cloud whirling into nothingness. The great buildings about me now stood out clear and distinct, shining with the wet of the thunderstorm and picked out in white by the unmelted hailstones piled along their courses. I felt nakedly exposed to a strange world. I felt as perhaps a bird may feel in the clear air, knowing the hawk wings above and will swoop. My fear grew to frenzy. I took a breathing space, set my teeth, and again grappled fiercely, wrist and knee, with the machine. It gave under my desperate onset and turned over. My chin was struck violently. With one hand on the saddle and the other on this lever I stood, panting heavily, in attitude to mount again.

'But with this recovery of a prompt retreat my courage recovered. I looked more curiously and less fearfully at this world of the remote future. In a circular opening high up in the wall of the nearer house I saw a group of figures, clad in robes of rich soft colour. They had seen me, and their faces were directed towards me. From some distant point behind this building a thin blade of colour shot into the blue air and went skimming in a wide ascending curve overhead. A white thing, travelling crow-fashion with a rare flap of the wings, may have been a flying machine. My attention was called from this to earth again by voices shouting. Coming through the bushes by the white sphinx could be seen the heads and shoulders of several men running. One of these emerged in a pathway leading straight to the little lawn upon which I stood with my machine. His was a slight figure clad in a purple tunic, girdled at the waist with a leather belt. A kind of sandals of buskins seemed to be upon his feet—I could not clearly distinguish which. His legs were bare to the knees, and his head was bare. For the first time I noticed how warm the air was. He struck me as being a very beautiful and graceful figure, but indescribably frail. His flushed face reminded me of the more beautiful kind of consumptive, that hectic beauty of which we used to hear so much . . .'

'That,' said the medical man, 'entirely discredits your story.' He was sitting on the bench near the circular saw. 'It is so absolutely opposed to the probabilities of our hygienic science—'

'That you disbelieve an eye witness!' said the Philosophical Investigator.

'Well, you must admit the suggestion of pthisis, coupled with a warm climate—'

'Don't interrupt,' said the red-haired man. 'Have we not this battered machine here to settle our doubts?'

I turned to the Philosopher again, but he had taken the lamp and stood as if he would light us back through the passage. Apparently he was offended at the attempt to dispose of his story from internal evidence. The curtain fell abruptly upon our brief glimpse of A.D. 12,203, and the rest of the evening passed in an unsuccessful attempt on the part of the doctor to show that the physique of civilised man was better than that of the savage. I agreed with a remark of the Philosopher's: that even if this were the case, it was slender inference that the improvement would continue for the next ten thousand years.

THE REFINEMENT OF HUMANITY

A.D. 12,203
This man, who said he had travelled through time, refrained, after our first scepticism, from any further speech of his experiences, and in some subtle way his silence, with perhaps a certain change we detected in his manner and in his expressed opinion of existing things, won us at last to

a doubt of our own certain incredulity. Besides, even if he had not done as he said, even if he had not, by some juggling along the fourth dimension, glimpsed the world ten thousand years ahead, yet there might still be a sufficiently worthy lie wasting in his brain. So that some conversational inducements began to be thrown towards him, and at last he partially forgave us and produced some few further fragments of his travel story.

'Of the fragile beauty of these people of the distant future,' said he, 'I bear eye-witness, but how that beauty came to be, I can only speculate. You must not ask me for reasons.'

'But did they not explain things to you?' asked the red-haired man.

'Odd as it may seem, I had no cicerone. In all the narratives of people visiting the future that I have read, some obliging scandal-monger appears at an early stage, and begins to lecture on constitutional history and social economy, and to point out the celebrities. Indeed so little had I thought of the absurdity of this that I had actually anticipated something of the kind would occur in reality. In my day-dreams, while I was making the machine, I had figured myself lecturing and being lectured to about the progress of humanity, about the relations of the sexes, and about capital and labour, like a dismal Demological Congress. But they didn't explain anything. They couldn't. They were the most illiterate people I ever met.

'Yes, I was disappointed. On the other hand there were compensations. I had been afraid I might have to explain the principles of the Time Machine, and send a perfected humanity on experimental rides, with some chance of having my apparatus stolen or lost centuries away from me. But these people took it for granted I was heaven-descended, a meteoric man, coming as I did in a thunderstorm, and so soon as they saw me appear ran violently towards me, and some prostrated themselves and some knelt at my feet. "Come," said I, as I saw perhaps fifty of these dainty people engaged in this pleasing occupation; "this at least is some compensation for contemporary neglect." A feeling of fatherly exaltation replaced the diffidence of my first appearance. I made signs to them that they should rise from the damp turf, and therewith they stood smiling very fearlessly and pleasantly at me. The height of them was about four feet, none came much higher than my chest, and I noticed at once how exquisitely fine was the texture of their light garments, and how satin smooth their skins. Their faces—I must repeat—were distinctly of the fair consumptive type, with flushed cheeks, and without a trace of fulness. The hair was curled.'

The medical man fidgeted in his chair. He began in a tone of protest: 'But *a priori*—'

The Philosophical Investigator anticipated his words. 'You would object that this is against the drift of sanitary science. You believe the average height, average weight, average longevity will all be increased, that in the future humanity will breed and sanitate itself into human

Megatheria. I thought the same until this trip of mine. But, come to think, what I saw is just what one might have expected. Man, like other animals, has been moulded, and will be, by the necessities of his environment. What keeps men so large and strong as they are? The fact that if any drop below a certain level of power and capacity for competition, they die. Remove dangers, render physical exertion no longer a necessity but an excrescence upon life, abolish competition by limiting population: in the long run—'

'But,' said the medical man, 'even if man in the future no longer need strength to fight against other men or beasts, he will still need a sufficient physique to resist disease.'

'That is the queer thing,' said the Time Traveller; 'there was no disease. Somewhen between now and then your sanitary science must have won the battle it is beginning now. Bacteria, or at least all disease causing bacteria, must have been exterminated. I can explain it in no other way.

'Certainly there had been a period of systematic scientific earth culture between now and then. Gnats, flies, and midges were gone, all troublesome animals, and thistles and thorns. The fruits of this age had no seeds, and the roses no prickles. Their butterflies were brilliant and abundant, and their dragonflies flying gems. It must have been done by selective breeding. But these delicious people had kept no books and knew no history. The world, I could speedily see, was perfectly organised—finished. It was still working as a perfect machine, had been so working for ages, but its very perfection had abolished the need of intelligence. What work was needed was done out of sight, and modesty, delicacy, had spread to all the necessary apparatus of life. The inquiries about their political economy I subsequently tried to make by signs, and by so much of their language as I learnt, were not understood or were gently parried. I saw no one eating. Indeed for some time I was in the way of starvation till I found a furtive but very pleasant and welcome meal of nuts and apples provided me in an elegant recess. They were entirely frugivorous, I found—like the Lemuridae. There was no great physical difference in the sexes, and they dressed exactly alike.'

The medical man would have demurred again.

'You are so unscientific,' said the Philosophical Inventor. 'The violent strength of a man, the distinctive charm and relative weakness of a woman, are the outcome of a period when the species survived by force and was ever in the face of danger. Marriage and the family were militant necessities before the world was conquered. But humanity has passed the zenith of its fierceness, and with an intelligent and triumphant democracy, willing to take over the care of offspring and only anxious to save itself from suffocation by its own increase, the division of a community into so many keenly competitive households elbowing one another for living room must sooner or later cease. And even now there is a steady tendency to assimilate the pursuits of the sexes. A very little refinement in our thinking, and even we should see that distinctive costume is an indelicate advertisement of facts it is the aim of all polite people to ignore.

'The average duration of life was about nineteen or twenty years. Well—what need of longer? People live nowadays to threescore and ten because of their excessive vitality, and because of the need there has been of guarding, rearing, and advising a numerous family. But a well-organised civilisation will change all that. At any rate, explain it as you will, these people about the age of nineteen or twenty, after a period of affectionate intercourse, fell into an elegant and painless decline, experienced a natural Euthanasia, and were dropped into certain perennially burning furnaces wherein dead leaves, broken twigs, fruit peel, and other refuse were also consumed.

'Their voices, I noticed, even at the outset, were particularly soft and their inflections of the tongue, subtle. I did a little towards learning their language.' He made some peculiar soft cooing sounds. 'The vocabulary is not very extensive.'

The red-haired man laughed and patted his shoulder.

'But I am anticipating. To return to the Time Machine. I felt singularly reassured by the aspect of these people and by their gentle manner. Many of them were children, and these seemed to me to take a keener interest in me than the fully grown ones. Presently one of these touched me, at first rather timidly, and then with more confidence. Others followed his or her example. They were vastly amused at the coarseness of my skin and at the hair upon the back of my hands, particularly the little ones. As I stood in the midst of a small crowd of them, one came laughing towards me, carrying a chain of some beautiful flowers altogether new to me, and put it about my neck. The idea was received with melodious applause; and presently they were running to and fro for flowers, and laughingly flinging them upon me until I was almost smothered with blossom. You, who have never seen the like, can scarcely imagine what delicate and wonderful flowers ten thousand years of culture had created. A flying machine, with gaily painted wings, came swooping down, scattering the crowd right and left, and its occupant joined the throng about me. Then someone suggested, it would seem, that their new plaything should be exhibited in the nearest building; and so I was beckoned and led and urged, past the Sphinx of white marble, towards a vast grey edifice of fretted stone. As I went with them, the memory of my confident anticipations of a profoundly grave and intellectual posterity came, with irresistible merriment, to my mind.'

THE SUNSET OF MANKIND

'We have no doubt of the truth of your story,' said the red-haired man to him that travelled through time; 'but there is much in it that is difficult to understand.'

'On the surface,' said the Time Traveller.

'For instance, you say that the men of the year twelve thousand odd were living in elaborate luxury, in a veritable earth garden; richly clothed they were and sufficiently fed. Yet you present them as beautiful—well!—idiots. Some intelligence and some labour, some considerable intelligence I should imagine, were surely needed to keep this world garden in order.'

'They had some intelligence,' said the Time Traveller, 'and besides—'

'Very little though; they spoke with a limited vocabulary, and foolishly took you and your Time Machine for a meteorite. Yet they were the descendants of the men who had organised the world so perfectly, who had exterminated disease, evolved flowers and fruits of indescribable beauty, and conquered the problem of flying. Those men must have had singularly powerful minds—'

'You confuse, I see, original intelligence and accumulated and organised knowledge. It is a very common error. But look the thing squarely in the face. Were you to strip the man of to-day of all the machinery and appliances of his civilisation, were you to sponge from his memory all the facts which he knows simply as facts, and leave him just his coddled physique, imperfect powers of observation, and ill-trained reasoning power, would he be the equal in wit or strength of the paleolithic savage? We do, indeed, make an innumerable multitude of petty discoveries nowadays, but the fundamental principles of thought and symbolism upon which our minds travel to these are immeasurably old. We live in the thought edifice of space, time and number, that our forefathers contrived. Look at it fairly: we invent by recipe, by Bacon's patent method for subduing the earth. The world is moving now to comfort and absolute security, not so much from its own initiative as from the impetus such men as he gave it. Then the more we know the less is our scope for the exercise of useful discovery, and the more we advance in civilisation the less is our need of a brain for our preservation. Man's intelligence conquers nature, and in undisputed empire is the certain seed of decay. The energy revealed by security will run at first into art—or vice. Our descendants will give the last beautifying touch to the edifice of this civilisation with the last gleam of their waning intelligences. With perfect comfort and absolute security, the energy of advance must needs dwindle. That has been the history of all past civilisation, and it will be the history of all civilisations. Civilisation means security for the weak and indolent, panmyxia of weakness and indolence, and general decline. The tradition of effort that animates us will be forgotten in the end. What need for education when there is no struggle for life? What need of thought or strong desires? What need of books, or what need of stimulus to creative effort? As well take targe and dirk and mail underclothing into a City office. Men who retain any vestige of intellectual activity will be restless, irked by their weapons, inharmonious with the serene quiescence which will fall upon mankind. They will be ill company with their mysterious questionings, unprosperous in their love-making, and will leave no offspring. So an end comes at last to all these things.'

'I don't believe that,' said the common-sense person; 'I don't believe in this scare about the rapid multiplication of the unfit, and all that.'

'Nor do I,' said the Time Traveller. 'I never yet heard of the rapid multiplication of the unfit. It is the fittest who survive. The point is that civilisation—any form of civilisation—alters the qualifications of fitness, because the organisation it implies and the protection it affords, discounts the adventurous, animal, and imaginative, and puts a premium upon the mechanical, obedient, and vegetative. An organised civilisation is like Saturn, and destroys the forces that begat it.'

'Of course that is very plausible,' said the common-sense person, in the tone of one who puts an argument aside, and proceeded to light a cigar without further remark.

'When do you conceive this civilising process ceased?' asked the red-haired man.

'It must have ceased for a vast period before the time of my visit. The great buildings in which these beautiful little people lived, a multitude together, were profoundly time-worn. Several I found collapsed through the rusting of the iron parts, and abandoned. One colossal ruin of granite, bound with aluminium, was not very distant from the great house wherein I sheltered, and among its precipitous masses and confusion of pillars were crowded thickets of nettles—nettles robbed of their stinging hairs and with leaves of purple brown. There had been no effort apparently to rebuild these places. It was in the dark recesses of this place, by-the-by, that I met my first morlock.'

'*Morlock*! What is a morlock?' asked the medicine man.

'A new species of animal, and a very peculiar one. At first I took it for some kind of ape—'

'But you slip from my argument,' interrupted the red-haired man. 'These people were clothed in soft and beautiful raiment, which seems to me to imply textile manufactures, dyeing, cutting out, skilled labour involving a certain amount of adaptation to individual circumstance.'

'Precisely. Skilled labour of a certain traditional sort—you must understand there were no changes of fashion—skill much on the level of that required from a bee when it builds its cell. That occurred to me. It puzzled me very much at first to account for it. I certainly found none of the people at any such work. But the explanation—that is so very grotesque that I really hesitate to tell you.'

He paused, looked at us doubtfully. 'Suppose you imagine machines—'

'Put your old shoes in at one end and a new pair comes out at the other,' laughed the red-haired man. 'Frankenstein Machines that have developed souls, while men have lost theirs! The created servant steals the mind of its creator; he puts his very soul into it, so to speak. Well,

perhaps it is possible. It is not a new idea, you know. And you have said
something about flying-machines. I suppose they were repaired by similar
intelligent apparatus. Did you have a chat with any of these machine-
beasts?'

'That seems rather a puerile idea to me,' said the Time Traveller,
'knowing what I do. But to realise the truth, you must bear in mind that
it is possible to do things first intelligently and afterwards to make a habit
of them. Let me illustrate by the ancient civilisation of the ants and bees.
Some ants are still intelligent and originative; while other species are
becoming mere automatic creatures, to repeat what were once intelligent
actions. The working bees, naturalists say, are almost entirely automatic.
Now, among these men—'

'Ah, these morlocks of yours!' said the red-haired man. 'Something
ape-like! Human neuters! But—'

'Look here!' suddenly interrupted the very young man. He had been
lost in profound thought for some minute or so, and now rushed headlong
into the conversation, after his manner. 'Here is one thing I cannot fall
in with. The sun, you say, was hotter than it is now, or at any rate the
climate was warmer. Now the sun is really supposed to be cooling and
shrinking, and so is the earth. The mean temperature ought to be colder
in the future. And besides this, the Isthmus of Panama will wear through
at last, and the Gulf Stream no longer impinge upon our shores with all
its warmth.'

'There,' said the Time Traveller, 'I am unable to give you an explanation. All I know is that the climate was very much warmer than it is
now, and that the sun seemed brighter. There was a strange and beautiful
thing, too, about the night, and that was the multitude of shooting stars.
Even during the November showers of our epoch I have never seen anything quite so brilliant as an ordinary night of this coming time. The sky
seemed alive with them, especially towards midnight, when they fell
chiefly from the zenith. Besides this the brilliance of the night was increased by a number of luminous clouds and whisps, many of them as
bright or brighter than the Milky Way; but, unlike the Milky Way, they
shifted in position from night to night. The fall of meteorites, too, was
a comparatively common occurrence. I think it was the only thing these
delightful people feared, or had any reason to fear. Possibly this meteoric
abundance had something to do with the increased warmth. A quantity
of such bodies in the space through which the solar system travelled might
contribute to this in two ways: by retarding the tangential velocity of the
earth in its orbit, and so accelerating its secular approach to the sun, and
by actually falling into the sun and so increasing its radiant energy. But
these are guesses of mine. All I can certainly say is that the climate was
very much warmer, and had added its enervating influence to their too
perfect civilisation.'

'Warmth and colour, ruins and decline,' said the red-haired man. 'One might call this age of yours the Sunset of Mankind.'

THE UNDERWORLD

'I have already told you,' said the Time Traveller, 'that it was customary on the part of the delightful people of the upper world to ignore the existence of these pallid creatures of the caverns, and consequently when I descended among them I descended alone.

'I had to clamber down a shaft of perhaps two or three hundred yards. The descent was effected by means of hooks projecting from the sides of the well, and since they were adapted to the needs of a creature much smaller and lighter than myself I was speedily cramped and fatigued by the descent. And not simply fatigued. My weight suddenly bent one of the hooks and almost swung me off it into the darkness beneath. For a moment I hung by one hand, and after that experience I did not dare to rest again, and though my arms and back were presently acutely painful, I continued to climb with as quick a motion as possible down the sheer descent. Glancing upward I saw the aperture a mere small blue disc above me, in which a star was visible. The thudding sound of some machine below grew louder and more oppressive. Everything save that minute circle above was profoundly dark. I was in an agony of discomfort. I had some thought of trying to get up the shaft again, and leave the underworld alone. But while I turned this over in my mind I continued to descend.

'It was with intense relief that I saw very dimly coming up a foot to the right of me a long loophole in the wall of the shaft, and, swinging myself in, found it was the aperture of a narrow horizontal tunnel in which I could lie down and rest. My arms ached, my back was cramped, and I was trembling with the prolonged fear of falling. Besides this the unbroken darkness had a distressing effect upon my eyes. The air was full of the throbbing and hum of machinery.

'I do not know how long I lay in that tunnel. I was roused by a soft hand touching my face. Starting up in the darkness I snatched at my matches, and, hastily striking one, saw three grotesque white creatures similar to the one I had seen above ground in the ruin, hastily retreating before the light. Living as they did, in what appeared to me impenetrable darkness, their eyes were abnormally large and sensitive, just as are the eyes of the abyss fishes or of any purely nocturnal creatures, and they reflected the light in the same way. I have no doubt that they could see me in that rayless obscurity, and they did not seem to have any fear of me apart from the light. But so soon as I struck a match in order to see them, they fled incontinently, vanishing up dark gutters and tunnels from which their eyes glared at me in the strangest fashion.

'I tried to call them, but what language they had was apparently a different one from that of the overworld people. So that I was left to my own unaided exploration.

'Feeling my way along this tunnel of mine, the confused noise of machinery grew louder, and presently the wall receded from my hand, and I felt I had come to an open space, and striking another match saw I had entered an arched cavern, so vast that it extended into darkness at last beyond the range of my light. Huge machines with running belts and whirling fly-wheels rose out of the obscurity, and the grey bodies of the Morlocks dodged my light among the unsteady shadows. Several of the machines near me were disused and broken down. They appeared to be weaving machines, and were worked by leather belts running over drums upon great rotating shafts that stretched across the cavern. I could not see how the shafts were worked. And very soon my match burned out.'

'That was a pity,' said the red-haired man.

'I was afraid to push my way down this avenue of throbbing machinery in the dark, and with my last glimpse I discovered that my store of matches had run low. It had never occurred to me until that moment that there was any need to economise them, and I had wasted almost half the box in astonishing the above-ground people, to whom fire was a novelty. I had four left then. As I stood in the dark a hand touched mine, then some lank fingers came feeling over my face. I fancied I detected the breathing of a number of these little beings about me. I felt the box of matches in my hand being gently disengaged, and other hands behind me plucking at my clothing.

'The sense of these unseen creatures examining me was indescribably unpleasant. The sudden realisation of my ignorance of their ways of thinking and possible actions came home to me very vividly in the darkness. I shouted at them as loudly as I could. They started away from me, and then I could feel them approaching me again. They clutched at me more boldly, whispering odd sounds to each other. I shivered violently and shouted again, rather discordantly. This time they were not so seriously alarmed, and made a queer laughing noise as they came towards me again.

'I will confess I was frightened. I determined to strike another match and escape under its glare. Eking it out with a scrap of paper from my pocket, I made good my retreat to the narrow tunnel. But hardly had I entered this when my light was blown out, and I could hear them in the blackness rustling like wind among leaves, and pattering like rain as they hurried after me, In a moment I was clutched by several hands again, and there was no mistake now that they were trying to draw me back. I struck another light and waved it in their dazzled faces. You can scarcely imagine how nauseatingly unhuman those pale chinless faces and great pinkish grey eyes seemed as they stared stupidly, suddenly blinded by the light.

'So I gained time and retreated again, and when my second match had ended struck my third. That had almost burnt through as I reached the opening of the tunnel upon the well. I lay down upon the edge, for the throbbing whirl of the air-pumping machine below made me giddy, and felt sideways for the projecting hooks. As I did so, my feet were grasped from behind, and I was tugged violently backwards. I lit my last match ... and it incontinently went out. But I had my hand on the climbing bars now, and, kicking violently, disengaged myself from the clutches of the Morlocks, and was speedily clambering up the shaft again. One little wretch followed me for some way, and captured the heel of my boot as a trophy.'

'I suppose you could show us that boot without the heel,' said the red-haired man, 'if we asked to see it?'

'What do you think they wanted with you?' asked the common-sense person.

'I don't know. That was just the beastliness of it.'

'And is that all you saw of the Morlocks?' said the very young man.

'I saw some once again. Frankly, I was afraid of them. I did not even look down one of those wells again.'

'Have you no explanation to offer of those creatures?' said the red-haired man. 'What were they really? In particular, what was their connection with the upperworld people, and how had they been developed?'

'I am a traveller, and I tell you a traveller's tale. I am not an annotated edition of myself.'

'Cannot you hazard something? I am puzzled by your statement, that human beings will differentiate into two species without any separation. Would not intermarriage prevent this?'

'Oh no! a species may split up into two without any separation into different districts. This matter has been worked out by Gulick. He uses the very convenient word "segregation" to express his idea. Imagine, for instance, the more refined and indolent class of people to intermarry mainly among themselves, and the operative or business class—the class of operatives aspiring to rise to business influence and finding their interests mainly in the satisfaction of a taste for industrial and business pursuits—also marrying mainly in their own class. Might there not be a widening separation? Indeed, since this time-journey of mine I have fancied that there is such a split going on even now in our English society, a split that began some two hundred and fifty years ago or more. I do not mean any split between working people and rich—families drop and rise from toil to wealth continually—but between the sombre, mechanically industrious, arithmetical, inartistic type, the type of the Puritan and the American millionaire and the pleasure-loving, witty, and graceful type that gives us our clever artists, our actors and writers, some of our gentry, and many an elegant rogue. Conceive such types drifting away from one another each in its own direction. Along the former line we should get at last a colourless love of darkness, dully industrious and productive, and along the latter, brilliant weakness and gay silliness. But this is a mere theory of mine. The fact remains that humanity had differentiated into two very distinct species in the coming time, explain it as you will. Such traditional industries as still survived remained among the Morlocks, but the sun of man's intelligence had set and the night of humanity was creeping on apace.'

THE TIME-TRAVELLER RETURNS

'After my glimpse of the underworld my mind turned incessantly towards this age again. The upper-world people, who had at first charmed me with their light beauty, began to weary and then to irritate me by their insubstantiality. And there was something in the weird inhumanity of the undermen that robbed me of my sense of security. I could not imagine that they regarded me as their fellow creature, or that any of the deep reasonless instincts that keep man the servant of his fellow man would intervene in my favour. I was to them a strange beast. When I thought of the soft cold hands clutching me in the subterranean darkness I was filled with horrible imaginings of what might have been my fate.

'Then these creatures, being now aware of my existence, and possessing far more curiosity than the upper-world people, began to trouble my nights. Their excessive sensibility to light kept me safe from them during the days, but after the twilight I found it advisable to avoid the deep shadows of the buildings and to sleep out under the stars. And even in the open, when the sky was overcast, these pallid little monsters ventured to approach me.

'I could see very dimly their grey forms approaching through the black masses of the bushes, and could hear the murmuring noises that stood to them in the place of articulate speech.

'I think they were far more powerfully attracted by the Time Machine than by myself. Their minds were essentially mechanical. That, indeed, was one of the dismal thoughts that came to me—that possibly they would try to take me to pieces and investigate my construction. The only thing that kept me in the future age after I had begun to realise what had happened to humanity was my interest in the present one. I was reluctant to go until I had seen enough to tell you some definite facts about your descendants. But the near approach of these Morlocks was too much for me. As one came forward in the obscurity and laid his hand upon the bars of the time Machine, I cried aloud and vaulted into the saddle, and in another moment that strange world of the future had swept into nothingness, and I was reeling down the time dimension to this age of ours again. And so my visit to the year 12,203 came to an end.'

He paused. For some minute or so there was silence.

'I do not like your vision,' said the common-sense person.

'It seems to me just the Gospel of Despair,' said the financial journalist.

The Time Traveller lit a cigar.

'Why there should be any particular despair for you in the contemplation of a time when our kind of beast—' he glanced round the room with a faint smile—'has ceased to exist, I fail to see.'

'We have always been accustomed to consider the future as in some peculiar way ours,' said the red-haired man. 'Your story seems to rob us of our birthright.'

'For my part I have always believed in a steady Evolution towards something Higher and Better,' said the common-sense person; and added, 'and I still do.'

'But still essentially human in all respects?' asked the Time Traveller.

'Decidedly,' said the common-sense person.

'In the past,' said the Time Traveller, 'the evolution has not always been upward. The land animals, including ourselves, zoologists say, are the descendants of almost amphibious mudfish that were hunted out of the seas by the ancestors of the modern sharks.'

'But what will become of Social Reform? You would make out that everything that ameliorates human life tends to human degeneration.'

'Let us leave social reform to the professional philanthropist,' said the Time Traveller. 'I told you a story; I am not prepared to embark upon a political discussion. The facts remain . . .'

'*Facts*!' said the red-haired man *sotto voce*.

'That man has been evolved from the inhuman in the past—to go no further back, even the paleolithic men were practically inhuman—and that in the future he must sooner or later be modified beyond human sympathy.'

'Leaving us,' said the red-haired man, 'a little island in time and a little island in space, the surface of the little globe out of all the oceans of space, and a few thousands of years out of eternity.'

'The limits are still large enough for me to be mean in,' said the Time Traveller.

'And after man?' said the medical man.

'A world with a continually longer day and a continually shorter year, so the astronomers tell us. For the drag of the tides upon the spin of the earth will bring this planet at last to the plight of Mercury, with one face turned always to the sun. And the gradual diminution of the centrifugal component of the earth's motion due to interplanetary matter will cause it to approach the sun slowly and surely as the sun cools, until the parent body has recovered its offspring again. During the last stages of the sunward movement over those parts of the earth that are sunward there will be an unending day, and a vast red sun growing ever vaster and duller will glow motionless in the sky. Twice already it will have blazed into a transient period of brilliance as the minor planets, Mercury and Venus, melted back into its mass. On the further side of the earth will be perpetual night and the bitterest cold, and between these regions will be belts of twilight, of perpetual sunset, and perpetual afternoon. Whether there will be any life on the earth then we can scarcely guess. Somewhere in the belts of intermediate temperature, it may be, that strange inconceivable forms of life will still struggle on against the inevitable fate that awaits them. But an end comes. Life is a mere eddy, an episode, in the great stream of universal being, just as man with all his cosmic mind is a mere episode in the story of life—'

He stopped abruptly. 'There is that kid of mine upstairs crying. He always cries when he wakes up in the dark. If you don't mind, I will just go up and tell him it's all right.'

APPENDIX IV

The *New Review Time Machine*: Two Excerpts

I. THE INVENTOR

The man who made the Time Machine—the man I shall call the Time Traveller—was well known in scientific circles a few years since, and the fact of his disappearance is also well known. He was a mathematician of peculiar subtlety, and one of our most conspicuous investigators in molecular physics. He did not confine himself to abstract science. Several ingenious and one or two profitable patents were his: very profitable they were, these last, as his handsome house at Richmond testified. To those who were his intimates, however, his scientific investigations were as nothing to his gift of speech. In the after-dinner hours he was ever a vivid and variegated talker, and at times his fantastic, often paradoxical, conceptions came so thick and close as to form one continuous discourse. At these times he was as unlike the popular conception of a scientific investigator as a man could be. His cheeks would flush, his eyes grow bright; and the stranger the ideas that sprang and crowded in his brain, the happier and the more animated would be his exposition.

Up to the last there was held at his house a kind of informal gathering, which it was my privilege to attend, and where, at one time or another, I have met most of our distinguished literary and scientific men. There was a plain dinner at seven. After that we would adjourn to a room of easy chairs and little tables, and there, with libations of alcohol and reeking pipes, we would invoke the God. At first the conversation was mere fragmentary chatter, with some local *lacunæ* of digestive silence; but towards nine or half-past nine, if the God was favourable, some particular topic would triumph by a kind of natural selection, and would become the common interest. So it was, I remember, on the last Thursday but one of all—the Thursday when I first heard of the Time Machine.

I had been jammed in a corner with a gentleman who shall be disguised as Filby. He had been running down Milton—the public neglects poor Filby's little verses shockingly; and as I could think of nothing but the relative status of Filby and the man he criticised, and was much too timid to discuss that, the arrival of that moment of fusion, when our several conversations were suddenly merged into a general discussion, was a great relief to me.

"What's that nonsense?" said a well-known Medical Man, speaking across Filby to the Psychologist.

"He thinks," said the Psychologist, "that Time's only a kind of Space."

"It's not thinking," said the Time Traveller; "it's knowledge."

"Foppish affectation," said Filby, still harping upon his wrongs; but I feigned a great interest in this question of Space and Time.

"Kant," began the Psychologist—

"Confound Kant!" said the Time Traveller. "I tell you I'm right. I've got experimental proof of it. I'm not a metaphysician." He addressed the Medical Man across the room, and so brought the whole company into his own circle. "It's the most promising departure in experimental work that has ever been made. It will simply revolutionise life. Heaven knows what life will be when I've carried the thing through."

"As long as it's not the water of Immortality I don't mind," said the distinguished Medical Man. "What is it?"

"Only a paradox," said the Psychologist.

The Time Traveller said nothing in reply, but smiled and began tapping his pipe upon the fender curb. This was the invariable presage of a dissertation.

"You have to admit that time is a spatial dimension," said the Psychologist, emboldened by immunity and addressing the Medical Man, "and then all sorts of remarkable consequences are found inevitable. Among others, that it becomes possible to travel about in time."

The Time Traveller chuckled: "You forget that I'm going to prove it experimentally."

"Let's have your experiment," said the Psychologist.

"I think we'd like the argument first," said Filby.

"It's this," said the Time Traveller: "I propose a wholly new view of things based on the supposition that ordinary human perception is an hallucination. I'm sorry to drag in predestination and free-will, but I'm afraid those ideas will have to help. Look at it in this way—this, I think, will give you the gist of it: Suppose you knew fully the position and the properties of every particle of matter, of everything existing in the universe at any particular moment of time: suppose, that is, that you were omniscient. Well, that knowledge would involve the knowledge of the condition of things at the previous moment, and at the moment before that, and so on. If you knew and perceived the present perfectly, you would perceive therein the whole of the past. If you understood all natural laws the present would be a complete and vivid record of the past. Similarly, if you grasped the whole of the present, knew all its tendencies and laws, you would see clearly all the future. To an omniscient observer there would be no forgotten past—no piece of time as it were that had dropped out of existence—and no blank future of things yet to be revealed. Perceiving all the present, an omniscient observer would likewise perceive all the past and all the inevitable future at the same time. Indeed, present and past and future would be without meaning to such an observer: he would always perceive exactly the same thing. He would see, as it were, a Rigid Universe filling space and time—a Universe in which things were always the same. He would see one sole unchanging series of cause and effect to-day and to-morrow and always. If 'past' meant anything, it would mean looking in a certain direction; while 'future' meant looking the opposite way."

"H'm," said the Rector, "I fancy you're right. So far."

"I know I am," said the Time Traveller. "From the absolute point of view the universe is a perfectly rigid unalterable apparatus, entirely predestinate, entirely complete and finished. Now, looking at things, so far as we can, from this standpoint, how would a thing like this box appear? It would still be a certain length and a certain breadth and a certain thickness, and it would have a definite mass; but we should also perceive that it extended back in time to a certain moment when it was made, and forward in time to a certain moment when it was destroyed, and that during its existence it was moved about in space. An ordinary man, being asked to describe this box, would say, among other things, that it was in such a position, and that it measured ten inches in depth, say, three in breadth, and four in length. From the absolute point of view it would also be necessary to say that it began at such a moment, lasted so long, measured so much in time, and was moved here and there meanwhile. It is only when you have stated its past and its future that you have completely described the box. You see, from the absolute standpoint—which is the true scientific standpoint—time is merely a dimension, quite analogous to the three dimensions in space. Every particle of matter has length, breadth, thickness, and—duration."

"You're perfectly right," said the Rector. "Theologians threshed all that out ages ago."

"I beg your pardon," said the Psychologist, "nothing of the sort. Our first impression, the very foundation of our mental life, is order in time. I am supported—"

"I tell you that psychology cannot possibly help us here," said the Time Traveller, "because our minds do not represent the conditions of the universe—why should they?—but only our necessities. From my point of view the human consciousness is an immaterial something falling through this Rigid Universe of four dimensions, from the direction we call 'past' to the direction we call 'future.' Just as the sun is a material something falling through the same universe towards the constellation of Hercules."

"This is rather abstruse," said Filby under his breath to me.

"I begin to see your argument," said the Medical Man. "And you go on to ask, why *should* we continue to drift in a particular direction? Why *should* we drive through time at this uniform pace? Practically you propose to study four-dimensional geometry with a view to locomotion in time."

"Precisely. *Have* studied it to that end."

"Of all the wild extravagant theories!" began the Psychologist.

"Yes, so it seemed to me, and so I never talked of it until—"

"Experimental verification!" cried I. "You are going to verify *that?*"

"The experiment!" cried Filby, who was getting brain-weary.

"Let's see your experiment anyhow," said the Psychologist, "though it's all humbug, you know."

The Time Traveller smiled round at us. Then, still smiling faintly, and with his hands deep in his trousers pockets, he walked slowly out of the room, and we heard his slippers shuffling down the long passage to his laboratory.

XII. THE FURTHER VISION

"I have already told you of the sickness and confusion that comes with time travelling. And this time I was not seated properly in the saddle, but sideways and in an unstable fashion. For an indefinite time I clung to the machine as it swayed and vibrated, quite unheeding how I went, and when I brought myself to look at the dials again I was amazed to find where I had arrived. One dial records days, another thousands of days, another millions of days, and another thousands of millions. Now, instead of reversing the levers I had pulled them over so as to go forward with them, and when I came to look at these indicators I found that the thousands hand was sweeping round as fast as the seconds hand of a watch— into futurity. Very cautiously, for I remembered my former headlong fall, I began to reverse my motion. Slower and slower went the circling hands until the thousands one seemed motionless and the daily one was no longer a mere mist upon its scale. Still slower, until the grey haze around me became distincter and dim outlines of an undulating waste grew visible.

"I stopped. I was on a bleak moorland, covered with a sparse vegetation, and grey with a thin hoarfrost. The time was midday, the orange sun, shorn of its effulgence, brooded near the meridian in a sky of drabby grey. Only a few black bushes broke the monotony of the scene. The great buildings of the decadent men among whom, it seemed to me, I had been so recently, had vanished and left no trace, not a mound even marked their position. Hill and valley, sea and river—all, under the wear and work of the rain and frost, had melted into new forms. No doubt, too, the rain and snow had long since washed out the Morlock tunnels. A nipping breeze stung my hands and face. So far as I could see there were neither hills, nor trees, nor rivers: only an uneven stretch of cheerless plateau.

"Then suddenly a dark bulk rose out of the moor, something that gleamed like a serrated row of iron plates, and vanished almost immediately in a depression. And then I became aware of a number of faint-grey things, coloured to almost the exact tint of the frost-bitten soil, which were browsing here and there upon its scanty grass, and running to and fro. I saw one jump with a sudden start, and then my eye detected perhaps a score of them. At first I thought they were rabbits, or some small breed of kangaroo. Then, as one came hopping near me, I perceived that it belonged to neither of these groups. It was plantigrade, its hind legs rather the longer; it was tailless, and covered with a straight greyish hair that thickened about the head into a Skye terrier's mane. As I had understood that in the Golden Age man had killed out almost all the other animals, sparing only a few of the more ornamental, I was naturally curious about the creatures. They did not seem afraid of me, but browsed on, much as rabbits would do in a place unfrequented by men; and it occurred to me that I might perhaps secure a specimen.

"I got off the machine, and picked up a big stone. I had scarcely done so when one of the little creatures came within easy range. I was so lucky as to hit it on the head, and it rolled over at once and lay motionless. I ran to it at once. It remained still, almost as if it were killed. I was surprised to see that the thing had five feeble digits to both its fore and hind feet—the fore feet, indeed, were almost as human as the fore feet of a frog. It had, moreover, a roundish head, with a projecting forehead and forward-looking eyes, obscured by its lank hair. A disagreeable apprehension flashed across my mind. As I knelt down and seized my capture, intending to examine its teeth and other anatomical points which might show human characteristics, the metallic-looking object, to which I have already alluded, reappeared above a ridge in the moor, coming towards me and making a strange clattering sound as it came. Forthwith the grey animals about me began to answer with a short, weak yelping—as if of terror—and bolted off in a direction opposite to that from which this new creature approached. They must have hidden in burrows or behind bushes and tussocks, for in a moment not one of them was visible.

"I rose to my feet, and stared at this grotesque monster. I can only describe it by comparing it to a centipede. It stood about three feet high, and had a long segmented body, perhaps thirty feet long, with curiously overlapping greenish-black plates. It seemed to crawl upon a multitude of feet, looping its body as it advanced. Its blunt round head with a polygonal arrangement of black eye spots, carried two flexible, writhing, horn-like antennae. It was coming along, I should judge, at a pace of about eight or ten miles an hour, and it left me little time for thinking. Leaving my grey animal, or grey man, whichever it was, on the ground, I set off for the machine. Halfway I paused, regretting that abandonment, but a glance over my shoulder destroyed any such regret. When I gained the machine the monster was scarce fifty yards away. It was certainly not a vertebrated animal. It had no snout, and its mouth was fringed with jointed dark-coloured plates. But I did not care for a nearer view.

"I traversed one day and stopped again, hoping to find colossus gone and some vestige of my victim; but, I should judge, the giant centipede did not trouble itself about bones. At any rate both had vanished. The faintly human touch of these little creatures perplexed me greatly. If you come to think, there is no reason why a degenerate humanity should not come at last to differentiate into as many species as the descendants of the mud fish who fathered all the land vertebrates. I saw no more of any insect colossus, as to my thinking the segmented creature must have been. Evidently the physiological difficulty that at present keeps all the insects small had been surmounted at last, and this division of the animal kingdom had arrived at the long awaited supremacy which its enormous energy and vitality deserve. I made several attempts to kill or capture another of the greyish vermin, but none of my missiles were so successful as my first; and, after perhaps a dozen disappointing throws, that left my arm aching, I felt a gust of irritation at my folly in coming so far into futurity without weapons or equipment. I resolved to run on for one glimpse of the still remoter future—one peep into the deeper abysm of time—and then to return to you and my own epoch. Once more I re-mounted the machine, and once more the world grew hazy and grey.

"As I drove on, a peculiar change crept over the appearance of things. The unwonted greyness grew lighter; then—though I was travelling with prodigious velocity—the blinking succession of day and night, which was usually indicative of a slower pace, returned, and grew more and more marked. This puzzled me very much at first. The alternations of night and day grew slower and slower, and so did the passage of the sun across the sky, until they seemed to stretch through centuries. At last a steady twilight brooded over the earth, a twilight only broken now and then when a comet glared across the darkling sky. The band of light that had indicated the sun had long since disappeared; for the sun had ceased to set—it simply rose and fell in the west, and grew ever broader and more red. All trace of the moon had vanished. The circling of the stars, growing slower and slower, had given place to creeping points of light. At last, some time before I stopped, the sun, red and very large, halted motionless upon the horizon, a vast dome glowing with a dull heat, and now and then suffering a momentary extinction. At one time it had for a little while glowed more brilliantly again, but it speedily reverted to its sullen red-heat. I perceived by this slowing down of its rising and setting that the work of the tidal drag was done. The earth had come to rest with one face to the sun, even as in our own time the moon faces the earth.

"I stopped very gently and sat upon the Time Machine, looking round.

[Chapter concludes as in Atlantic edition, chapter 11.]

APPENDIX V

Correlation of the Holt Edition with the *New Review* Version (NR) and the Atlantic Edition (A)

The title of the Holt edition is *The Time Machine: An Invention*. Title-page gives the author's name as "H. S. Wells" and includes an epigraph from Browning:

> Fool! All that is at all
> Lasts ever past recall.

Opposite verso of title page appears the following "Author's Note," signed "H.S.W.":

> *The Time Traveler's Story* and a part of the introductory conversation appeared as a serial in the *New Review*. Several descriptive passages in the story had previously appeared in dialogue form in the *National Observer*, and the explanation of the "principles" of Time Travelling given in this book is inserted from the latter paper. I desire to make the usual acknowledgements.

The following correlation ignores minor textual variants.

Chapters in Holt	*Correlate with*
1. The Inventor	(NR) 1. The Inventor From "The man who made the Time Machine" to " 'It's this,' said the Time Traveller." Followed by (A) "You must follow me carefully" to "I was never more serious in my life."
2. The Time Traveler Returns	2. (A)
3. The Story Begins	3. (A)*
4. The Golden Age	4. (A) "In another moment" to "I never met people more easily fatigued."
5. Sunset	4. (A) "A queer thing I soon

discovered" to 5 (A) "I could feel it grip me at the throat and stop my breathing."

6. The Machine is Lost

5. (A) "In another moment I was in a passion of fear" to "things got back to the old footing."

7. The Strange Animal

5. (A) "I made what progress I could" to "I solemnly burned a match."

8. The Morlocks

6. (A)

9. When the Night Came

7. (A)

10. The Palace of Green Porcelain

8. (A)

11. In the Darkness of the Forest

9. (A)

12. The Trap of the White Sphinx

10. (A)

13. The Further Vision

11. (A) "I have already told you" to 12. (A) "tap with it nervously upon the bars of the grate."

14. After the Time Traveler's Story

12. (A) "There was a momentary stillness" to "The Time Traveller vanished three years ago."** Holt ed. concludes thereafter with the following text:

Up to the present he has not returned, and when he does return he will find his home in the hands of strangers and his little gathering of auditors broken up forever. Filby has exchanged poetry for playwriting, and is a rich man—as literary men go—and extremely unpopular. The Medical Man is dead, the Journalist is in India, and the Psychologist has succumbed to paralysis. Some of the other men I used to meet there have dropped as completely out of existence as if they, too, had traveled off upon some similar anachronisms. And so, ending in a kind of dead wall, the story of the Time Machine must remain for the present at least.

*A minor variant of special interest occurs in 3. Atlantic ed. has "blow myself and my apparatus out of all possible dimensions—into the Unknown." This passage in Holt appears as "blow myself and my apparatus out of the Rigid Universe— out of all possible dimensions—into the the Unknown." The passage in Holt is a survival from an essay by Wells that had provided a "frame" for the *New Review* Time Machine. See further *Experiment in Autobiography* (1934, 172) and Publication section of Introduction to this edition.
**Holt specifies that the "daily paper" the outer narrator reads is the *New Review*.

APPENDIX VI

Correlation of the Heinemann Edition and the Atlantic Edition

Minor textual variants are ignored.

Chapters in Heinemann	Correlate with Atlantic
1. Introduction	1. "The Time Traveller (for so it will be convenient to speak of him)" to "Filby's anecdote collapsed."
2. The Machine	1. "The thing the Time Traveller held" to "he winked at me solemnly."
3. The Time Traveller Returns	2
4. Time Travelling	3
5. In the Golden Age	4. "In another moment" to "people more indolent or more easily fatigued."
6. The Sunset of Mankind	4. "A queer thing I soon discovered" to "as most wrong theories are!"
7. A Sudden Shock	5. "As I stood there musing" to "round the point of my arrival."
8. Explanations	5. "So far as I could see" to "I solemnly burned a match."
9. The Morlocks	6
10. When Night Came	7
11. The Palace of Green Porcelain	8
12. Into the Darkness	9
13. The Trap of the White Sphinx	10
14. The Further Vision	11
15. The Time Traveller's Return	12. "So I came back" to "now I am telling you the story."
16. After the Story	12. "'I know,' he said, after a pause" to end of the Epilogue.

The Time Traveller Visits the Past

The following material, which does not appear in any previously published edition of *The Time Machine*, is preserved in MS. as sheaf D in
the H. G. Wells Collection, Rare Book Room, University of Illinois Library
at Urbana-Champaign. Sheaf D contains two chapters of *The Time Machine*, "XIII. The Further Vision" and "XIV. The Return of the Time
Traveller" (the latter is D12 through D25), a passage on different paper
describing the experience of return time travelling (D26), and a detached
episode (D27 and D28) which provides another version of the novella's
ending in which the Time Traveller (named "Bayliss") loses his Time
Machine after being ejected from it. What follows is the text of chapter
XIV as it appears in sheaf D and the description of reverse time travel.
Letter drafts on the versos of D14 and D15 (XIV) bear the date 4/10/94.
The two footnotes are by Wells.

XIV. THE RETURN OF THE TIME TRAVELLER

When I recovered I found myself upon the machine. & with my hands
resting upon the dials. The old confusion & tumult was around me &
the old blinking alternation of night & day. But now that I was travelling
back in time the sun was hopping from west to east, from its setting to
its rising, and the circles of the stars spun in the reverse direction.

My sole object was now to return. My curiosity was sated; I was in
pain. I longed for this age, for this house, for you human beings that I
have known with an almost passionate longing.

I turned to the dials. For a moment I could scarcely credit my eyes.
Then I remember[ed] that my hand had rested upon the slender rod con-
necting them with the rest of the machine. This was displaced. The dials
simply recorded the extent of my voyage.

Now to you that may seem an inconvenient accident, a little trouble
to meet. To me it was—not even excepting the visit to the Morlocks &
the fight in the forest—the most awful thing of all that happened in my
time journey. The strange sickness that had come upon me by that desolate beach of the dying Earth, still clung to me. Now I was lost in time!
It was weak of me, no doubt—the fact of it is I was hurt & weak physically
at that time—but I began to cry like a child. So conceive [of] me the Time

Traveller, the discoverer of futurity, clinging nerveless to his Time Machine and choking with sobs & with the tears streaming down his face. full of a terrible fear that he would never see humanity again or enter again into the delights of life. In my passion I drove back, I do not know how far. A childish persuasion came into my mind that I should stop when the country was submerged, & sink plump into the water of some of those vanished oceans whose sediments form the dry land of today.

So I travelled back through time. At last my heaping wretchedness grew to agony. Anything was better than that horrible suspense. In a suicidal mood I turned to the levers. Slower & slower I travelled. I began to see a flat green sward about me & the leaden gleam of waters. This gave me heart. I stopped completely & the Time Machine subsided with a succulent sound upon a bed of marshy gamboge green weed. Around me were stumpy trees not unlike willows. The sky was clear & very blue[,] the air hazy & the glowing western sky betokened a recent sunset. The yellow ground upon which I stood was perfectly flat & but little raised above the level of the waters that flowed on either side. A smell of decaying vegetation was in the air & the soil that showed between the litter of green weed was black. I judged I stood on a part of the delta of some large river.

A number of small white birds were running about on the green a few score yards away. They were picking about amidst the slime, & carried their wings, which appeared to me to be webbed, extended. Now & then one would flutter up into the air. They were not unlike gulls. Beyond this & some shells like large water snails I saw at first no living things.

Then I felt thirsty & descending from the machine I went to the edge of the water, stooped down & taking some in the hollow of my hand tasted it. It was brackish but quite drinkable. I took a draught & bathing my hands and face, felt very considerably refreshed.

I stood up & as I did so saw a pair of brown bodies swimming towards me & perhaps forty yards away. They looked like floating lumps of brown leather. For a moment I wondered what these things might be & then as they approached I saw they were the protuberant eyes and nostrils of a large hippopotamus. At that I hastily retreated to my machine. The monster came partly out of the water, then stopped & stared at me. Then with a grunt he turned back to the water again & swam away.

I was hungry but saw no means of satisfying my hunger in this desolate spot. My courage was now creeping back to me by slow degrees. I looked facts squarely in the face. So far as my knowledge of geology* went this river might be the great flood that deposited what is now the London Clay.

*The Time Traveller's knowledge of geology was scarcely on a level with his mechanical acquirements. A distinguished geologist assures me that this supposition was quite inaccurate. The birds puzzled this authority, but the hippopotamus—if it was a true hippopotamus—would indicate the much more recent epoch of the Pliocene period.

I sat under the warm sunset musing upon my position. I peered through the thin haze to see any forms of life that I could identify from my geological reading & that would give me some idea of my position in time. Far away through the drifting mist some huge great creatures followed one another in a line but I could not imagine what they were. I looked at the fluttering birds & at the willows. Then I remembered that the deciduous trees came after the Cretaceous period. At any rate I had not that oceanic period between me & my own time.

I determined to travel forward two million years & see what came of it. I connected the dials with the mechanism again & pulled over the levers.

When I stopped again it was very cold. It was night & the stars were shining, & a softly undulating mantle of white lay upon the earth. I was on a hillside & a river gleamed dimly among the black tree stems below. Then suddenly as a [sic] looked at the sky my heart came into my throat. For high above circled the old familiar constellation of the Great Bear.

I shouted at that & held out my arms to the dear old stars. For I knew from that grouping I was near my own time.

I began calling their names & pointing to them, "Cassiopeia" I cried; "with your chair there! back again in the sky! The Seven! Polaris! The white stream of the Milky Way!"

Then suddenly I heard a crackling among the bushes & footsteps. "Hallo!" said a voice hoarsely.

I turned my head and saw coming through the trees the black figure of a man carrying a many-paned lantern. The pink light from this lay in a circle on the snow round him & showed his nearer leg, clad in a kind of inflated knee breeches, black hose & buckled shoes.

"Hallo!" cried I.

He stopped abruptly and lifted the lantern to the level of his head. The black shadows in the tree stems whirled as he did so. The pink light fell on his ear & I saw his hair was close cropped & his hat square of outline & straight of brim. An expression of extreme astonishment came over his face as he saw me.

I wanted to say something but I was speechless with excitement. I tried to gesticulate.

Abruptly he dropped the lantern which was extinguished as it hit the ground & I heard his heels clattering up the hill & saw the sparks fly from the pebbles.

I sat there for some time in silence under the starlight, speculating how the thing might seem to this worthy. I judged him a seventeenth century puritain [sic] so that I had very nearly hit the mark—quite by accident as it happened. My impression had been that I was thirty or forty million years away from our time. That is the period I think some geologists give for the London Clay.* I was thinking of going on another

---

*The Time Traveller's geology was extremely elementary.

hundred years & stopping. But now I was in no great hurry or anxiety. There were now no nameless terrors in the air.

Then I saw a pink glimmer coming through the trees & heard several voices, & the noise of stumbling feet. Several men seemed shouting together. Scraps of their talk came drifting down to me.

"One must go forward with the lantern for me to take my aim by."

"Not me". . . .

"Even so are all Warlocks". . . .

I saw their light now [:] a pink cylindrical lantern, & two torches showering sparks & carried by boys. In front of the advancing crowd came a tall man whose head glinted like metal in the flickering light. He had a sandy coloured jacket drawn in at the waist by a leather belt, big leather gloves, & huge riding boots. He carried a lumpish piece of artillery with a heavy stock & a brass barrel, broadening at the muzzle.

They became silent when they saw me & halted. Then one stood a little in front of the rest—a tall man with white bands upon his chin — & lifting up his right hand to heaven & pointing his left to me this person began shouting at me in a loud voice.

"Hence Satain [sic]! I command thee. Get thee hence & be no more seen!"

I shouted back. "Can you tell me the date please?"

This seemed to disconcert him a little. He began again [.] "Avaunt. You spirit of mischief!"

I put my hands to the sides of my mouth. "I am no spirit of mischief, but an honest English gentleman, I tell you. I ask you a simple question."

He lowered his hand. A man standing in the shadow behind him said something I did not catch. & the preacher—for such I judge he was [—] turned & began to argue with him, every now & then glancing at me.

The soldier fumbled with his musket.

The boys with the torches drew near each other.

The night was bitter cold. I felt my teeth [illegible: ?near] chattering. "Cannot you answer a plain question?" I said.

"Who be you?" said the soldier sullenly.

"What are you doing out here at midnight with that devilry?" said the preacher pointing to my machine.

""I tell you I am an honest English gentleman & this is no devilry at all. Will you, in the name of charity, tell me the date?"

"It's some devilish trick—" began the preacher.

"New Year's Eve, sixteen hundred & forty five" piped out one of the little boys. *"Now,* who are you?"

The preacher gripped him by the collar.

"Well I," said I, "am a Chronic Argonaut, an explorer of epochs, a man for all time, a Morlock fighter, a—"

"*Horrible* blasphemy! screamed the preacher gesticulating. "Shoot him! Avaunt! Avaunt!"

The soldier hastily clapped his gun to his shoulder & as hastily I pulled over the lever. I heard the dull bang of the musket & the twang of the silver button by my ear.

But I did not care what they thought or did: I was coming home now. I rushed headlong down through the intervening two hundred & fifty years & in my excitement overshot the mark by a decade. I swung round & came back more deliberately. The hands on the dials ran back again.

[REVERSE TIME TRAVELLING]

I saw one thing that seemed odd to me for a moment. I think I have told you that when I set out before my velocity became very high[.] Mrs. Watchett had walked across the room, travelling as it seemed to me like a rocket. As I returned I passed again across that minute when she traversed the laboratory. But now every motion appeared to be the exact inversion of the previous one. The door at the lower end opened & she glided quietly up the laboratory back foremost & disappeared behind the door by which she had previously entered.

The hand upon the dial for the days went slower & slower & so I stopped.

APPENDIX VIII

How to Construct a Time Machine

Alfred Jarry

I. THE NATURE OF THE MEDIUM

A Time Machine, that is, a device for exploring Time, is no more difficult to conceive of than a Space Machine, whether you consider Time as the fourth dimension of Space or as a locus essentially different because of its contents.

Ordinarily, Time is defined as the locus of events, just as Space is the locus of bodies. Or it is defined simply as succession, whereas Space—(this will apply to all spaces: Euclidean or three-dimensional space; four-dimensional space implied by the intersection of several three-dimensional spaces; Riemannian spaces, which, being spheres, are closed, since the circle is a geodesic line on the sphere of the same radius; Lobatchevski's spaces, in which the plane is open; or any non-Euclidean space identifiable by the fact that it will not permit the construction of two similar figures as in Euclidean space)—Space is defined by simultaneity.

Every simultaneous segment of Time is extended and can therefore be explored by machines that travel in Space. The present is extended in three dimensions. If one transports oneself to any point in the past or the future, this point will be present and extended in three directions as long as one occupies it.

Reciprocally, Space, or the Present, has the three dimensions of Time: space traversed or the past, space to come or the future, and the present proper.

From *Selected Works of Alfred Jarry*, edited by Roger Shattuck and Simon Watson Taylor. New York: Grove Press, 1965. Reprinted here by permission of Grove Press, Inc. The piece originally appeared in the February 1899 issue of the *Mercure de France* under the title: "Commentaire pour servir à la construction pratique de la machine à explorer le temps."

Keith Beaumont comments: "This lengthy article—whose author was given, in the *Mercure*, as 'Dr. Faustroll'—was inspired by H. G. Wells's *The Time Machine* which had recently appeared in a French translation by Henry Davray. Where Wells was interested primarily in the uses to which such a machine might be put, Jarry was fascinated by the *idea* of the machine. He was of course as aware as anyone of the inherent contradictions, not to say absurdities, of such a notion; but far from wishing to expose such contradictions, he set out to play with them" (Keith Beaumont, *Alfred Jarry: A Critical and Biographical Study*. New York: St. Martin's Press, 1984, pp. 333–34).

Space and Time are commensurable. To explore the universe by seeking knowledge of points in Space can be accomplished only through Time; and in order to measure Time quantitatively, we refer to Space intervals on the dial of a chronometer.

Space and Time, being of the same nature, may be conceived of as different physical states of the same substance, or as different modes of motion. Even if we accept them only as different forms of thought, we see Space as a solid, a rigid system of phenomena; whereas it has become a banal poetic figure to compare Time to a flowing stream, a liquid in uniform rectilinear motion. Any internal obstruction of the flow of the mobile molecules of the liquid, any increase in viscosity is nothing other than consciousness.

*

Since Space is fixed around us, in order to explore it we must move in the vehicle of Duration. In kinematics Duration plays the part of an independent variable, of which the coordinates of the points considered are a function. Kinematics is a geometry in which events have neither past nor future. The fact that we create that distinction proves that we are carried along through them.

We move in the direction of Time and at the same speed, being ourselves part of the Present. If we could *remain immobile in absolute Space* while Time elapses, if we could lock ourselves inside a Machine that isolates us from Time (except for the small and normal "speed of duration" that will stay with us because of inertia), all future and past instants could be explored successively, just as the stationary spectator of a panorama has the illusion of a swift voyage through a series of landscapes. (We shall demonstrate later that, *as seen from the Machine*, the Past lies beyond the Future.)

II. THEORY OF THE MACHINE

A Machine to isolate us from Duration, or from the action of Duration (from growing older or younger, the physical drag which a succession of motions exerts on an inert body) will have to make us "transparent" to these physical phenomena, allow them to pass through us without modifying or displacing us. This isolation will be sufficient (in fact it would be impossible to design it any more efficiently) if Time, in overtaking us, gives us a minimal impulse just great enough to compensate for the deceleration of our habitual duration conserved by inertia. This slowing down would be due to an action comparable to the viscosity of a liquid or the friction of a machine.

To be stationary in Time means, therefore, to pass with impunity through all bodies, movements, or forces whose locus will be the point of space chosen by the Explorer for the point of departure of his *Machine of Absolute Rest or Time Machine.* Or one can think of oneself as being traversed by these events, as a projectile passes through an empty window frame without damaging it, or as ice re-forms after being cut by a wire, or as an organism shows no lesion after being punctured by a sterile needle.

The Time Explorer's Machine must therefore:

1) Be absolutely rigid, or in other words, absolutely elastic, in order to penetrate the densest solid as easily as an infinitely rarified gas.

2) Have weight in order to remain stationary in Space, yet remain sufficiently independent of the diurnal movement of the Earth to maintain an invariable orientation in absolute Space; and as a corollary, although it has weight, the Machine must be incapable of falling if the ground gives way beneath it in the course of the voyage.

3) It must be nonmagnetic so as not to be affected (we shall see why later on) by the rotation of the plane of polarization of light.

An ideal body exists which fulfills the first of these conditions: the Luminiferous Ether. It constitutes a perfect elastic solid, for wave motion is propagated by it at the well-known speed; it is penetrable by any body or penetrates any body without measurable effect, since the Earth gravitates within it as in empty space.

But—and here lies its only similarity to the *circular body* or Aristotelian ether—it is not by nature heavy; and, as it turns as a whole, it determines the magnetic rotation discovered by Faraday.

Now one common machine known to us all provides a perfect model for the luminiferous ether and satisfies the three postulates.

Let us briefly recall the constitution of the luminiferous ether. It is an ideal system of material particles acting on one another by means of springs without mass. Each molecule is mechanically the envelope of a coil spring whose ends are attached to those of neighboring molecules. A push or a pull on the last molecule will produce a vibration through the entire system, exactly as does the advancing front of a luminous wave.

The structure of this system of springs in analogous to the circulation without rotation of infinitely extensive liquids through infinitely small openings, or to a system consisting of rigid rods and rapidly rotating fly-wheels mounted on all or some of those rods.[†]

The system of springs differs from the luminiferous ether only because it has weight and does not turn as a whole, any more than would the ether in a field without magnetic force.

If one keeps increasing the angular velocity of the flywheels, or if one keeps tightening the springs, the periods of elementary vibrations will become shorter and shorter and the amplitude weaker and weaker.

[†]Cf. William Thomson [Lord Kelvin], *On a Gyrostatic Adynamic Constitution for Ether* (C. R. 1899; Proc. R. Soc. Ed., 1890). [Author's note.]

The movements will increasingly resemble those of a perfectly rigid system formed of material points mobile in Space and turning according to the well known law of rotation of a rigid body having equal moments of inertia around its three principal axes.

In sum, the element of perfect rigidity is the *gyrostat* or *gyroscope*.

Everyone is familiar with those square or round copper frames containing a flywheel spinning rapidly around an interior axis. By virtue of its rotation, the gyrostat maintains its equilibrium in any position. If we displace the center of gravity a little out of the vertical of the point of support, it will turn in azimuth *without falling*. The azimuth is the angle subtended between the meridian and a plane determined by the vertical and a given fixed point—a star for example.

When a body rotates around an axis one of those points is carried along with the diurnal motion of the earth, the direction of its axis remains fixed in absolute Space; so that for an observer carried along without his awareness in this diurnal motion, that axis appears to turn uniformly around the axis of the earth, exactly as would a parallactic telescope constantly pointed at a particular star low down on the horizon.

Three rapidly rotating gyrostats with shafts parallel to the three dimensions of space would produce a condition of cubic rigidity. The Explorer seated in the machine would be mechanically sealed in a cube of absolute rigidity, capable of penetrating any body without modification just like the luminiferous ether.

We have just seen that the Machine maintains an invariable orientation in absolute Space, but related to the diurnal movement of the Earth so as to have a reference point to determine time traveled.

Finally, the Machine has no magnetized parts as its description will show.

III. DESCRIPTION OF THE MACHINE

The Machine consists of an ebony frame, similar to the steel frame of a bicycle. The ebony members are assembled with soldered copper mountings.

The gyrostats' three *tori* (or flywheels), in the three perpendicular planes of Euclidean space, are made of ebony cased in copper, mounted on rods of tightly rolled quartz ribbons (quartz ribbons are made in the same way as quartz wire), and set in quartz sockets.

The circular frames or the semicircular forks of the gyrostats are made of nickel. Under the seat and a little forward are located the batteries for the electric motor. There is no iron in the Machine other than the soft iron of the electromagnets.

Motion is transmitted to three flywheels by ratchet-boxes and chain-drives of quartz wire, engaged in three cogwheels, each of which lies on the same plane as its corresponding flywheel. The chain-drives are connected to the motor and to each other through bevel gears and driveshafts. A triple brake controls all three shafts simultaneously.

Each turn of the front wheel triggers a lever attached to a pulley system, and four ivory dials, either separate or concentric, register the days in units, thousands, millions, and hundreds of millions. A separate dial remains in contact with the diurnal movement of the Earth through the lower extremity of the axis of the horizontal gyrostat.

A lever, controlled by an ivory handle and moving in a longitudinal or parallel direction to the Machine, governs the motor speed. A second handle slows the advance of the Machine by means of an articulated rod. It will be seen that a return from future to present is accomplished by slowing down the Machine, and that travel into the past is obtained by a speed even greater than that used for movement into the future (so as to produce a more perfect *immobility of duration*). In order to stop at any determined point in Time, there is a lever to lock the triple brake.

When the Machine is at rest, two of the circular frames of the gyrostats are tangential to the ground. In operation, since the gyrostatic cube cannot be drawn into rotation or at least is held to the angular motion determined by a constant couple, the Machine swings freely in azimuth on the extremity of the horizontal gyrostatic axis.

IV. FUNCTIONING OF THE MACHINE

By gyrostatic action, the Machine is *transparent to successive intervals of time*. It does not endure or "continue to be," but rather conserves its contents outside of Time, sheltered from all phenomena. If the Machine oscillates in Space, or even if the Explorer is upside down, he still sees distant objects normally and constantly in the same position, for since everything nearby is transparent, he has no point of reference.

Since he experiences no duration, no time elapses during a voyage no matter how long it is, *even if he has made a stop outside the Machine.* We have said that he does not undergo the passage of time except in the sense of friction or viscosity, an interval practically equivalent to that he would have passed through without even entering the Machine.

Once set in motion, the Machine always moves toward the future. The Future is the normal succession of events; an apple is on the tree; it will fall. The Past is the inverse order: the apple falls—from the tree. The Present is non-existent, a tiny fraction of a phenomenon, smaller than an atom. The physical size of an atom is known to be 1.5×10^{-8} centimeters in diameter. No one has yet measured the fraction of a solar second that is equal to the Present.

Just as in Space a moving body must be smaller than its containing medium, the Machine, in order to move in duration, must be shorter in duration than Time, its containing medium—that is, it must be more immobile in the succession of events.

Now the Machine's immobility in Time is directly proportional to the rate of rotation of its gyrostats in Space.

If t stands for the future, the speed in space or the slowness of duration necessary to explore the future will have to be a temporal quantity, V, such that

$$V < t.$$

Whenever V approaches o, the Machine veers back to the Present.

Movement into the Past consists in the perception of the reversibility of phenomena. One sees the apple bounce back up onto the tree, the dead man come to life, and the shot re-enter the cannon. This *visual* aspect of succession is well known to be theoretically obtainable by outdistancing light waves and then continuing to travel at a constant speed equal to that of light. The Machine, by contrast, transports the explorer through actual duration and not in search of images preserved in Space. He has only to accelerate to a point where the speed indicator (recall that the speed of the gyrostats and the slowness in duration of the Machine, that is the speed of events in the opposite direction, are synonymous) shows

$$V < -t.$$

And he will continue with a rate of uniform acceleration that can be controlled almost according to Newton's formula for gravitation. For a past anterior to $-t$ may be indicated by $< -t$, and to reach it he must obtain on the dial a reading equivalent to

$$V < (< -t).$$

V. TIME AS SEEN FROM THE MACHINE

It is worth noting that the Machine has *two Pasts:* the past anterior to our own present, what we might call the real past; and the past *created by the Machine* when it returns to our Present and which is in effect the reversibility of the Future.

Likewise, since the Machine can reach the real Past only after having passed through the Future, it must go through a point symmetrical to our Present, a dead center between future and past, and which can be designated precisely as the *Imaginary Present.*

Thus the Explorer in his Machine beholds Time as a curve, or better as a closed curved surface analogous to Aristotle's Ether. For much these same reasons in another text (*Exploits and Opinions of Doctor Faustroll,* Book VIII) we make use of the term *Ethernity*. Without the Machine an observer sees less than half of the true extent of Time, much as men used to regard the Earth as flat.

From the operation of the Machine there can easily be deduced a definition of Duration. Since it consists in the reduction of t to o and of o to $-t$, we shall say:

Duration is the transformation of
a succession into a reversion

In other words:

THE BECOMING OF A MEMORY.

—Translated by Roger Shattuck

Professor Shattuck writes that Paul Valéry "at the beginning of his career (in an essay inspired by H. G. Wells) developed his theory of the symbol as a " 'time machine' that fuses and embodies different states" (Paul Valéry, *Occasions*, translated by Roger Shattuck and Frederick Brown with an Introduction by Roger Shattuck [Princeton: at the University Press, 1970], xxix).

APPENDIX IX

Robert Paul and *The Time Machine*

Terry Ramsaye

[Inventor Robert] Paul's attention was arrested by a conspicuous piece of fiction entitled *The Time Machine*, which appeared in 1894. There was a striking relation between the fancy of the story and the fact of the motion picture. The author of this story was H. G. Wells, a science teacher who had turned from the class room and lecture platform to fiction for his expression. His story *The Time Machine* was helping mightily to establish him as a writer. Remember this was thirty years ago. Wells had only fairly begun to write of his speculations and forecasts in the evolution of the doctrines and social opinion which today make him world famous.

In this story Paul saw an opportunity to use the special properties of the motion picture in a new and perhaps especially effective method of narration. He wrote to Wells, who went to confer with Paul at his laboratory at 44 Hatton Garden.

A reading of *The Time Machine*, even now, leaves one with a strong impression that the story was born of the direct suggestion of the behavior of a motion picture film. Wells, in a letter to the writer in 1924, said he was unable to remember details of the relation. But the evidence is such that if the story was not evolved directly from the experience of seeing the Kinetoscope, it was indeed an amazing coincidence.

The Time Machine is a fanciful tale of the adventures of a physicist who built a machine which could travel in time just as an airplane travels in space. The *Time Traveler* tells his story in the first person. In the third chapter of the Wells story he says:

> I drew a breath, set my teeth, gripped the starting lever with both my hands, and went off with a thud. The laboratory got hazy and went dark. Mrs. Wachett came in, and walked, apparently without seeing me, toward the garden door. I suppose it took her a minute or so to traverse the place, but to me she seemed to shoot across the room like a rocket.

In that paragraph one does not have to stretch his fancy to see what must be taken as the motion picture influence at the bottom of Wells' concept. The operation of the *Time Traveler* was very like the starting of the peep-show Kinetoscope, and the optical effect experienced by the fictional adventurer was identical with that experienced in viewing a speeding film.

But even more strongly is the motion picture character of the *Time Machine* idea evidenced in Wells' chapter thirteen, where the *Time Traveler*, nearing the end of his narrative, recites:

> I saw one little thing that seemed odd to me. I think I have told you that when I set out, before my velocity became very high, Mrs. Wachett had walked across the room, travelling, it seemed to me, like a rocket. As I returned, I passed again across that minute when she traversed the laboratory. But now every motion appeared to be the direct inverse of her previous ones. The door at the lower end opened and she glided quietly up the laboratory, back foremost, and disappeared behind the door by which she had previously entered.

This paragraph details precisely the effect of running a film backward with consequent exact reversal of the action. It is hard to believe that Wells did not take his notion directly from the peep show film. One of the earliest novelty effects sought in the Kinetoscope in the days when it was enjoying scientific attention was in exactly this sort of reversal of commonplace bits of action. It continues today a somewhat hackneyed bit of trick camera work. In the early days we saw runners backing up at high speed and backing locomotives swallowing their smoke in reverse gear. Nowadays we see Venuses in half-piece bathing suits spring from the pool and retrace the parabola of the dive to alight on the springboard. Such is the progress of art.

Returning to Wells, there is additional evidence of the motion picture root of the *Time Machine* idea in that he stresses the picture reversal effect in the phrase: "she glided quietly." Wells seems to have been thinking in terms of the picture exclusively. He for the moment ignored the fact that his *Time Traveler* in recrossing a moment of time should have experienced the sounds as well as the sights of that moment, both reversed. Mrs. Wachett might just as well also have been heard backing up and closing the door. The thing had already done in experimental reversals of the phonograph. It would seem pretty definite that the *Time Traveler* was all eyes and the story all motion picture.

Out of the author-scientist collaborations in Hatton Garden came a screen project to materialize the human wish to live in the Past, Present and Future all at once. It is all set forth in clear terms in a British patent application, No. 19984, drawn up by Paul under date of October 24, 1895, reading:

A NOVEL FORM OF EXHIBITION OR ENTERTAINMENT,
MEANS FOR PRESENTING THE SAME

My invention consists of a novel form of exhibition whereby the spectators have presented to their view scenes which are supposed to occur in the future or past, while they are given the sensation of voyaging upon a machine through time, and means for presenting these scenes simultaneously and in conjunction with the production of the sensations by the mechanism described below, or its equivalent.

The mechanism I employ consists of a platform, or platforms, each of which contain a suitable number of spectators and which may be enclosed at the sides after the spectators have taken their places, leaving a convenient opening towards which the latter face, and which is directed towards a screen upon which the views are presented.

In order to create the impression of traveling, each platform may be suspended from cranks in shafts above the platform, which may be driven by an engine or other convenient source of power. These cranks may be so placed as to impart to the platform a gentle rocking motion, and may also be employed to cause the platform to travel bodily forward through a short space, when desired, or I may substitute for this portion of the mechanism similar shafts below the platforms, provided with cranks or cams, or worms keyed eccentrically on the shaft, or wheels gearing in racks attached to the underside of the platform or otherwise.

Simultaneously with the forward propulsion of the platform, I may arrange a current of air to be blown over it, either by fans attached to the sides of the platform, and intended to represent to the spectators the means of propulsion, or by a separate blower driven from the engine and arranged to throw a regulated blast over each of the platforms.

After the starting of the mechanism, and a suitable period having elapsed, representing, say, a certain number of centuries, during which the platforms may be in darkness, or in alternations of darkness and dim light, the mechanism may be slowed and a pause made at a given epoch, on which the scene upon the screen will come gradually into view of the spectators, increasing in size and distinctness from a small vista, until the figures, etc., may appear lifelike if desired.

In order to produce a realistic effect, I prefer to use for the projection of the scene upon the screen, a number of powerful lanterns, throwing the respective portions of the picture, which may be composed of,

(1) A hypothetical landscape, containing also the representations of the inanimate objects in the scene.

(2) A slide, or slides, which may be traversed horizontally or vertically and contain representations of objects such as a navigable balloon etc., which is required to traverse the scene.

(3) Slides or films, representing in successive instantaneous photographs, after the manner of the kinetoscope, the living persons or creatures in their natural motions. The films or slides are prepared with the aid of the kine-

tograph or special camera, from made up characters perfoming on a stage, with or without a suitable background blending with the main landscape.

The mechanism may be similar to that used in the kinetoscope, but I prefer to arrange the film to travel intermittently instead of continuously and to cut off the light only during the rapid displacement of the film as one picture succeeds another, as by this means less light is wasted than in the case when the light is cut off for the greater portion of the time, as in the ordinary kinetoscope mechanism.

(4) Changeable coloured, darkened, or perforated slides may be used to produce the effect on the scene of sunlight, darkness, moonlight, rain, etc.

In order to enable the scenes to be gradually enlarged to a definite amount, I may mount these lanterns on suitable carriages or trollies, upon rails provided with stops or marks, so as to approach to or recede from the screen a definite distance, and to enable a dissolving effect to be obtained, the lantern may be fitted with the usual mechanism. In order to increase the realistic effect I may arrange that after a certain number of scenes from a hypothetical future have been presented to the spectators, they may be allowed to step from the platforms, and be conducted through grounds or buildings arranged to represent exactly one of the epochs through which the spectator is supposed to be traveling.

After the last scene is presented I prefer to arrange that the spectators should be given the sensation of voyaging backwards from the last epoch to the present, or the present epoch may be supposed to have been accidentally passed, and a past scene represented on the machine coming to a standstill, after which the impression of traveling forward again to the present epoch may be given, and the re-arrival notified by the representation on the screen of the place at which the exhibition is held, or of some well-known building which by the movement forward of the lantern can be made to increase gradually in size as if approaching the spectator.

ROBT. W. PAUL

Paul, inspired by Wells' story, in this document of three decades ago exactly anticipated the photoplay, which was not to be born yet for many a year.

It was, viewed from the easy facility of the slowly evolved screen technique of to-day, a clumsy collection of mechanical expedients. He did not and could not know then that everything sought by way of revolving stages, combined stereopticons, projection machines, scenic settings, masked seating sections and platform rocking devices to simulate travel motion, would one day be done entirely on the screen. The photoplay of to-day moves backward and forward through Time with facile miracle from the Present into the Past and Future by the cutback, flashback and vision scenes. The Paul patent notion of sliding projection machines to enlarge or diminish the size of the picture is executed by the camera of to-day while the projector stands still in its theatre booth. Most amazingly, too, Paul and Wells in 1895 plainly had the idea of not only the cutback and close-up but also the fade-in and fade-out, the overlap-dissolving of scenes into each other and all of the supplemental tonal effects of sunshine, fog, rain, moonlight and the like, now common to the screen drama.

Many years of reading Wells' works have rather accustomed us to thinking of him as the forecaster of most of the scientific wonders which have become commonplaces of civilization, as for instance the airplane. But even that is no preparation for the surprising discovery in this long forgotten patent application that Wells and Paul forecast something infinitely more complex than any machine—no less than a whole art form.

The Wells-Paul feat of 1895 surpasses event that remarkable anticipation by which Savinien Cyrano de Bergerac completely described the phonograph, two centuries before its invention, in his *Histoire Comique des États et Empires de la Lune* published in 1656, the year after his death in Paris.

The anticipations of the phonograph by de Bergerac in the middle of the seventeenth century and of the screen drama in the end of the nineteenth are given still more interest when we realize that these two desires of sight and sound were fused in the one mind of Edison, and that through his single agency they were both materialized. The line between Art and Science is narrow indeed.

But the Wells-Paul idea, embodied in the patent application, contained gropings for a greater and new liberty for art. It sought to liberate the spectator from the instant of Now. The Now to which our consciousness is chained is but a mathematical point of no dimensions traveling ever forward, describing the line which extends behind us as the Past and ahead of us as the Future.

The same impulse of cosmic adventure which has colored Wells' writing feats of fancy in tales of other worlds and of hypothetical ages was at work here. He wanted free range to lead his audiences at will back and forth along the infinite hyperdimensional line of Time. It was a plan to give the spectator possession, on equal terms, of *Was* and *To Be* along with *Is*. The motion picture was to cut away the hampering fog of the complex sequence of tenses of thought just as it was to cut back to reality through the misty attenuations of language.

This motion picture Time-machine idea was artistically at one with Ouspensky's mathematically mysterious philosophy and Einstein's philosophically mysterious mathematics. It was a promise of a more concrete application of their remote intellectual abstractions. The author and the philosopher alike often in their flights come beating against the walls of Space and Time. They are just expressions of the human wish to be liberated from the cage of the eternal Now.

Way back in the early '70's Nicolas Camille Flammarion, student of stars and dreamer of dreams, in France, wrote a scientific fantasy tale embodying related concepts, concerning the adventures of an interstellar race, masters of Time and Space. Flammarion's story was widely translated and circulated. In the United States, by coincidence, two editions were published in the '90's just before the birth of the motion picture. The peculiar possibilities of the motion picture's ability to petrify and preserve moments of fleeting time were here and there recognized even in the earliest days of the peep show. Witness the following fragment of an editorial from the *St. Louis Post Dispatch*:

KINETOSCOPE MARVELS

The kinetoscope, we are told, has recently been made to run backwards, and the effects of this way of running it are truly marvelous. In his remarkable romance, *Lumen*, the imaginative French astronomer, Flammarion, conceives of spiritual beings who, by traveling forward on a ray of light, see, with the keen vision of the spirit, all that ray of light carried from the beginning of creation. By reversing the process and traveling in the contrary direction, they witness the events of history reversed, so that men appear to be rising from the grave, growing young and finally disappearing in the process of birth.

It now seems that the kinetoscope is to make this wondrous vision possible to us. Already, by allowing it to turn backwards, the actions can be seen in reverse order. The effect is said to be almost miraculous. In the process of eating food is taken from the mouth and placed on the plate.

It has taken the motion picture more than a quarter of a century to grow from the Edison Kinetoscope into the photoplay's modern approximation of the *Time Machine* and the Paul-Wells concept of 1895!

Wells was the first writer, in other words the first professional recreator of events, to come into contact with the motion picture. This circumstance led nearly to the attainment, at a single stroke, of the photoplay construction which has since come only by tedious evolution.

No writer or dramatist has since made so bold a gesture with reference to the screen as resulted from this tentative joining of Paul's invention and Wells' fancy. They were hampered by no precedent or built-up tradition of the screen industry, such as has affected the thought of every writer or dramatist of subsequent connection with the art. When, more than a decade later, the screen reached for the aid of the writing craft, it had established an audience and precedents of practice which did not permit the scenario writer to be a free agent of expression. The project of '95 conceived the motion picture as a tool and servant in the business of story telling, while the writers who came in after the lapse of years were to be the tools and servants of the then intrenched motion picture business.

The actual processes of the evolution which was to realize some measure of this early vision did not well begin until some thirteen years later, in 1908, when D. W. Griffith began to assemble the mechanical and optical properties of the motion picture into a new dramatic technique peculiar to the screen.

The extraordinary machinery of the Past, Present and Future embodied in the Paul patent application was never built because there was no money available to carry out the daring idea. Paul dropped the project and did not proceed with the formalities necessary to the issuance of the patent. It was utterly forgotten until the researches of this history caused Paul to bring it to light to establish an incidental date. In the third specification of the proposed methods of the patent Paul defined the intermittent principle of the motion picture projection device included. The patent application therefore establishes the fact that it was some time prior to October 25, 1895, that he arrived at the idea of an intermittent motion in screen projection.

When the Wells-Paul Past-Present-Future machine came to naught the whole Paul screen notion became dormant for a period awaiting the vitalizing influence to developments to come.

Some months later Paul, who was still inclined to view his machine as a scientific instrument, decided to show it to a scientific audience. On February 20, 1896, Paul's projector was demonstrated before an audience at Finsbury Technical College, and on February 28 it was shown in the library of the Royal Institution. These showings were accepted with due and grave appreciation. After two whole generations a British scientist had demonstrated an application of certain elements of that paper on *Persistence of Vision with Regard to Moving Objects* read by Dr. Peter Mark Rôget before the Royal Society. That was that, and the Royal Society proceeded with the regular order of business.

To the student of contemporary literature this near motion picture adventure of Wells is of interest in that it appears to have been a part of his experience when he was laying down the foundations of his writing career, which became an outgrowth of his work and considerations as a teacher of science. He broke from the class room for the greater liberty of the printed page. If he had given attention to the motion picture and its larger opportunity of mastery over Time by translations into the Present he might have set the screen's progress forward many a year.

The Past and the Future are at best mere fictions of Art. This is unconsciously understood by the more primitive minds uncontaminated with culture. The standard daily argot of the melting pot commonalty of the United States recognizes only one real tense, the present progressive. Witness the accurate recordings in the Americanese of Ring Lardner. Or collect your own samples in any subway crowd:

"I'm off with him now—we has a date last Sunday and he stands me up. Next time I sees him I says you cake eater you don't get away with that kinda stuff on me."

Purveying to the same audience, the sports writer gives his graphic narrative of the fight-by-rounds and the baseball-game-by-innings in the same progressive present.

The motion picture is a triumph over tenses. It is a Time machine in which we all ride with Lumen.

APPENDIX X

Hinton and Newcomb
on the Fourth Dimension

1. CHARLES H. HINTON

Evidence of a Fourth Dimension

... Let us investigate the conception of a four-dimensional existence in a simpler and more natural manner—in the same way that a two-dimensional being should think about us, not as infinite in the third dimension, but limited in three dimensions as he is in two. A being existing in four dimensions must then be thought to be as completely bounded in all four directions as we are in three. All that we can say in regard to the possibility of such beings is, that we have no experience of motion in four directions. The powers of such beings and their experience would be ampler, but there would be no fundamental difference in the laws of force and motion.

Such a being would be able to make but a part of himself visible to us, for a cube would be apprehended by a two-dimensional being as the square in which it stood. Thus a four-dimensional being would suddenly appear as a complete and finite body, and as suddenly disappear, leaving no trace of himself, in space, in the same way that anything lying on a flat surface, would, on being lifted, suddenly vanish out of the cognizance of beings, whose consciousness was confined to the plane. The object would not vanish by moving in any direction, but disappear instantly as a whole. There would be no barrier, no confinement of our devising that would not be perfectly open to him. He would come and go at pleasure; he would be able to perform feats of the most surprising kind. It would be possible by an infinite plane extending in all directions to divide our space into two portions absolutely separated from one another; but a four-dimensional being would slip round this plane with the greatest ease.

To see this clearly, let us first take the analogous case in three dimensions. Suppose a piece of paper to represent a plane. If it is infinitely extended in every direction, it will represent an infinite plane. It can be divided into two parts by an infinite straight line. A being confined to this plane could not get from one part of it to the other without passing

Excerpted from Charles H. Hinton, "What is the Fourth Dimension?" in *Scientific Romances* by Hinton. London: Swan Sonnenschein & Co., 1884–85. (See this edition of *The Time Machine*, chapter 1, note 11.)

through the line. But suppose another piece of paper laid on the first and extended infinitely, it will represent another infinite plane. If the being moves from the first plane by a motion in the third dimension, it will move into this new plane. And in it it finds no line. Let it move to such a position that when it goes back to the first plane it will be on the other side of the line. Then let it go back to the first plane. It has appeared now on the other side of the line which divides the infinite plane into two parts.

Take now the case of four dimensions. Instead of bringing before the mind a sheet of paper conceive a solid of three dimensions. If this solid were to become infinite it would fill up the whole of three-dimensional space. But it would not fill up the whole of four-dimensional space. It would be to four-dimensional space what an infinite plane is to three-dimensional space. There could be in four-dimensional space an infinite number of such solids, just as in three-dimensional space there could be an infinite number of infinite planes.

Thus, lying alongside our space, there can be conceived a space also infinite in all three directions. To pass from one to the other a movement has to be made in the fourth dimension, just as to pass from one infinite plane to another a motion has to be made in the third dimension.

Conceive, then, corresponding to the first sheet of paper mentioned above, a solid, and as the sheet of paper was supposed to be infinitely extended in two dimensions, suppose the solid to be infinitely extended in its three dimensions, so that it fills the whole of space as we know it.

Now divide this infinite solid in two parts by an infinite plane, as the infinite plane of paper was divided in two parts by an infinite line. A being cannot pass from one part of this infinite solid to another, on the other side of this infinite plane, without going through the infinite plane, *so long as he keeps within the infinite solid.*

But suppose beside this infinite solid a second infinite solid, lying next to it in the fourth dimension, as the second infinite plane of paper was next to the first infinite plane in the third dimension. Let now the being that wants to get on the other side of the dividing plane move off in the fourth dimension, and enter the second infinite solid. In this second solid there is no dividing plane. Let him now move, so that coming back to the first infinite solid he shall be on the other side of the infinite plane that divides it into two portions. If this is done, he will now be on the other side of the infinite plane, without having gone through it.

In a similar way a being, able to move in four dimensions, could get out of a closed box without going through the sides, for he could move off in the fourth dimension, and then move about, so that when he came back he would be outside the box.

Is there anything in the world as we know it, which would indicate the possibility of there being an existence in four dimensions? No definite answer can be returned to this question. But it may be of some interest to point out that there are certain facts which might be read by the light of the fourth-dimensional theory.

To make this clear, let us suppose that space is really four dimensional, and that the three-dimensional space we know is, in this ampler space, like a surface is in our space.

We should then be in this ampler space like beings confined to the surface of a plane would be in ours. Let us suppose that just as in our space there are centers of attraction whose influence radiates out in every direction, so in this ampler space there are centers of attraction whose influence radiates out in every direction. Is there anything to be observed in nature which would correspond to the effect of a center of attraction lying out of our space, and acting on all the matter in it? The effect of such a center of attraction would not be to produce motion in any known direction, because it does not lie off in any known direction.

Let us pass to the corresponding case in three and two dimensions, instead of four and three. Let us imagine a plane lying horizontally, and in it some creatures whose experience was confined to it. If now some water or other liquid were poured on to the plane, the creatures, becoming aware of its presence, would find that it had a tendency to spread out all over the plane. In fact it would not be to them as a liquid is to us—it would rather correspond to a gas. For a gas, as we know it, tends to expand in every direction, and gradually increase so as to fill the whole of space. It exercises a pressure on the walls of any vessel in which we confine it.

The liquid on the plane expands in all the dimensions which the two-dimensional creatures on the plane know, and at the same time becomes smaller in the third dimension, its absolute quantity remaining unchanged. In like manner we might suppose that gases (which by expansion become larger in the dimensions that we know) become smaller in the fourth dimension.

The cause in this case would have to be sought for in an attractive force, acting with regard to our space as the force of gravity acts with regard to a horizontal plane.

Can we suppose that there is a center of attraction somewhere off in the fourth dimension, and that the gases, which we know are simply more mobile liquids, expanding out in every direction under its influence. This view receives a certain amount of support from the fact proved experimentally that there is no absolute line of demarcation between a liquid and a gas. The one can be made to pass into the other with no moment intervening in which it can be said that now a change of state has taken place.

We might then suppose that the matter we know extending in three dimensions has also a small thickness in the fourth dimension; that solids are rigid in the fourth as in the other three dimensions; that liquids are too coherent to admit of their spreading out in space, and becoming thinner in the fourth dimension, under the influence of an attractive center lying outside of our space; but that gases, owing to the greater mobility of their particles, are subject to its action, and spread out in space under its influence, in the same manner that liquids, under the influence of gravity, spread out on a plane.

Then the density of a gas would be a measure of the relative thickness of it in the fourth dimension; and the diminution of the density would correspond to a diminution of the thickness in the fourth dimension. Could this supposition be tested in any way?

Suppose a being confined to a plane; if the plane is moved far off from the center of attraction lying outside it, he would find that liquids had less tendency to spread out than before.

Or suppose he moves to a distant part of the plane so that the line from his position to the center of attraction lies obliquely to the plane; he would find that in this position a liquid would show a tendency to spread out more in one direction than another.

Now our space considered as lying in four-dimensional space, as a plane does in three-dimensional space, may be shifted. And the expansive force of gases might be found to be different at different ages. Or, shifting as we do our position in space during the course of the earth's path round the sun, there might arise a sufficient difference in our position in space, with regard to the attractive center, to make the expansive force of gases different at different times of the year, or to cause them to manifest a greater expansive force in one direction than in another.

But although this supposition might be worked out at some length, it is hard to suppose that it could afford any definite test of the physical existence of a fourth dimension. No test has been discovered which is decisive. And, indeed, before searching for tests, a theoretical point of the utmost importance has to be settled. In discussing the geometrical properties of straight lines and planes, we suppose them to be respectively of one and two dimensions, and by so doing deny them any real existence. A plane and a line are mere abstractions. Every portion of matter is of three dimensions. If we consider beings on a plane not as mere idealities, we must suppose them to be of some thickness. If their experience is to be limited to a plane this thickness must be very small compared to their other dimensions. Transferring our reasoning to the case of four dimensions, we come to a curious result.

If a fourth dimension exists there are two possible alternatives.

One is, that there being four dimensions, we have a three-dimensional existence only. The other is that we really have a four-dimensional existence, but are not conscious of it. If we are in three dimensions only, while there are really four dimensions, then we must be relatively to those beings who exist in four dimensions, as lines and planes are in relation to us. That is, we must be mere abstractions. In this case we must exist only in the mind of the being that conceives us, and our experience must be merely the thoughts of his mind—a result which has apparently been arrived at, on independent grounds, by an idealist philosopher.

The other alternative is that we have a four-dimensional existence. In this case our proportions in it must be infinitely minute, or we should be conscious of them. If such be the case, it would probably be in the ultimate particles of matter, that we should discover the fourth dimension, for in the ultimate particles the sizes in the three dimensions are very minute, and the magnitudes in all four dimensions would be comparable.

The preceding two alternative suppositions are based on the hypothesis of the reality of four-dimensional existence, and must be conceived to hold good only on that hypothesis.

It is somewhat curious to notice that we can thus conceive of an existence relative to which that which we enjoy must exist as a mere abstraction.

Apart from the interest of speculations of this kind they have considerable value; for they enable us to express in intelligible terms things of which we can form no image. They supply us, as it were, with scaffolding, which the mind can make use of in building up its conceptions. And the additional gain to our power of representation is very great.

Many philosphical ideas and doctrines are almost unintelligible because there is no physical illustration which will serve to express them. In the imaginary physical existence which we have traced out, much that philosophers have written finds adequate representation. Much of Spinoza's *Ethics*, for example, could be symbolized from the preceding pages.

Thus we may discuss and draw perfectly legitimate conclusions with regard to unimaginable things.

It is, of course, evident that these speculations present no point of direct contact with fact. But this is no reason why they should be abandoned. The course of knowledge is like the flow of some mighty river, which, passing through the rich lowlands, gathers into itself the contributions from every valley. Such a river may well be joined by a mountain stream, which, passing with difficulty along the barren highlands, flings itself into the greater river down some precipitous descent, exhibiting at the moment of its union the spectacle of the utmost beauty of which the river system is capable. And such a stream is no inapt symbol of a line of mathematical thought, which, passing through difficult and abstract regions, sacrifices for the sake of its crystalline clearness the richness that comes to the more concrete studies. Such a course may end fruitlessly, for it may never join the main course of observation and experiment. But, if it gains its way to the great stream of knowledge, it affords at the moment of its union the spectacle of the greatest intellectual beauty, and adds somewhat of force and mysterious capability to the onward current.

2. SIMON NEWCOMB

Modern Mathematical Thought

... Now it is a fundamental principle of pure science that the liberty of making hypotheses is unlimited. It is not necessary that we shall prove the hypothesis to be a reality before we are allowed to make it. It is legitimate to anticipate all the possibilities. It is, therefore, a perfectly legitimate exercise of thought to imagine what would result if we should not stop at three dimensions in geometry, but construct one for space having four. As the boy, at a certain stage in his studies, passes from two to three dimensions, so may the mathematician pass from three to four dimensions with equal facility. He does indeed meet with the obstacle that he cannot draw figures in four dimensions, and his faculties are so limited that he cannot construct in his own mind an image of things as they would look in space of four dimensions. But this need not prevent his reasoning on the subject, and one of the most obvious conclusions he would reach is this: As in space of two dimensions one line can be drawn perpendicular to another at a given point, and by adding another dimension to space a third line can be drawn perpendicular to these two; so in a fourth dimension we can draw a line which shall be perpendicular to all three. True, we cannot imagine how the line would look, or where it would be placed, but this is merely because of the limitations of our faculties. As a surface describes a solid by continually leaving the space in which it lies at the moment, so a four-dimensional solid will be generated by a three-dimensional one by a continuous motion which shall constantly be directed outside of this three-dimensional space in which our universe appears to exist. As the man confined in a circle can evade it by stepping over it, so the mathematician, if placed inside a sphere in four-dimensional space, would simply step over it as easily as we should over a circle drawn on the floor. Add a fourth dimension to space, and there is room for an indefinite number of universes, all alongside of each other, as there is for an indefinite number of sheets of paper when we pile them upon each other.

From this point of view of physical science, the question whether the actuality of a fourth dimension can be considered admissible is a very interesting one. All we can say is that, so far as observation goes, all legitimate conclusions seem to be against it. No induction of physical science is more universal or complete than that three conditions fix the position of a point. The phenomena of light show that no vibrations go outside of three-dimensional space, even in the luminiferous ether. If

Excerpted from Simon Newcomb, "Modern Mathematical Thought," *Nature*, February 1, 1894, 325–29. This was based on Newcomb's address to the New York Mathematical Society, December 28, 1893. (See this edition of *The Time Machine*, chapter 1, note 14.)

there is another universe, or a great number of other universes, outside of our own, we can only say that we have no evidence of their exerting any action upon our own. True, those who are fond of explaining anomalous occurrences, by the action of beings that we otherwise know nothing about, have here a very easy field for their imagination. The question of the sufficiency of the laws of nature to account for all phenomena is, however, too wide a one to be discussed at present.

As illustrating the limitation of our faculties in this direction, it is remarkable that we are unable to conceive of a space of two dimensions otherwise than as contained in one of three. A mere plane, with nothing on each side of it, is to us inconceivable. We are thus compelled, so far as our conceptions go, to accept three dimensions and no more. We have in this a legitimate result of the universal experience through all generations being that of a triply extended space. . . .

APPENDIX XI

Beowulf and *The Time Machine*:
A Note On Analogues

Harry M. Geduld

A relationship between *Beowulf* and *The Time Machine* seems, on the face of it, to be patently unlikely. Apart from the difference of genre, the epic poem and the prose narrative deal with subject matter that is literally separated by eons. The *Beowulf* poet recounts a pre-Norman Conquest tale of monsters and marvelous deeds of heroism. Wells's scientific romance, on the other hand, ranges in time from London in the 1890s through the year 802,701 A.D. to a "further vision" of the world's end. In *Experiment in Autobiography*, Wells nowhere displays any interest in Anglo-Saxon literature. Yet significant similarities between the epic and his novella do exist. Whether there was an actual influence of one on the other is likely to remain a matter of speculation. However, lack of confirmatory evidence should not prevent us from noticing the striking parallels that exist between the poem and the story.

The numerous analogues are either direct or approximate, and are evident in incident and circumstance as well as in description. The hero's journey is fundamental to both works. Poem and story pay particular attention to the vessel or vehicle (machine), emphasizing certain details and its direction by a skilled individual—in one case a warrior, in the other an inventor. In each work, the hero comes to a "new world" uninvited from afar (in space or time—to encounter horrific predators)—although it is only in *The Time Machine* that the predators are unexpected. Both groups—the Morlocks in Wells's story and Grendel and his mother in *Beowulf*—are pointedly traced to a common ancestry with those they devour. The Time Traveller comes to the conclusion (in chapter 5) that Morlocks and the Eloi are the evolutionary outcome of a radical, degenerative bifurcation of the human species, while we learn from *Beowulf* that Grendel and his mother are descendants of Cain and are thus progeny of Adam equally with the Geats, the Danes, and the Swedes. Thus, in effect, the Time Traveller's paradoxical slaughter of his own descendants, the Morlocks, parallels Beowulf's destruction of his monstrous kinfolk.

However, the most striking analogues are observable between the predatory habits of the monsters, their cannibalism, their earliest appearance to the heroes, and their encounters with them. It is difficult to believe that Wells was not thinking of *Beowulf* immediately before writing his description of the great communal house of the Eloi. For here we have a "future" domicile equivalent to the hall Heorot and its mead-benches: joyous places of feasting and gaiety by day but shelters that are fitfully insecure from murder and cannibalism by night. The Eloi—like the Danes—eat together and sleep communally. They fear the Morlocks who rise up at night, like grey ghosts, from the old subterranean machine-shops—just as Hrothgar and his Spear-Danes fear Grendel who emerges nightly from the depths of his mere and stalks the misty moors.

Ignorant of the dangers that lurk at night, the Time Traveller sleeps apart from the Eloi. He is awakened about dawn by the groping hands of a Morlock. Similarly, Grendel clutches at the apparently sleeping Beowulf, supine in the shadows of the hall Heorot. In each case it is the hero's first encounter with his adversary: a decisive encounter for Beowulf—for he wrenches Grendel's arm from its socket, mortally wounding the enemy of the Spear-Danes. The Time Traveller's glimpse of his future enemies is vague and almost meaningless at the time, but following that encounter and the next he wonders if he has seen ghosts—a notion that recalls many passages descriptive of Grendel and Grendel's mother slinking ghostlike through the early morning mists. None of the Morlocks loses an arm, but later in Wells's narrative, an "iron arm," a lever, is used by the Time Traveller to batter many of them to death. The weapon is acquired in an emergency just a Beowulf obtains the sword he uses to slay Grendel's mother in her home below the mere. Previously, the Time Traveller had protected himself solely by his own ingenuity and strength, for he has been temporarily deprived of his Time Machine, his effective means of escape—and also the symbol of his intellectual superiority and power. From this latter standpoint the Time Machine may be regarded as an equivalent of Beowulf's sword, symbolizing that hero's *physical* superiority, a symbol Beowulf voluntarily discards before battling with Grendel.

Crucial episodes in both poem and story are those concerning the hero's descent to the subterranean haunts of his adversaries. The Time Traveller descends a shaft or well to explore the domain of the Morlocks; Beowulf plunges deep into a dark mere to seek out Grendel's mother whose depredations have replaced those of her dead offspring. In the underworld, both heroes are almost overcome by their adversaries—but both survive to return to the sunlight.

Just as the brute strength of the hero is a characteristic of both works, so is the means of first presenting it to the listener or reader. Beowulf, after describing his endurance and intrepidity in a swimming contest, resolves to perform heroic deeds for Hrothgar and his people. His story earns the admiration of the Danish queen Wealhtheow. Through another swimming feat, the Time Traveller, a man of exceptional strength by the standards of 802,701, earns the gratitude and devotion of Weena. Significantly, these swimming episodes occur at corresponding points in both poem and story, that is, before the first encounters with the predators and after a parallel sequence of episodes dealing with the departure and arrival of vessel/machine and the "removal" of the symbols of prowess or intellectual superiority—Beowulf's sword and the Time Machine.

Wells's hero, having finally escaped the clutches of the Morlocks, travels onward to an even more remote future when man has become as extinct as the dinosaur. At one point he stops under "the huge hull of the sun, red and motionless" with his machine standing on "a sloping beach" surrounded by rocks "of a harsh reddish color"—the scene recalls the territory devastated by the dragon in the final episode of *Beowulf*. And 'dragons' of a kind are indeed present: "I saw that, quite near, what I had taken to be a reddish mass of rock was moving slowly towards me. Then I saw the thing was really a monstrous crab-like creature."

Lamed but not mortally wounded like Beowulf, the Time Traveller returns briefly to his own time before vanishing forever into the unknown—without the final glory of the epic hero.

There are, of course, numerous folkloric and literary analogues to *Beowulf*, beginning with the Icelandic saga of *Grettir the Strong*, that might have come to Wells's attention even if he had never looked into the Old English epic. Although, as I noticed at the outset, there is no evidence of Wells's familiarity with *Beowulf* in particular, the strong flavor of "Welsh superstition" that characterizes parts of *The Chronic Argonauts* (see Appendix I) points to his early interest in myth and legend generally. The name "Morlock" (from warlock: see chapter 5, note 46) is an unmistakable mark of this interest on the later versions of *The Time Machine*.

The Heaven of the Time-Machine

Louis Untermeyer

I

You must imagine a vast laboratory—a tremendous affair of several thousand miles—stretching its spotless length of Albalune (a by-product of moon-dust that had superseded all woodwork and tilings since 2058), reflecting only the purest of celestial colors. An intricate network of rapidly moving runways spanned the stars; myriads of spinning platforms threaded the upper reaches which were reserved for aerocars traveling at speeds of three hundred miles an hour and upward. The introduction of a dozen new metals in 1970—especially Maximite, Kruppium and Luxpar, to name the three chief members of the important Iridio-Aluminoid family—had revolutionized aerial traffic and when a half century later the full power of atomic energy was released and exploited, land travel ceased entirely. The whirling streets flashed by in a maelstrom of sound. Huge trumpets, grotesquely curved to resemble calla lilies, blared eternity's oldest ethics and its newest advertisements with an impartial clamor. "Harrumph! Harrumph! Baroom! Look slippy! All the latest styles in latter-day creeds! Special Bargains Today in Neo-Paganism! Large Assortment! Baroom! Ham's Halos for Happiness! Ask Adam—He Knows! Harrumph! Harrumph!"

II

Down one of these runways, seated on a machine not unlike a twentieth-century bicycle but far more delicate and equipped with dozens of sensitive antennæ, advanced a figure. You had to look twice at his fantastic costume to assure yourself that this was a man. You figure him a sallow, plumpish person, a little over middle size and age, bespectacled, and with a thinning of the hair on his dolicocephalic head—a baldness, if one examined closely, that might have been covered by a shilling. His clothes, conforming to the ethereal fashion, were loosely draped rather than tubular; woven of some bright semipneumatic material, ingeniously inflated to suggest a sturdiness not naturally his. All vestiges of facial hair had been extracted by a capillotomist in his youth and a neat head-dress, not unlike a Phrygian liberty cap, was fastened to his scalp by means of suction. You must picture him borne down one of these ribbons of traffic, past the harr and boom of the Blare Machines, to a quiet curve (corners and all dust-collecting angles had long since vanished from architecture) half screened off by a translucent substance resembling milky glass. . . . In the center of this chamber, on a pedestal of weights and measures, stood a crystal ball that seemed to have a luminous quality of its own. Clouds, colors, half-defined shapes writhed within it; a faint humming seemed to emanate from its now sparkling, now nebulous core. Fastening three of the web-like filaments of the machine to the globe, he pressed a series of studs along what seemed to be the crank-shaft, spun the sphere with a gyroscopic motion and brought it gradually to where a violet ray pierced the ramparts. The light within the crystal ball grew brighter. It turned orange, then flame-color, then prismatic in its fire, exhausting the spectrum until it assumed an unwavering brilliance. This play of colors was reflected in the features of the crystal-gazer. His expression, almost kaleidoscopic in its changes, was, in quick succession, imaginative, philosophic, extravagant, metaphysical, romantic, quizzical, analytic, middle-class, historical, prophetic.

("Who is it?" I whispered in an awe-struck undertone to my super-terrestrial companion. "Am I actually gazing on God, the Invisible King?"

"Scarcely," replied the unabashed angel. "Those varying features belong to a more local divinity: Wells, the Divisible God."

"But look—" I exclaimed, "he is drawing nearer. . . . He is stopping immediately beneath us. . . . We can even see what is happening inside the crystal. . . . Look—")

III

It is very hard to tell precisely what period was registering itself in the heart of that amazing crystal. One saw walls quite plainly, a table with shaded lamp, books, chairs. From the conversation between the two men—they were both in their aggressive thirties—the place seemed to be England some time in the Nineteen Twenties. The older one, whose name was something incongruously like Fulpper, had a trick of waving his arms whenever words failed him, finishing his expansive sentences with a rush of onomatopoetic sound.

"We can't wait for wisdom, Balsmeer," he was saying; "life goes too damn fast. We start off at a fair pace, increase our speed a little, lag behind, try to catch up and, first thing you know—*whooosh!*" That's what the whole business is: an immense and hideous scramble, an irresistible race ending in heart-break and—*whooosh!*

"But isn't there such a thing as the scientific temperament; something that is not carried away so passionately?" inquired Balsmeer.

"Meaning—?"

"Well," continued the younger chap, "I'm what you might call a serious sociological student. I'm earnest straight through. No humor to speak of. No romance. I stumble over bright and beautiful things . . . missing most of 'em, I dare say, but getting on fairly well without 'em. I know there are high ecstasies in the world—splendid music, extraordinary women, stupendous adventures, great and significant raptures—but they are just so many abstractions to me. Scientific truth is the least accessible of mistresses. She disguises herself in unlovely trappings; she hides in filthy places; she is cold, hard, unresponsive. But she can always be found! She is the one certainty, the one radiance I have found in a muddle of dirt and misery and disease."

"And don't you see," pursued Fulpper with exuberant warmth, "that this same Science of yours is the very Romance you're running away from? This whole mechanistic age with its oiled efficiency, its incalculable energy and speed and—*whizz*. . . . What's it all for, anyway? Just to make traffic go quicker? to get the whole mess revolving faster? Not a bit of it. Your Research and my Romance are blood-brothers or dual personalities, to be more exact. . . . I seem to see—wait a minute—I seem to see a time when this Science will be revealed not so much as the God from the Machine as a god within it. A socialized thing. A lessener of stupid and unnecessary labor. A force to end the criminal exploitation of man by man. A power to finish, once and for all, the muddle and waste and confusion that destroy finest human possibilities."

"Yes," Balsmeer conceded, "but—"

"I'm coming to that," continued Fulpper. "That's where Love and Refined Thinking—grrr!—meet as enemies. Mr. and Mrs. Grundy won't be able to debase the latter and foul the former. Knowledge—a full, frank knowledge—is going to change all that."

"But innocence—"

"It may go. We've tasted the fruit of the tree. You can't have your apple and eat it, any more than Adam could. But there's something better than innocence. There's a fiercer virginity, a more courageous and affirmative purity in wisdom. No more dark whispering. No more poisonous insinuations, nasty suggestiveness. No more music-hall smut. No French-farce allusions. No more smirching of impulses that are as beautiful as art and as clean as chemistry. No more nightmares of adolescence. No more muddling up to sex. . . . This, please my God or your Science, will cease to be the world of the bully, the enslaved woman, the frightened child—the domain of the mud-pelter, the hypocrite, the professional diplomat. It will no longer be the world of the underworld, the cesspool, the liver-fluke. . . ."

His voice trailed off, incontinently. . . .

IV

The crystal became suddenly opaque. For a few minutes there was absolute silence. Then a faint clicking began; invisible pistons tapped out a delicate rhythm. The tympani increased both in volume and speed. A lever shot out from the very heart of the mechanism and the dials of the Time Machine began to register new eras. The radiometer clicked off years, decades, centuries, millennials. . . . Presently the hands stopped. The diffused light within the ball resolved itself; a gray-blue mist lifted from a strange landscape as the magnetic arrow pointed to 5,320,506.

V

It was, as I have said, a strange landscape. There was no color, no motion, not a sign of vegetation. Even as the darkness disappeared, the sun, a great greenish disc half the size of the heavens, sprang out of the icy sea. The planets were drawing nearer together for the final *débâcle*. The rocks on the shore were covered with frozen rime; the shadow of Mars, a dark clinker as round as the forgotten moon, covered the ground. It fell on the faces of the two who sat, as if carved, at the mouth of their subterranean tunnel. . . . They were swathed in bands of thermic electrons; what showed of their faces was bloodless. Their lips did not move—the organs of speech had disappeared during the second stage of telepathic communication—and only the minute dilations of the pupils during some emotional passage animated their chiseled immobility.

"The waste of it . . . the hideous waste of it," you figure him flashing this to her, "what's the whole push and struggle for? Is every generation to be at the beginning of new things, never at a happy ending? Always prodded or prodding itself on with dreams, half-perceived vistas?"

"My dear . . ." her eyes remonstrated.

"It's you and I against the world," he telepathed. "I guess it's always been that. Two alone against the welter of mud and ugliness, dullness, obstinacy; two tiny rebels against a world frozen with hate and hypocrisy. . . . The pity and shame of it. . . . The shabbiness of it all. . . ."

"But, dear," she challenged, "the human race is still so young. It is still learning to progress."

"Progress!" his pupils contracted. "We are as sunk in apathy and ignorance as our mythical ancestors in the prehistoric twentieth century. Progress is a shibboleth. It's worse—a religion that every one professes and nobody believes in. Where are we now? Education has lost itself in the schools. Sex has been buried in lies and lingerie. Science is fuddling over its dead bones, trying to reconstruct the braincells of the Post-Wilsonian man. . . . Progress! . . . Until this icy earth falls at last into a solid sun, millions of us will come out of our burrows to question what it all means. . . . Here—at the very mouths of our underground tunnels—man once walked, warm and careless and secure. And here, before that, life ran prodigally on every inch of the surface. . . . Here, in some obscure and forgotten epoch, the long-necked Brontosaurus waded and the Diplodocus thrashed his thirty-foot tail among the muggers. Here the giant Moa screamed as the Hesperornis, that strange wingless bird, pursued the fishes through the Mesozoic waters. Here the Protohippus pranced on his three toes and the Tyrannosaurus, buoyed up by fertile mud, preyed on the happy herbivores. . . . And all for what? . . ."

"For something it will be hard to answer but harder to deny," she communed intensely, "for some transfiguration, some sort of world cleansed of its crippling jealousies, its spites, its blunderings. . . . After all, there is a long time ahead. Man has existed for little more than ten or twelve million years. We are still so new. . . . The future is so enormous, so staggering, so superb. Life is forever young . . . forever eager. . . . Men will, in some distant maturity, adjust their scattered dreams and energies. I see the time when life will have unified meaning, when even death will be a part of the great integration. And, whether we die or live, mankind is in the making. . . . Old worlds are being exchanged for new. Utopias, anticipations, unguessed brotherhoods, the last conquest of earth and the stars. . . . All so slowly but so confidently in the making. . . ."

VI

The picture faded out, dissolving imperceptibly, until the ball paled to a mere glassy transparency. . . . The figure in the machine suddenly became energetic. He wheeled about, took his hands from the controlling levers and touched a series of buttons on delicate, jointed rods which terminated in a set of metal hieroglyphs. First one was struck, then another, then a swift succession of notes. The fingers flew faster, as though they sought to wrest some harmony from the heart of the machine. . . . For some time, nothing else was heard but tap, click—tap, tap, tap—click—tap—*ping!*— as the incessant typewriter was driven mercilessly on through space and time.